D0690260

The Latina's Bible

The Latina's Bible

THE NUEVA LATINA'S GUIDE TO

Love,
Spirituality,
Family,
AND
La Vida

SANDRA GUZMÁN

Northern Plains Public Library
Ault Colorado

THREE RIVERS PRESS • NEW YORK

Grateful acknowledgment is made to the following for permission to reprint material:

Alejandro Anreus: the poem "My Daughter" from the unpublished collection of poetry *In This Our Exile* by Alejandro Anreus. Copyright © by Alejandro Anreus. Reprinted by permission of the author.

Aunt Lute Books: the poem "No Se Raje, Chicanita/Don't Give In, Chicanita" from *Borderlands/La Frontera: The New Mestiza*, by Gloria Anzaldua. Copyright © 1987, 1999 by Gloria Anzaldua. Reprinted by permission of Aunt Lute Books.

Copyright © 2002 by Sandra Guzmán

All rights reserved. No part of this book may be reproduced or transmitted in any form or by any means, electronic or mechanical, including photocopying, recording, or by any information storage and retrieval system, without permission in writing from the publisher.

Published by Three Rivers Press, New York, New York.
Member of the Crown Publishing Group, a division of Random House, Inc.

www.randomhouse.com

THREE RIVERS PRESS and the Tugboat design are a registered trademarks of Random House, Inc.

Printed in the United States of America

Design by Joy O'Meara

Library of Congress Cataloging-in-Publication Data
Guzmán, Sandra.
The Latina's bible : the Nueva Latina's guide to love, sex, spirituality, and
la Vida/Sandra Guzmán.
1. Feminism—United States.   2. Hispanic American women—Social
conditions.   I. Title.
HQ1421 .G89 2002
305.48'868073—dc21

2001049138

ISBN 0-609-80696-3

10   9   8   7   6   5   4   3   2   1

First Edition

This book is dedicated to the fierce *mujeres* in my life
who nurture, support, and inspire the warrior woman in me:
mi madre and *maestra*, Lydia;
my two big sisters, Wandi and Mari; and my best friend, Ana.
To the next generation of Nueva Latinas and Latinos in my life,
my nieces Christina, Lianna, and Serena.
And to the one young man
who has taught me much about love, life, and womanhood,
my son, BJ.

Acknowledgments

I am humbled when I look back and see how all the forces of the universe conspired on my behalf in the name of love to make this book happen. This book was truly a community and family project.

A most profound thanks to Cleyvis Natera, my researcher, reader, partner, and main sister on this journey. I am forever grateful for your dedication to this book. You were by my side during the entire adventure and walked the mountain with me. Your fierceness inspires my soul. Pa'lante. Thank you to another angel in my life who guided me through the writing process, the talented wordsmith Richard Simon, who I swear was a Latina in a previous life. Thanks for encouraging the writer in me, making me smile and shine. *Gracias de todo corazón a la fabulosa editora,* Becky Cabaza, my editor at Three Rivers Press. Latinas like Becky are a reminder of the power of having women of courage, vision, and cultural pride in publishing. She is Mexican by heritage, was raised in Texas, and educated in an elite "white" public school. I am Puerto Rican born and raised in the northeast and educated in an urban public school system. Our U.S. Latina experiences could not be more different, but the minute we met, she knew we were sisters under the skin. That in a nutshell is how Becky described our first meeting and why today I am a published author. Becky gets it and I pray that God continues to bless her with strength and unwavering passion and commitment to La Raza! Thank you, Tanya Mc Kinnon—agent extraordinaire. You saw the book from our first breakfast meeting and were as passionate about its vision and mission as I. Your business savvy and faith in me were God-sent.

Thanks to the people in my life who give me unconditional love and support, my *famillia: Mami,* Wandi, Mari, Mike, Alex, Cynthia, Myra, Victor, Rafael, Tuto, Cheylene, Bebe, Anthony, Chichi, Christina, Liana, Mikey Jr., Markus, *el gordito de titi,* my niece and godchild Serena. Thanks for putting up with me during stressful moments and my super-duper lengthy conversations about the joys of Nueva Latinas. You guys are the best! I want to especially thank you, my son BJ, for being so understanding when you had to go without the company of your mommy when she had to retreat to the solitude of writing. My *papi chulo* and *rey,* Willie, I thank for the love, the tuna avocado salads, and for keeping the music hot. Your magic changed me forever. Ana, *mi amiga del alma,* your friendship is priceless; thanks for always being there for me.

Mi amiga Rossana is the one who always replenished the energizer battery in me. Thanks to you I look at life with a certain detachment and see how it all makes sense. Ani, I couldn't have asked for a better adoptive mother. Your love feeds my soul. Wanda, you are a true survivor girl. I love it that you always say you got it and then do it. Thanks for all the last-minute technical assistance. Belisa, your wisdom and *cariño* are contagious. Thank you for sharing it, even in those awkward places—buying shoes, or weird hours—your therapy made sense. A shout out to my *hermanas, las reinas* of sóloella.com, Edna, Luz María, Teba, Adriana, Erica, Christine, Ceci, Gonzalo, and Clara. The A-team if there ever was one. Father Barrios, I really wish that you had been my priest growing up but I am glad that you are in my life now. You restored my faith in "the church." My girls Lee, Sandra Garcia, Tania, Nina, Marta Lucia, Mari; the fabulous Lipsters, especially Elaine, Mia, Evelyn, Gloria; the *mujeres* of Grupo de Café, Jessie, Yexenia, Arlene and Amparo Silva, Margaret, and Dr. Emilio Carrillo. Dr Yvette Martas, you outdid yourself. Thank you to the hundreds of Latinas and Latinos I met along the way who took the time to humor me and share the joyful, sad, and frustrating stories of your lives. Cashiers, bank tellers, waitresses, cab drivers, accountants, nurses, ice cream vendors, social workers, teachers, cops, secretaries, flight attendants, and so many others. Complete strangers who just opened up to me. Thanks for the love and the conversations. Every single one of you confirmed why this book had to be written.

Thank you, Christy H. and Ed Lewis, for giving me the opportunity to lead *Latina Magazine*. And thank you to Ada and Johan for giving me the chance to help create a cyber-space for us in sóloella.com.

Thanks to my team at Three Rivers Press. What a professional and fabulous group of talented publishing gladiators. Carrie Thornton, the warrior, held the fort down when Becky went off to become a *mamá*. I knew I was blessed then. I could not have asked for a more supportive and talented ally. You are a true pro and an "*hermana*" under the skin. Thanks also to Trisha Howell, Lauren Dong, Joy Sikorski, Phillip Patrick, Brian Belfiglio, Melissa Kaplan, Pamela Roskin, Debbie Koenig, Lindsay Mergens, Andrea Rosen, and Jill Flaxman.

Finally, I must acknowledge and give thanks to Dios, los Santos, and my ancestors who guide me and send *bendiciones del más allá*. Every day you confirm and affirm my faith.

Bendiciones, God bless!

Contents

INTRODUCTION

The Joy of Being Nueva Latina

For most of our lives the lesson is to love ourselves even more deeply, especially because we are the survivors of colonization…that's our fight against injustice!

PATRISIA GONZÁLES, CHICANA-KIKAPU WRITER

I am a proud Latina. I am a proud American. I am *not* exotic. I am two cultures in one fabulous, curvaceous, *café-con-leche* body. I own English. I dream in Spanish. On most days, I'm delighted to explain this marvelous heritage to the curious and clueless who ask questions like, "So Sandra, what *are* you?" Other days I just repeat to myself, "I am what I am."

But I want to tell *you* what I am, because I think once I do, you'll understand why I've written this book–*para ti, mujer!*

As a Puerto Rico–born and U.S.-raised woman, I am layers of history that speak of beaches and snowflakes, rain forests and tenements, Spanish and English, spicy food and fast food, hip-hop and congas, apple pie and flan. I have two homes–an America that sometimes refuses to accept me as a legitimate daughter, and a Puerto Rico that sometimes denies me when my Spanish fails me.

For as long as I can remember, I always yearned to belong neatly to just one of them. But greater forces were at play. Puerto Rico is a U.S. territory with unresolved political and identity issues that date back more than a century. It's neither a state nor a sovereign nation, but an in-between political entity called a "commonwealth"–a euphemism for "colony." Puerto Rico is still trying to answer profound political questions about who it is as a nation—as a people and as a collection of individuals. We are simultaneously part of the United States and a member nation of the twenty countries that make up Spanish-speaking Latin America. When I think of Puerto Rico's political dilemma, I am reminded of an old Mexican *dicho:* "Poor Mexico—so close to the U.S., so far from God."

I am a Latina who was born into a borderland and raised in a cultural middle. When I was a little girl, my family—my mom, two sisters, and two brothers—made its way north. My mother was a seamstress, but when the factory where she made sneakers (Pro-Keds) closed down, she packed up suitcases full of tropical clothes and we left El Tuque, the small fishing village we called home. We moved to the immigrant working-class town of Jersey City, New Jersey, where some of our other relatives had settled years earlier. Some say that the best thing Jersey City has to offer is a view of Manhattan, but it was there that I became a Jerseyrican—a combination of American and *boricua* from New Jersey.

There was no such thing as bilingual education in my public school, or even English as a Second Language; it was strictly sink or swim. (Ironically, the school was named in honor of Roberto Clemente, the Puerto Rican baseball legend. Go figure!) But as the daughter of strong and clever people, I learned English quickly. Unfortunately, I also learned to forget Spanish—though I picked up a lot of Spanglish. Lunch, for example, became *lonche;* roof, *rufo;* the building's superintendent, *el super.*

Though I was quickly absorbing mainstream *americana* ways, everything in my Jersey home spoke fluent Latino. The food, the music, the language, *la familia*'s deep religious fervor, *las fiestas, las novelas,* the traditions. Even the house decor screamed Latino—from the plastic-covered sofas and the pictures of *virgencitas* to the thousands of ceramic figurines of elephants, angels, and *coquís,* Puerto Rico's thumb-size singing frogs.

My barrio friends were fellow *boricuas,* Dominicans, Cubans,

Ecuadorians, and other South and Central Americans, but also Irish, Polish, Asians, and Italians. It wasn't so much a melting pot as a big mixed *ensalada*.

My Latino friends and I had different accents when we spoke our broken Spanish, but we shared the same basic cultural Latino customs: family is blood, have faith in *Dios* and church, all *viejitos* are respected, girls are of the home, boys not. English was like a glue for us; it held the different Latin American *banderas* together. I remember a lot of warmth and *cariño* in this very diverse Latino immigrant community.

Before long, I became the family translator. And just as quickly as I was learning to own the English language, I was embracing American behaviors—the attitude, the fashions, the music, and, *ay, Dios mio,* the independent and "unbecoming" *gringita* habit of always expressing my opinion! Growing up, I found it a challenging task to explain myself to *Mami*. It didn't help that she never really learned English and I was quickly losing my Spanish; she never accepted what she called this *americana* in me. She wanted me to be her idea of a good Puerto Rican girl forever.

But I was becoming something else: a new breed, a new woman, a confluence of Pan-Latino consciousness and American influences: *yo me convertí en una nueva latina.*

Identifying as Latina was a politically conscious move on my part. I understood "Hispanic" to be a term made up by the U.S. government, so I didn't want anyone labeling me that way. On the other hand, the friendlier "*puertorriqueña*" and "Jerseyrican" described only parts of me, not the whole.

As a Nueva Latina I am a combination of all of the Latinos I came of age with: Mexican Americans, Cuban Americans, Tejanas, Chicanas, Dominicans, and Central and South Americans, as well as the African Americans, Asian Americans, and Anglos who I call friends. As a Nueva Latina, I am three languages: English, Spanish, and Spanglish. I embrace fast food as well as (and more often than) home-cooked feasts. My opinion counts—within my family and out-

> Immigrant parents send their children to school (simply, they think) to acquire the skills to "survive" in America. But the child returns home as America.
>
> —RICHARD RODRÍGUEZ, *DAYS OF OBLIGATION: AN ARGUMENT WITH MY MEXICAN FATHER*

side it. I stand up to authority when I need to, with my eyes firmly planted on those I challenge. I refuse to look away in shame or fear. I never walk with my head bowed, like those campesinos made so famous by the great painter Diego Rivera. Blood is sacred. I honor it by honoring me. I own my body; as much as I believe in God, it is not his place to tell me when and with whom I shall share it. I am neither a martyr nor a *sirvienta*. I refuse to be defined solely by how well I cook a plate of arroz con pollo or how nicely I can keep house. My Latina femaleness is beyond the walls of my *casa* and womb. Are you feeling me yet? I am—we are—indeed a new breed. We are new women. Calling myself Latina (instead of, say, "Puerto Rican" or—*no lo quiera Dios*—"Puerto Rican American") means validating and celebrating the fact that I feel closer kinship with a Chicana raised in Los Angeles or a Tejana raised in San Antonio than I do with a Puerto Rican woman raised in Ponce, where I was born. Everything, from our survival in America's schools to Univision and *The Brady Bunch,* has made us *comadres.* Not long ago my son reminded me of this powerful reality experienced by so many of us.

He was watching a kids' show on television and started screaming that the Puerto Rican kid had won a pie-eating contest. I rushed to the living room and saw that a boy named Luis Jiménez, draped in a Mexican flag, had devoured fifteen pies in two minutes.

I said, "Listen, baby, this kid isn't Puerto Rican. He has the Mexican flag draped over him, so I think we can safely assume that he's Mexican American."

My son looked at me with a cocked eye, as only a little kid can, and said, "It's the same thing, Mom!" He understood the difference— he knows the colors of both the Cuban flag (his dad's side) and the Puerto Rican flag—but he saw parts of himself in that other little brown boy, and could celebrate the boy's victory as his own. This is what has happened to us, the sons and daughters of Latin America's immigrants—a feeling of Pan-Latino consciousness and kinship. We are an *hecho en América* reality.

So sure, as I said at the get-go, Latinas in the United States battle racism, discrimination, border harassment, racial profiling, police brutality, invisibility, and exploitation. We battle old-country traditions that sometimes stifle us. Yet despite—or maybe because of—all the external and internal *luchas,* U.S. Latinas are among the fiercest and strongest women I know. We or our foremothers crossed oceans, rivers, and time zones and survived nightmares to get to America, and we continue to survive and thrive *en América.* We raise families in homes and neighborhoods deemed dysfunctional by society, and look great while we're doing it. We've made up a new language, Spanglish. We've made up a new culture with a synergy of rhythms old and new. We've made up new rules that combine Mom and Abuela's old ways with new and more modern ones. We are true survivors. And that is because U.S. Latinas—those of us who speak Spanish and those of us who don't—are a new breed, and the diversity of our faces, values, and traditions is at the heart of the American future.

As a Nueva Latina I pledge allegiance to both parts of my soul, the "American" *and* the Latin American within. But no matter how warmly I embrace my inner Anglo or African American *chica,* there are some things that I can do only in my native tongue: I curse, dream, and make love in *español.* And it's physical, too—I can go only so many days before my body craves *pasteles, arroz con habichuelas, mole* chicken, and anything with chiles; or my soul yearns for an Ismael "Maelo" Rivera salsa or Juan Gabriel ballad.

Comadre connection

There are a total of 140,154,000 women in the United States.

> 98,584,000 are non-Hispanic white.
> 25,201,000 are non-Hispanic other.
> 16,369,000 are Latinas.

There are 16,369,000 Latinas.

> 10,582,000 are Mexican.
> 2,526,000 are Central and South American.
> 1,496,000 are Puerto Rican.
> 669,000 are Cuban.
> 1,095,000 are other Hispanic.

> 30 percent of the Latina population is under fifteen years old.
> 70 percent of the Latina population is fifteen years and older.

The biggest single group is thirty-five to forty-four-year-old Latinas who comprise 15.2 percent (2,493,000) of the Latina population.

Coming to terms with my cultural identity—and feeling comfortable with the different parts of me that make me who I am—has been an emotional roller-coaster ride. During my adolescence, surrounded by my very Latino neighborhood and family, identity was a nonissue; my struggles then were around acculturation. I was not allowed to date, unlike my non-Latina friends; I was expected to stay a virgin until I married. And even if I went to college and embarked on some fabulous career, if I ever hoped to be a complete woman I'd have to marry, have kids, and cook a mean *arroz con gandules*.

It wasn't until I got to college, when I encountered a larger America, that being a Latina came to feel like a burden. I continually had to explain myself to strangers. I often felt that I had to choose sides: white or black. This country's obsession with race and nationality didn't allow me to celebrate the joy of being Latina.

Many of us go around unaware that we carry baggage that prevents us from being proud of *la raza* and feeling entitled to the riches this country has to offer. Too many of us adopt a form of cultural denial—for instance, by not using an accent on our name, either because we never knew it carried one or because "it doesn't look right." We even go to lengths to Americanize our Latino surnames: Garcia becomes something that sounds more like Garsha, or Jiménez is pronounced "JIM-uh-nez." We are quick to claim our Spaniard *abuela* and deny the *india* or *africana* one. And for those of us who grow up in the suburbs with very few Latino families around, the burden to fit in, the discomfort that sometimes we are made to feel because we are Latino, is even greater.

The Compadre Connection

There are 133,933,000 men in the United States.

95,049,000 are non-Hispanic white.
22,448,000 are non-Hispanic other.
16,435,000 are Hispanic.

There are 16,435,000 Latinos.

11,120,000 are Mexican.
2,216,000 are Central and South American.
1,463,000 are Puerto Rican.
631,000 are Cuban.
1,005,000 are other Hispanic.

31.1 percent (5,108,000) of Latino men are under fifteen years old.
68.9 percent (11,327,000) of Latino men are fifteen years old and over.

I understand why some of us have trouble being proud of our heritage. We've grown up in an America that sees us in terms of negative stereotypes or doesn't see us at all. And it doesn't matter how much our *familias* hammer on about "*raza* pride" either. At some point or another, we start to doubt that our heritage is all that great.

I have a friend who grew up in a border town in Texas, the state we all know was once part of Mexico. When she was growing up her parents did not want her to speak Spanish outside the home. They didn't want her to be a victim of the vicious discrimination that they had to endure, so Spanish became a secret family language that no one besides *la familia* should know about. Ultimately, she was taught to forget her people's language, but her parents' good intentions didn't spare her anything. Gringos assumed she could speak Spanish; Latinos questioned her identity because she couldn't roll her *r*'s. Today my *amiga* is in Spanish-language immersion classes, trying to claim a heritage that was denied her. And what happened to her is far from unique.

Portrait of Our Latino Nation: Spicing up the U.S. of A.

In the year 2000, out of a total U.S. population of 281,421,906 people, Hispanics comprised 12.5% of the population, or 35.3 million people.

There are:
   211 million whites, or 75.1%;
   35.3 million Hispanics, or 12.5%; and
   34.7 million blacks, or 12.3%.

Watch us grow
The number of Latinos increased by a whopping 12.9 million between 1990 and 2000. In other words, our population grew by 58 percent in ten years. (Of course, this takes into account only those the government counted.)

According to projections, the Latino population will nearly triple, from 35.3 million in 2000 to 98.2 million in 2050. Under this scenario, one in every four Americans will be descended from a Latino.

THE COCONUT I WAS, THE MANGO I'VE BECOME

As a college student, I tried changing my name to Sandi Rodgers (Rodríguez is my maiden name). When I told my mom of my decision, I think she thought alien professors had abducted her *hija*. My

Latinos in the U.S.A.

Out of the 35.3 million Hispanics:
   20.6 million are Mexican;
   10 million are South and Central
     American;
   4 million are Dominican or other
     Hispanics*
   3.4 million are Americans of Puerto Rican
     descent; and
   1.2 million are of Cuban ancestry.

*"Others" are Hispanics who did not specify a nationality.

brothers and sisters, who'd stayed in Jersey City, thought I was trying to "go white." In the pain and process of finding myself, I just wanted to blend in. I thought with a different name, a less Latino name, I could erase history and everything that made me feel "less than." I hated always being "other," or "exotic." (I certainly never saw myself as exotic, even though others did, and still do!) Any of these feelings sound familiar?

So for several years I was a coconut—brown on the outside, "white" on the inside. In other words, I had a serious *blanquita* complex. I even picked up a silly California Valley girl accent to cover up my Spanish-Jersey-urban rhythm. Can you imagine? All this because I wanted to "fit in." Later, still trying to find my way, I adopted a so-called black attitude and embraced everything urban and black. I felt closer to the cause and pain of my African American sisters. And I could certainly claim African heritage, since my father is Afro-Boricua. I claimed anything but Puerto Rican heritage, anything but Latino roots.

Thank God my mother, my friends, and my family finally knocked some sense into me! Through them, I got history lessons; doses of my native culture through art, music, and storytelling; trips to my homeland and other Latin American destinations; and, more important than anything, love—love of myself and my people, which helped me heal the wounds of cultural battle. Today I can proudly reclaim my culture, and I do—every day.

I finally came to understand that this cultural amalgam is a gift, a marvelous and exquisite joy. I can take pleasure in this Pan-Latino joy within and all around me: the music, the families, the racial diversity— *las indias, las mestizas, las negras, las rubias, las morenas, las bajitas, las flacas, las gorditas*—the *novelas,* the food. *Ay, que rico,* our food! Driving in my car, I flip from *salsa* to rock 'n' roll to *boleros* to *rancheras* to ele-

So, you *no hablas español?*

Maybe you are a Latina who does not speak Spanish. And because of this you have been penalized by purists who refuse to accept you as a legitimate Latina daughter. Maybe you have been called a fake Latina because your last name is Rodríguez but you can't roll your r's. Too many of us have accepted the line put out by these cultural police—that it's sad or even disgusting that a Latina *no habla español*. But here is the truth: you alone have the power to define yourself a genuine Latina. No one else is entitled to make that judgment. It's your right to feel included in the larger *familia* of Latinos, and to claim that heritage. It doesn't matter how many generations your family has been here, no matter how much of an accent you have or don't have, no matter what corner of America you were born or raised in, and no matter how much Latino blood makes up your lineage—a quarter, half, or the whole *enchilada*! The bottom line is that our Latina-ness goes beyond borders and the ability to speak Spanish.

Sometimes it's our own people who seek to divide, to define who can rightly claim Latino heritage. Those purists have it all wrong. Spanish is indeed a way to connect with our heritage. It unlocks family secrets, *raza* secrets, and soulful *secretos*. But as special and important as speaking Spanish may be, too much hurt and discomfort has been caused to those of us who, for reasons that can fill another book, simply don't speak it. Spanish is only one among a slew of cultural connections.

To me, the question of language is a personal one. If you want to speak it, to better connect to your lineage or to discover the joy of reading Gabriel García Márquez in Spanish, *hechale con ganas*—I guarantee you a new world of personal joy. (There is also an economic benefit to speaking Spanish. The United States is currently the fifth-largest Spanish-speaking nation in the world, so speaking, writing, and understanding Spanish *will* open new career doors—see chapter 10.) But if you don't want to take it up, or you have tried and "failed," or you want to but don't have the time right now, you are still as legitimately part of the *familia* as those who speak our mother tongue. This book is not about who doesn't belong; it's about who belongs. And if you have picked up this book and it speaks to you, *hermana*, you belong.

The median age for Hispanics: 25.9 years. The median age for the entire U.S. population: 35.3 years. Within our group, this is the breakdown, *los más viejitos son los Cubanos:*

Mexican	24.2 years
Puerto Rican	27.3 years
Central American	29.2 years
Dominican	29.5 years
South American	33.1 years
Spanish	36.4 years
Cuban	40.7 years
Other	24.7 years

vator music to hip-hop, and it feels great that a little of me lives in of all these diverse worlds. I find joy in the laughter, the ancient spirits, the *bochinche* or *chisme,* the cadence, the *cariño,* and the *chistes* of our people.

For so many years I worried that my *latinidad* was a handicap, an obstacle I'd have to climb over or walk around every day in my career. Now I see that accepting myself—Latina hips, skin, accent, and everything else—has been the key to my personal and professional success. The power that self-affirmation has had in my career and personal life is nothing less than remarkable. There is extraordinary power in embracing, openly, publicly, and proudly, one's *latinidad.*

Soy Latina, si—but I'm different from Latinas a generation ago. My lifestyle reflects a combination of Old World beliefs and new American ways. I light candles to my *santos* and *virgencitas,* and have parties for my dead ancestors. I've taught my son to leave grass and water for pretend camels and their Three Kings, who in turn leave presents under his bed. While I celebrate the individual warrior in me—as the "me generation" was taught to do—my family is still like a fortress. They lift me and ground me; they're as important to my life as water is to a growing flower. Mom, sisters, brothers, and best friends go into the equation when I have to make major life decisions. Sometimes blood comes first, even at the expense of my personal priorities. So much of me is comfortable with Old World values.

But the schizophrenia kicks in when that Old World clashes with my New World. I am an unabashed feminist. I employ a cleaning lady. I have hired a nanny. I am not defined by the house that I keep nor the man and son that I so deeply love. I am not my mother or *abuelas,* nor do I want to be, though I love and respect them dearly.

I do not believe that being a *sacrificada* is a noble thing. I am deeply spiritual, but I don't go to church three times a week, as Mom does. I have learned to challenge those in positions of power over me (first teachers, then college professors, and finally bosses) when I'm not treated fairly. When I worked in television, if I hadn't looked my boss in the eye and told her why I should produce the next special, I would not have won an Emmy in 1995.

Diosas de las Américas

Mama Kilya (or **Mama Quilla**) is an Incan goddess who regulates the festival calendar and all matters of time. She is also a prophetic *diosa*, often warning of impending danger through eclipses. She is the daughter of Viracocha, the Supreme God and creator of all that is Incan. She is the wife of Inti, the sun god. When the moon was under an eclipse, the people viewed this as a time when Mama Kilya was in danger. They felt she was under attack from a mountain lion or snake, and they would scream at the top of their lungs and whip their dogs so they would bark and howl, in hopes of scaring off the predator. They would also throw their spears and shoot their arrows at the moon to try to frighten away the beasts attacking her.

I see ways in which old Latino traditions and values have morphed with my new Latina American lifestyle in almost every area of my life. And as uncomfortable and challenging as that constant reconciling can be, I have no desire to reject it—that daily synthesizing makes me me; and it makes you you. You are a special blend of *tradición* and the modern. Today's Latinas are blessed to live in a time when it doesn't have to be either/or, because it can be both: American y Latina, career woman and good *hija*. We have choices, and can carve out lifestyles that fulfill our individual dreams and goals without *peros* or, *ay, bendito,* shame or guilt.

Where we hang our hats, by state

California	10,966,556
Texas	6,669,666
New York	2,867,583
Florida	2,682,715
Illinois	1,530,262
Arizona	1,295,617
New Jersey	1,117,191

The fastest-growing county in the fastest-growing state, Clark County, Nevada, home to Las Vegas, doubled in size to 1.4 million, largely from a Hispanic influx.

We are so racially diverse that for non-Latinos, and surprisingly even some Latinos, this diversity can be confusing. Our skin color ranges from the whitest shade of pale to the darkest shade of ebony, including everything in between. I happen to be a *café con leche* shade. What are you? And then there's the range of our body shapes. From the Selena and Jennifer Lopez big *nalgonas* type to the plumpness you see in Botero's paintings to the *flacas* you see in some women's magazines and on TV (if not in real life!). And our hair texture is just as varied: it is Chinese-straight to African curly; it is blond, red, brown, black, and any shade made by Clairol!

Unfortunately, many of us still have superficial prejudices about who "qualifies" as Latina. My friend, a psychologist, told me that after she dyed her hair blond, someone called the office asking to speak to a Latina doctor and the receptionist told the caller that there were no Latinas in the office—my friend did not qualify as Latina since she was a "blond." Dark Latinas get it in other ways. Another *amiga,* a marketing director, gets so frustrated when she meets fellow Latinos who marvel at how this "black woman" speaks such great Spanish—they think it's so cool that a "sister" has learned their tongue! My friend constantly has to explain, *"Pero, soy Latina!"*

The fact is, Latinas embody every difference in the world. Some of us are married (to men or to women), some are single and happy, some are housewives, some are single moms, and some are childless by choice. We are straight, gay, bi, and undecided. Some of us live in the barrio where our great-grandparents settled; others have moved to the suburbs or across the country. We are descendants of people who were here before this country was a country, or just recently arrived from south of the border. Some of our parents speak no English, some speak not a lick of *español,* and many others switch easily between Spanish and English. (I fall into that last category. Where are you in the language spectrum?) We are many women, with many faces and many languages. But as different as we are, there are some things nearly all Latinas share no matter where we came from or when: *familia* (think how much we love our *abuelitas*); faith (think how much we love our *virgencitas* and *santos* and *papa Dios*); love of food; love of music; and the gender politics that insists *las mujeres son de la casa, los hombres de la calle* (no matter how much our lives as Nueva Latinas disprove it). *¿Me entiendes?*

Another thing we share is a particular ignorance of our own place and value in "the big picture." The truth is that Latinas and Latinos have inspired America. We have been instrumental in making it the powerful nation it is today, and we have changed American culture—not just since the "Latin Explosion" but from the very beginning. From California to New York, to Texas, Illinois, and Florida, our contributions to this nation in the arenas of politics, entertainment, sports, food, music, fashion, literature, and style have been enormous.

The Spanish-speaking nations of the Americas at a glance, por si acaso...

Argentina	Guatemala
Belize	Honduras
Bolivia	Mexico
Chile	Nicaragua
Colombia	Panama
Costa Rica	Paraguay
Cuba	Peru
Dominican Republic	Puerto Rico
Ecuador	Uruguay
El Salvador	Venezuela

España, of course, is *La Madre Patria,* part of the Old World in Europe.

We are the largest ethnic group in this nation. Demographers predict that by the year 2050, four out of every ten Americans will be of Latino descent. But we don't have to wait until then to be influential. Our buying power is already in the billions each year. Politically we can swing national elections. (Have you noticed how Anglo politicians love to drag out their one distant Latino relative to get our attention and—they *think*—our votes?) There is no need or reason to reject our language, culture, looks, music, or heritage, because all those things *are* America!

HOW TO USE THIS *LIBRO*

I first dreamed of having a book like this to turn to when I was in my teens. I felt that the Church was stifling me, I had ongoing battles with my mom, and I wanted to do all the normal things my non-Latina friends were doing: hanging out, dating, and wearing what my mom considered wild clothes. I felt as if I was different from everyone, all alone, and I wished there were a book to show me I wasn't; to show me that I was one of many, and that I belonged. This is the book I wished for.

In it, I share my experiences, the experiences of other Latinas, and the "rules" I've come up with for living a rich and rewarding Latina life. There's no "right way" to read this book: you can pick and choose chapters that interest you most or read from cover to cover. Along the way, you will find inspiring quotes, sidebars, quizzes, and interesting information about our Latino and Latina population. I suggest that you have a pen handy for making notes, and don't be afraid to write in this book. Make it yours by highlighting, underlining, and circling anything you want. Many of us don't write in our books because that was a cardinal rule in our public school days, but *mija*, this book is yours, for growth, for fun, and for reference. You can also keep a journal while reading it—there's no better way to see yourself grow than when you put pen to paper and reflect on your life. Because *your* Latina experience, like mine, is unique, this book can only guide you to the path of understanding and relishing that experience; only you can make the experience your own.

You will also find recipes, *remedios*, and *baños* of all sorts included in the various chapters. Many of these home remedies were shared by *viejitas, vecinas,* friends, and family members alive and gone, so I've given these *recetas* the names of the women who shared them with me. (Check out Fragancia's hair-growth recipe on page 71, which uses shoe sole and cinnamon. I know it sounds gross, but I've used it and it works!) There are also source lists and references to books I love, all at your fingertips. There are many regional and universal Spanish words and *dichos* peppered throughout the text. You know that there are some things that only Spanish can capture—those wonderful "*abuela*-isms" and bits of folk wisdom we all grew up with.

The first chapter of this "bible" is all about the generation gap between our parents—especially our mothers—and us, their grown-up, independent, and "*gringa*" *hijas*. If your mother is still alive, then you know how much Latina mothers meddle in their daughters' lives. You understand how challenging it can be to choose a lifestyle that may be very different from what they expect or want for us, and you know the role that "*el que dirán*," or "what will they say," plays in their lives, and thus, yours. You've probably wondered at least once how you can be true to yourself without having to ban your disapproving mother (father, *familia*) from your life. And while most of us ultimately survive the pressures of acculturation, a growing number of teenage Latinas feel themselves alone, not understood by their families and the larger society. This chapter addresses all these issues and offers suggestions for dealing with them; it also relates stories of women who've dealt with this, and what worked for them.

The second chapter explores the subject of beauty. Yes, Latinas are beautiful, not just in the racial and ethnic diversity I mentioned earlier but also in our much-imitated and admired sense of *estilo*. Yet so many of us still grow up feeling ugly. This chapter looks at the ways our sense of our own beauty is undermined and offers perspectives to help you fill in those potholes in your self-esteem. You also get my six-step soulful beauty makeover, an easy, do-it-yourself beauty treatment that works from the inside out *and* the outside in.

The third chapter is all about our health. Did you know that the more time we spend in this country, the worse our collective health gets? We top the charts for obesity, sexually transmitted diseases, and cancer, and it's all related to cultural taboos and lifestyle choices. Luckily, each of us has the power to change, and this chapter offers a gift basket of tried-and-true ways to make those changes. I'm living proof that they work, and if you aren't yet, you will be soon.

The fourth chapter, on friendship, is one of my favorites. One way to soften the blows and overcome the challenges we encounter is to surround ourselves with a strong network of Latina friends. This chapter helps you start a Latina "talk circle" in your city or town. My group is called LIPS—short for Latinas In Power, Sort of. What will you call your *grupito*?

Chapter 5 is called "Centering Your Soul: Spirituality Latina Style." Religion and spirituality are at the center of every Latino family, but so much has changed in the way that we, *las nuevas latinas,* practice religion. Do you have an altar? Have you forgotten what *virgencita* you should pray to if you want that job? Is your spiritual path far from the mainstream? Check out the fascinating sidebars that address the concerns of our spiritual lives.

Now, I know that most of you don't need my help in the dating scene. After all, it's true what they say: we are Latin lovers. We know how to catch and keep a good man. But I felt that it was important to let it be known that we do have our own dating rules in the barrio. So read chapter 6, "Secrets of Latina Dating," and let me know if I have missed any of your favorites.

Sexuality plays a big role in our lives, and yet as a community, talking openly and honestly about sex is still a rare occurrence in our families. If your mother was like mine, this topic, the subject of chapter 7, was never discussed except for the expectation that I had to remain a virgin until marriage. My vagina was always referred to by a euphemism. Check out the sidebar of the *cuchie* euphemisms gathered from all over the Spanish Americas! Do *popina, totito,* or *la cosita* ring a bell? In addition, because I feel so strongly that we must start to demystify our vaginas, I included another list of street *cuchie* names in each of our Latin American countries. My mother thought I was being very *sucia* when she overheard a conversation between my sister Mari and me about this sidebar. Mom cautioned that I should be a little more *sofisticada.* But that is the precisely my point, that we should be able to demystify and talk about our vaginas *sin vergüenza* or apologies.

Ay, Dios mio, on love and relationships there is so much to discuss, and I do that in chapter 8. I know that most of our struggles as Nueva Latinas center around relationships with our mates. As Mexican author Angeles Mastretta writes, intelligent women fall in love the way all women do—like complete idiots. The *sirvienta* we didn't know we were comes out too! Yes, I have been there. Have you? However, we have made new rules. And just like there are Nueva Latinas living *la vida buena* out there, there are our counterparts, this beast I call the Nuevo Latino. These Hispanic men have broken tradition and become partners of their Latina girlfriends and wives. Just as we have had to relearn and discard those stifling gender politics about where *las mujeres* belong, so too have many of our Latino brothers.

If you are part of the growing number of Latinas who are dating (or married) outside *la raza,* then chapter 9 is for you. Make sure you give your non-Latino *papi chulo* this quiz.

Chapter 10 is chock-full of information to help you find professional success. Do you have trouble challenging authority? I did, and this is but one of the self-imposed cultural *complejos* that can stymie our careers. So, go ahead: check out how you ask for that raise and promotion without shame.

Chapter 11, on going home, is really about the importance of reconnecting with your homeland—whether this land is now part of the United States or somewhere south of the border or the in the Spanish-speaking Caribbean islands. The land has a special way of allowing for profound spiritual connections. In addition, it allows you to explain yourself better to those who will undoubtedly ask, "So, where are you from?"

Finally, the last chapter is an ode to our little Latina girls. As I look at how much we have accomplished, I can only be saddened by the statistics that place our younger *hermanitas* in a cycle of teenage pregnancy, and by high school dropout charts. If each of us gives back a little of our time to one Latina girl who needs to know a real-life role model, then each of us is helping in their future and our collective Latino future.

It is my hope that this book is one you will share and grow with. Whenever you get that feeling of *Damn, this is hard, I feel so alone,* pick up this book. I guarantee you'll find that it addresses what you're dealing with, offers you tried-and-true suggestions, and steers you to other sources of help. Let this book offer you comfort in the knowledge that you, this Latina who lives simultaneously in two worlds, have a sister *and* a sisterhood of *hermanas* who share your challenges, frustrations, and joys.

While the specifics of your life and mine can't possibly be the same, you'll find that many of the thoughts, experiences, and feelings are; I hope you'll focus on what we share. I don't mind at all when people think I'm Mexican, Dominican, Cuban, Colombian, Chicana, Ecuadorian, Peruvian, Salvadorean, and so on—just like my son with the pie-eating champ, I'm much more interested in what we have in common than where we differ. If we look past the surface, we can all see deep parts of ourselves in one another.

So I encourage you to read with your heart. Some women have shared their lives with me on the condition that their names remain anonymous; many of their stories deal with issues still shrouded in taboo. I respected the anonymity and encouraged them to tell others about their experiences. Read with your heart, and I promise you that you will recognize parts of our collective story in your own life.

One last warning: Sometimes this book digs into subjects that "good" Latina girls aren't supposed to talk about. If these subjects generate sparks, I hope they light a flame of conversation, of caring dialogue between you and your family, friends, and lovers. Because as much as we're a culture of talkers, I don't believe we talk enough about what matters most. In the middle of all the lively

I am blessed to be able to share my story with you; it's my wish that more and more Latinas will be able to share theirs—and that you will share yours. Send me your stories, on family, love, career, motherhood, and faith, to www.thelatinasbible.com.

chatter, there is a culture of *silencio,* a refusal to talk about painful or embarrassing parts of our past. The intention of the silence is rarely to cause hurt, but secrets only make hurt go deeper. Let's start talking with one another, really talking. Let this book and its "rules" be your mentor, your *amiga,* and your *hermana*—and let us show the world that what they've seen of the Nueva Latina so far is just the tip of the iceberg!

Pa' lante, Orale—and go on, girl!

A fierce Latina who made U.S. history

 **Josefina Sierro de Bright** was born in a Mexican border town, Madera, California, in 1920. As the daughter of a *bordera* who served meals to migrant workers, she was exposed to the injustices of farm labor camps from a very early age. She abandoned her studies at UCLA to become a union organizer and soon developed a reputation as a gutsy, flamboyant, and tough-as-nails woman.

In the 1930s and '40s, Josefina organized a sophisticated and intricate underground railroad that returned safely hundreds of Mexican American citizens who had been illegally deported to Mexico by the United States. During the same time, she also served as the executive secretary of El Congreso, one of the first national Latino civil rights organizations in the United States. From this important position, she organized protests against racism in the Los Angeles school system, against the exclusion of Mexican American youths from public swimming pools, and against police brutality. In 1942, she was one of the key figures in organizing the Sleepy Lagoon Defense Committee. This committee was formed to support seventeen Chicano youths being held without bail and on little evidence of the alleged killing of another youth. She was instrumental in the coordination of El Congreso's support for Spanish-speaking workers in the furniture, shoe-manufacturing, electrical, garment, and longshoremen's unions.

CHAPTER ONE

SURVIVING YOUR MOTHER, *LA FAMILIA*, AND *EL QUE DIRÁN*
Without Going *Loca*!

SCENARIO 1: You're almost thirty years old, a college graduate with a nice job, your own apartment, and a love life out of *Sex and the City*. Your dad is coming over for a visit. Do you hide the condoms that are openly and neatly sitting in the bathroom bin or do you leave them right where they are? You decide it's high time that you stop pretending to be a virgin—no more *mentiritas*.

SCENARIO 2: You have been accepted by the college of your choice. The only problem is that the college is located an eight-hour drive away. Your mother begs you to stay, imploring you to not "abandon" her because she needs your help caring for your younger sisters. After her *ataque de nervios*, the pressure is so overwhelming that you forgo your dreams of experiencing dorm life. You end up living at home and commuting to the local college.

SCENARIO 3: You're married with two children, and you and your husband don't want to baptize either of them—you want to raise them in a less traditionally religious way. But every time you visit Mom, she reminds you that you are sinning, and *Dios los cuide*, if the children were to die, they wouldn't enter the kingdom of heaven. Their souls would wander in purgatory forever because of you! *Mala madre, mala hija!*

SCENARIO 4: Your traditional parents dislike your boyfriend. First of all, they think you're too young to have a *novio,* and even if you weren't, he's a bad influence. Despite their furious disapproval, you see him secretly. Then a gossipy *vecina* tells them she saw you French-kissing "that boy" two days ago. All hell breaks lose when you come home. You get a beating. You feel helpless, worthless, and ashamed. You see no escape. Though you have no place to go, you consider leaving home.

Unfortunately, these are not *telenovela* scenes but real life parent-child conflicts happening to Latinas today. You would think that in the forty years since the start of women's liberation, Latino parents would be hip to their daughters' dying their hair purple, piercing their belly buttons, having boyfriends, moving away to college, getting their own apartments, raising their kids with "new" rules, living with *novios,* coming out of the closet, or—yikes!—even having pre-marital sex at thirty. *No, señorita!* Intense melodramas and *cantaletas* are lived every day as more and more of us grow up and embrace "modern" lifestyles and *costumbres* that happen to offend the cultural sensibilities of our parents.

It's a given that every young woman has to deal with the generation gap and her parents, especially her mother, when she begins to *independizarse,* regardless of *raza* or religion. This is the classic *madre-hija* war, part of life's growing pains. But for Latina daughters, these growing pains are complicated by the fact that we have to cross a cultural bridge. We have to learn to deal with mothers (and dads) who were raised not only in a different era but with a different set of customs.

The key to crossing the bridge and surviving the wars without going *loca,* lying, or having to banish your overprotective and meddling traditional mother is understanding and respecting her generation and lifestyle.

UMBILICAL TIES THAT BIND

Our families tend to baby their kids longer than non-Latinos do. The way we nurture our children is one of the things I treasure in our culture. A Latina mother *nunca* kicks her adult daughter out of the house so she can "discover the world" or "be out on her own." In fact, quite the opposite: a good *hija* is expected to live under her family's roof, a virgin the whole time, until she is ready to marry and start a family. Latino parents are doting, loving, and very protective, especially of their girls. However, the downside of this "Latina momma nurturing" is when babying and nurturing extend through college and into our adult lives. No matter how grown up we are, they refuse to "let go." Is your mom like that? If she is, you're not alone—and you should know that the extended umbilical cord has an ancient tradition.

In an old custom practiced by the natives of the American Southwest and northern Mexico, the umbilical cord of a newborn girl is buried under the house so that she will never leave home or stray from her domestic duties. When I read about this, I checked with my mom to see if she'd ever heard of it. To my surprise, she told me that similar rites are performed regularly in Puerto Rico and most parts of the Spanish Caribbean, only it's the placenta of a newborn girl that's buried under the house to ensure that she'll grow up to love the home! My sister Mari, the only one of us not born in a hospital, suffered the effects of this *tradición.* My fisherman *abuelo* buried her placenta under his house a few hours after she was delivered, and, as it turns out, Mari is absolutely the most *hogareña* of my mother's three daughters—a real Martha Stewart type. My mom is convinced that the buried placenta is why Mari (unlike me and Wandi) is so "loving" of *la casa*. Mari only recently found out about the fate of her placenta and wants to plan a trip to unearth the remains! (The running joke in my family is that *my* placenta was thrown into the Caribbean.)

If you or your parents were born in the old country, it might be interesting for you to find out what they did with your placenta or *ombligo*. You may also want to find out if there are any rituals in your family that are meant to keep you close to the bosom or inside the kitchen. It might shed new light on your parents' expectations!

UNDERSTANDING *MAMÁ* AND CROSSING THE GAP

If your mother's identity is like my mother's identity, it's tightly woven to her kids, her grandchildren, her great-grandchildren, the food she cooks, and the house she keeps. My mother always worked outside the home, doing all kinds of odd jobs to put food on the table and clothes on our backs. At one time or another she worked as a hairstylist, a hotel maid, a *pastelera* (*tamalera* to some), and a sneaker seamstress. But her greatest sense of achievement is having raised her children—two boys and three girls—by herself, children who today have successful careers and families of their own. Her greatest joy is cooking up a storm and feeding her family in the home she built with her life's savings.

My mother is a *chingona,* as my Chicana sisters would say—a fierce *boricua* warrior who never takes no for an answer. Though she has a small and stocky frame, in my eyes she was always an *amazona*. She taught me, by her unbreakable strength, resistance, perseverance, and profound Christian faith, how to be the *luchadora* that I am today. I have seen parts of my mother in so many Latina mothers I have met. We have been raised by truly fearless *mujeres* who were in turn raised by awesome *abuelas*. They are emblems of our collective strength.

However—and this is a *big* however—I didn't always appreciate all that my mother was. In fact, my mother and I had so many *batallas* growing up, I thought that as soon as I hit eighteen, I'd never see her again.

As a young Latina coming of age in America, I kept making choices that went against the grain of *tradición*. Nothing I ever did, except excelling in school, seemed to make her happy. The clothing I wore was weird; the way I styled my hair was freaky; the music I listened to was horrible; the friends I had were never good enough; and the *malas costumbres* I was picking up were offensive. Many times I felt as if I were an alien in my own home. The fact that she didn't speak English and I was quickly losing my Spanish made our communication even more difficult. It was so hard to explain myself to *Mamá*. She didn't cut the umbilical cord for a very, very long time, and, bless her heart, she still hasn't stopped meddling in all of my affairs. Was your mom always in your business? Was she worried about *"el que dirán" la gente, la familia, los vecinos?*

When I was young I spent years resenting her and our life together. Now that age and understanding have tempered my anger and I can appreciate the wisdom of the past, I see her for who she is. More important, I'm peaceful enough within myself that I can *accept* her as she is. Are you where you want to be in your relationship with your mother? What do you think it would take for you to get there?

La Familia

In 1999:

> 68% of Hispanic families were married-couple families;
> 24% were maintained by a woman with no husband present;
> 8% by a man with no wife present.

Eight in ten Cuban families were maintained by a married couple in 1999, the highest percentage among Hispanic groups.

OUR MOTHERS OF THE SANDWICH GENERATION

A few months after I became the editor in chief of *Latina* magazine, I received a letter from California freelance writer Juana Vázquez-Gómez. She had written an article in Spanish titled *"Las mujeres de la*

Sandwich Generation"—in an effort to explain herself and her *amigas,* fifty- and sixty-year-old Latina mothers, to the younger readers of the magazine. After reading the article I realized that Juana had explained my mother to me.

"My husband tries to calm me and tells me that I shouldn't be so drastic. My *hija* says, 'Oh, Mother, I don't even want to hear it. Come on, you are strong, you can do it.' And my son consoles me, telling me, 'Come on, Mom, take a big breath, *otro,* another . . .'"

According to Juana, Latina mothers in their fifties, sixties, and above live in a perpetual state of *ansiedad,* pressured from five directions: by their more traditional husbands (our dads); by their mothers (our *abuelas*); by the culture of the country where they were born or raised (especially if they are first-generation immigrants); by their *americano* kids (us); and by the pressures of life in America. If you think you have it bad as a young Latina, *mija,* just think about what life must be like for your mom!

Juana's eloquent piece reminded me of my mom and the many mothers her age I have met over the years. They were raised in countries where Latinas were taught to be *sumisas,* to be dependent on males, and to find identity in their roles as mothers, wives, and

Diosas de las Américas

Yemayá's name in Yoruba means "Mother Whose Children Are the Fish." She is the sea goddess who lives and rules over the seas and lakes. She also rules over maternity, as she is the mother of all. Yemayá is the root of all the paths, or manifestations. She dresses herself in seven skirts of blue and white and, like the profound oceans, she is deep and unknowable. She is the *diosa* of the impenetrable, holding deep, dark, and mysterious secrets.

daughters. Even those who rejected this notion, as my mom did by getting divorced, had few alternative lifestyle possibilities.

Many of these women find themselves in a cultural abyss. We, the *liberada* generation, urge them to be stronger, to stand up to the old *machista* ways, to discover a world outside their homes. Yet they are also pressured by their mothers, and by husbands who don't want them to stray too far from the *mujer tradicional.* Our mothers are expected to toe the line and hold everything together, no matter what. I often wonder if we, *las hijas agrindadas,* who have been privy to a new world of possibilities for women, really understand our mothers' cultural plight. Do we honor their *ansiedad* as well as their *sacrificios*?

Our mothers, *luchadoras* in their own right, raised us to be independent women and to take advantage of the options outside the home. They have sacrificed a lot in search of a better future for us. In the past twenty years, they have seen the possibilities available to us double before their eyes. They have lived to enjoy watching Latina daughters break new barriers and serve as managers, teachers, soldiers, school principals, hospital

Easy Ways to Honor Your *Familia*

• Collect recipes from your eldest relatives and make a calendar or a book with the recipes, then distribute it to your family—it makes a great gift anytime!

• Create a website with family genealogy or family tree information, pictures, funny family anecdotes, *cuentos,* stories of leaving the old country and coming to a new one. Update it with new births, party pictures, and the like.

• Grab a tape recorder and ask your parents what their all-time favorite songs are and what memories those songs inspire. Find the songs and make a tape interspersing the songs with the "interviews." It's another great gift, but you're also recording family history—and what's a Latino family history without music?

• Make a home movie of all the elders sharing their favorite *chistes, cuentos,* riddles, dance moves, and so on. Nothing heavy—this is all for fun; but watch it ten years from now and see if it doesn't bring tears to your eyes.

• Create an address book that includes the birthdays and e-mail addresses of your entire—and I mean entire—family and extended family. Give it as a Christmas gift, or just because.

chiefs, engineers, newspaper publishers, reporters, doctors, university professors, lawyers, judges, governors, members of Congress, and more. They secretly and openly cheer us on, to do the many things they could not do because of cultural or economic circumstances. Go for it, *superate mija,* they encourage, but don't stray too far from home, the family, or the traditions. Despite how delighted they are for us, I can only imagine that these cultural changes are often scary for them. At the same time, the ones needing attention most desperately are in the generation of their granddaughters.

MAMÁ, IT'S LIFE AND DEATH

Some experts point to acculturation issues as central to the rising rate of attempted suicides among Hispanic teenage girls. According to the Centers for Disease Control, two out of ten Latina teenagers between the ages of fourteen and eighteen attempted suicide in 1996. That is double the rates for Anglo or African American teenage girls (21 percent of Hispanic girls, 10.8 percent of African American girls, and 10.4 percent of non-Hispanic white girls). Dr. Luis H. Zayas, a psychologist who heads the Center for Hispanic Mental Health at Fordham University in New York City, who has been studying the phenomenon since the 1980s, says that little is done to address the issue. But early speculation is that these Hispanic teenagers (first, second, and sometimes third generation), are caught in a cultural minefield as they straddle peer pressure and American freedoms while living with parents who are entrenched in Latin tradition.

"These young women are crying out for help," he says. "When things get really bad they feel like they have no alternative, no outlet, other than suicide. The only blessing here is that most of these suicide attempts are *not* successful." Even so, the fact of these attempts is a flashing DANGER sign. The sign is telling us that a new language has to be created so that these young women, who feel so isolated

Love Words That Honor Our Mothers and Grandmas

Even if you are a tenth-generation Latina who does not speak a lick of Spanish, when it comes to our *madres* and *abuelas,* many of us somehow remember the long-forgotten mother tongue, because calling them "Mom" or "Grandma" simply will not do. We make up the most beautiful nicknames for them. What do you call your mother? What about your grandma? Here is a sampling.

For Mother

- *Mami*
- *Mima*
- *Mamá*
- *Mamuchi*
- *Máh*
- *Memo*
- *Mamita*
- *Mamacita*
- *Madre*
- *Mimi*
- *Momo*
- *Vieja*
- *Viejita*
- *Progenitora*
- *Tutin-tanti*
- *Melo*
- *Mamucha*

For Grandmother

- *Abuela*
- *Guela*
- *Buela*
- *Mamagrande*
- *Mairande* (when the little ones couldn't fully pronounce *Mamagrande*)
- *Viejita*
- *Vieja*
- *Ague*
- *Vela* (from *Guela*)
- *Aguelita*
- *Aweca*
- *Awelucha*
- *Mamibuela*
- *Lela* (short for *Abuela*)
- *Lita* (short for *Abuelita*)
- *Nana*
- *Nanita*
- *Mauder* (Spanglish for Mother, from Texas)
- *Melo*
- *Tita*
- *Mami* or *Mamá* with her name

from their families, can be heard and understood without having to resort to suicide attempts.

Since communication is so clearly at the heart of our issues with our parents *and* our children, I cannot stress enough how important it is to give our loved ones the space and security to share with us. In the hopes of modeling a more productive intergenerational dialogue, I have written two letters. One a love letter from a daughter to her mother, asking to be heard. It's the kind of letter I wish I could have given to my mother when I was an adolescent. The second is a letter I wrote to my son, when he entered adolescence. Even though our conflicts are different, I see in our struggles some of the pain my mother felt, and I want to reach out to him in the way I wish my mother could have reached out to me.

Below are sample letters to get you started. (The third letter is a Spanish translation of the first, mom-daughter letter in case your parent—like my mother—does not read in English.) Since every situation is unique, I encourage you to tailor your handwritten letter to the issues that concern you and your loved one. Keep it simple, direct, honest, and loving. A personal touch makes all the difference, so make sure you write and not type or e-mail the letter. You can mail it or leave it in a more personal spot where your mother or the person to whom you are reaching out will find it. (For instance, you can place the letter on her pillow with a rose.) If she doesn't bring up the letter immediately—don't worry—allow several days to pass. Chances are the person is digesting the information. (Bring it up after one week in a moment when the two of you are alone.) While the issues you have with your parent or loved one will probably not be resolved in one letter or in one conversation, this can serve as the "olive branch" that both of you needed. *Suerte.*

Dear Mami,

Before I tell you anything else, I want you to know how very much I love you. But as much as I love you, I have to tell you that our recent fights have been extremely painful for me. I know you want to protect me, but what hurts me most is our inability to understand each other.

I know you're concerned with the recent decisions I've made, the friends and especially the boyfriend I've chosen, the music I love, and my taste in clothes. To you, most of my adult life seems like a misstep. I know that you want the best for me. But Ma, how am I going to learn if I don't make mistakes? I read somewhere that parents need to love their children but not control them; that being a good parent means letting a child make mistakes as well as find solutions on her own. As a mom, you don't always have to step in; just be there so you can come if and when _I_ ask you for help.

I know you don't want to see me suffer, but I suffer more when you don't let me make my own mistakes. Sometimes you're right, sometimes you're not. But it's hard to hear you, let alone obey you, when I feel like you're shaming me. I want you to share your wisdom, but I feel blamed and infantilized when you tell me, "I told you so."

I'm not entirely sure how we can reconcile our differences, but I am sure that I want to. Perhaps we could each take a small step. I promise to listen without judgment to what you have to say, if you promise to couch your <u>consejos</u> in the language of suggestion. Please don't be so accusatory.

I know this is hard; I know this dialogue we're attempting is not like any you ever had with your mother, and I also know that I can be a very difficult daughter. But I want so much for you to be proud of me for who I've grown into. I want to feel that I can share the truth of my everyday life with you. Can we each try to love each other enough to let go of the things that divide us? We have so much to give each other, and my fondest wish is that we learn to accept each other enough to accept those gifts.

With love,

Your hija

Dear BJ,

When I was your age and my mother and I would argue, I would always ask myself whether she loved me. It was such a scary thought to think that my _mami_ didn't love me that I never asked her. Now it seems silly to think that the woman who gave birth to me, who made _avena_ in the mornings and rice and beans at night, the woman who washed my clothes and blessed me every morning and night, didn't love me. But my doubt was real when we fought, or when I thought she was ashamed of me.

So the other night, when you asked me if I loved you, I was overjoyed. Your asking gave me the opportunity to tell you directly that the answer is a huge YES—I love everything about you! My love for you started a long time ago, when I first heard your little heartbeat inside my belly. When you were born and I saw what a funny, beautiful baby you were, I really thought I might burst from loving you. Then something happened: I watched you take your first baby steps and heard you say your first baby word ("Mama!"), and I loved you even more. Then you started preschool and put your underwear on all by yourself, and I loved you even _more._ Then you turned five, six, seven, eight, nine, ten . . . and every single day, as you got bigger, smarter, and funnier, I realized I loved you still more.

I want you to know that I love you when you're mad at me and when you're happy with me. I love you when you do your homework, and when you forget to study for a quiz. I love you when your room looks like a hurricane hit and when you clean it up so a friend can sleep over. I love you when you stink, when you smell good, when you dance, when you sleep. I love you when you're in school, when you're in the park, when you're with your friends. I love you when you are rushing to school and forget your Metro pass and I have to take you in a taxi, and I love you when you forget to walk Pepita and she makes it in one of my favorite shoes. I guess what I'm trying so desperately to say is that you're my beautiful, wonderful _hijo_ and I love you no matter what you're doing or not doing.

I admit that as you started to grow up it was hard for me to accept that you wouldn't always need me the way you did when you were a baby, but then I realized something equally wonderful. I realized that you don't belong to me. You belong to God and the universe, and mostly to yourself. And although realizing that was scary at first, I thank my lucky stars every day that the universe is sharing _you_ with me.

So I apologize for occasionally getting on your nerves! And even though we'll argue sometimes, I never want you to feel like you're alone or can't come to me for sympathy or understanding. Because, as I said before, I love you.

Mami

Mamá querida,

Antes que nada, quiero decirte cuánto te amo. Pero así como te amo, te tengo que decir que nuestras últimas peleas han sido súmamente dolorosas para mí. Sé que quieres protegerme, pero lo que más me duele es nuestra falta de comprensión.

Sé que te preocupan las decisiones que he tomado recientemente, los amigos, y en especial el novio que he elegido, la música que me encanta, y mi forma de vestir. Algunas veces siento que para ti, la mayor parte de mi vida parece haber sido un error. Sé que quieres lo mejor para mí. Pero mamá, ¿cómo voy a aprender si no cometo errores? Leí por ahí que los padres necesitan amar a sus hijos pero no controlarlos; que el ser buen padre significa permitir que tu hija cometa errores y encuentre soluciones por sí misma.

Sé que no quieres verme sufrir, pero yo sufro más cuando tú no me permites errar. A veces tienes razón, otras no. Pero es difícil escucharte—y más aún obedecerte—cuando siento que me quieres avergonzar, que me acusas y no me escuchas. Yo quiero que compartas tu sabiduría, pero siento que me culpas y me tratas como a una niña cuando me dices: "Te lo advertí".

No sé exactamente cómo podemos reconciliar nuestras diferencias, pero estoy segura que quiero lograrlo. Quizás ambas debamos dar un paso adelante. Para empezar, puedo prometerte escuchar sin juzgar, si tú prometes ofrecerme tus consejos como sugerencias y no como acusaciones.

Sé que esto es difícil; sé que el diálogo que estamos tratando de alcanzar no se parece en nada al tipo de comunicación que tuviste con tu mamá, y sé también que puedo ser una hija muy difícil. Pero anhelo tanto saber que te sientes orgullosa pues crecí y alcancé todo lo que he logrado hasta ahora. Quiero sentir que puedo compartir la verdad de mi vida diaria contigo. ¿Podríamos tratar de amarnos mútuamente lo suficiente como para deshacernos de las cosas que nos separan? Tenemos tanto que ofrecernos mútuamente. Y mi mayor anhelo es que aprendamos a aceptarnos lo suficiente como apreciar esos regalos.

Con amor,

Tu hija

ADIÓS MAMÁ, I'M OFF TO LIVE LIFE AS A GROWN-UP . . .

When you are among the eight out of ten who do manage to survive adolescence without attempting suicide, that does *not* mean life is smooth sailing. When a Latina daughter is ready to leave the family nest for college, a job across the country, a pad of her own, or a live-in situation with a boyfriend, there is bound to be high melodrama. Although there is some sadness when a daughter leaves her home to be a wife, there is also much pride, excitement, and happiness. But what do we do when our departure is less than traditional? *Vete pero no me olvides* are the words spray-painted on a wall in Tijuana, Richard Rodriguez reminds us in his memoir *Days of Obligation,* a profound reminder from Mother Mexico to all of her children crossing the border to *el norte* not to forget her as they search for a better life in America. That is in many ways what our mothers seem to be saying to their *hijas* as we come into womanhood.

I can remember the pain in my mother's eyes as she said good-bye, leaving me in my first dorm room in college. While I was dreaming of freedom, my mother was breathing *angustia.* She whispered *los hijos son de Dios, no son de uno.* And with those dramatic words, she reluctantly let me go.

College was the first time I had been away from home, but moving to a campus two hours away was not as traumatic for me as it had been for my older sister. As the first to attend college in my family, my sister Mari had to deal with our mother's fears about her daughter living somewhere else. My sister had never even been to a sleepover in anybody's house. Though a welcome opportunity for her children, college was a strange place for my mom. Daughters in Latino families live in the bosom and protection of our families until they marry a good man. So by the time I was ready to leave, my mother had already survived the pain of seeing my oldest sister become pregnant at fourteen and the next oldest go away to college. Although watching us leave home was hard, my mother, who didn't finish high school, saw college as a place of great opportunity. What she wasn't so happy about was campus life. In her mind I was going to live with *gente extraña.* She was convinced that without her influence, we would become strangers—that we would come back *hechas unas extrañas,* with strange *costumbres.*

A college education is still a big deal in our community. Only 53 percent of the Latino high school students who graduated in 2000 enrolled in a college the following fall. While that is a promising sign of progress, the reality is that the number accounts for a little more than a half since a staggering 47 percent don't attend college. (We all know the value of a college diploma in today's economy.) And even when we do go on to higher education, it's not piece of *pan dulce.* At the City University of New York, for example, a staggering three quarters of Puerto Rican students leave college within the first two years. And Latinas have the distinction of being the least likely of all women to complete a bachelor's degree, dropping out of college in the first two years.

So when one of us gets the opportunity to go away, it's a big celebration. However, that doesn't mean that our families—especially first-generation families—necessarily understand why we need to *move* three cities away to make it a reality.

My friend Lee tells me that she was determined to study at Georgetown University in Washington, D.C., but her father refused. He wanted her to attend a community college in New York City, close to home.

She remembers the melodrama to this day. "I was in the bathroom with my acceptance letter, crying. My dad didn't understand the difference between a city college and Georgetown. To him it was all the same," she says. When her dad, who had worked hard as an elevator operator to pay her

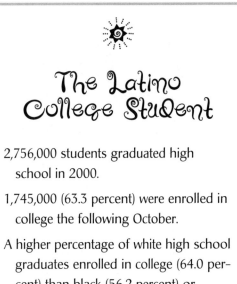

The Latino College Student

2,756,000 students graduated high school in 2000.

1,745,000 (63.3 percent) were enrolled in college the following October.

A higher percentage of white high school graduates enrolled in college (64.0 percent) than black (56.2 percent) or Hispanic (53.0 percent) high school graduates in 2000.

The College-Age Latina

In 2000, there were 1,289,000 Latinas between the ages of sixteen and twenty-four. Of those, 488,000 were enrolled in college, while 802,000 were not. On the other hand, there were 1,184,000 Latinos of the same age. Four hundred thousand were enrolled in college while a greater majority, or 784,000, were not.

The College Latino Student

In 2000, there were a total of 2,474,000 Hispanics (both sexes) aged sixteen to twenty-four.

Enrolled in college: 888,000
Enrolled full-time, 2-year college: 233,000
Enrolled part-time, 2-year college: 100,000
Enrolled full-time, 4-year college: 389,000
Enrolled part-time, 4-year college: 105,000
Enrolled in graduate school: 60,000
Enrolled in vocational schools: 36,000

Catholic school tuition, wouldn't see reason, Lee resorted to the lowest form of "compromise": blackmail. She gave her dad an ultimatum: "It's either Georgetown or I'm getting pregnant." When *that* didn't work, she enlisted the help of her mother, who was more understanding.

"It wasn't that Mom wanted me to go either, but she understood what it meant for me, she knew how hard I'd worked to get into the school. I remember my mother telling me, 'Give me a week, but don't say anything to your dad.'" A week later her dad relented, and Lee went to Georgetown.

"We made the college trip a family vacation. My dad, mom, and *abuela* went to campus. It was *Abuela*'s first visit to D.C., and she had a grand old time." Today, Lee is an attorney in the Manhattan district attorney's office, and her family couldn't be prouder.

Many college-bound Latinas still go through the pressure of the emotional melodrama that Lee and I lived twenty years ago. Our parents encourage a good education and a go-getter *superación* attitude. But when it comes down to reality, it's *superación* with limits. They can't let go of their *hijas,* and they don't want us to change. Going away to college is a really big issue for those of us who are first-generation daughters or the first in our families to attend university. It's a painful battle to fight, but a deeply necessary one. So if you are in the midst of the college war, check out the *consejitos* for college-bound Latinas sprinkled throughout the rest of this chapter.

EL QUE DIRÁN AND THE GROWN-UP LATINA

Moving away to a dorm is just the first step in living the life of a grown-up Latina. For a long time, every time I walked into *Mami*'s house I felt as if I were twenty-five years old going on twelve. In her eyes, I was still *su hija chiquita*, not a grown woman with a career, a child, and a dog. *¡Qué locura!*

Many of the women I've spoken with express the same thing. Even after they've moved out and started families of our own, the pressure to be a good *hija* doesn't let up.

"You have to pretend a lot," says Erica, who has been on her own since her twenty-third birthday. This is especially true, she says, about your sex life. And all of the grown women admit that the burden of living this double life is draining. Erica was the woman who left the condoms in the bathroom for her dad to see.

"I just felt that it was time that Dad got it. I'm a grown-up. There comes a time when you get tired of living the lies for their benefit," she said. As it turns out, her dad said nothing, choosing either to ignore his daughter's sexual choices or to simply deny the obvious.

Another friend, Carmen, tells me that the first morning her mom called her in her new apartment, she was lying naked in bed with her *novio*. Before she could shush her honey he said something. Her mother, with bionic ears at the other end of the line, immediately asked, "*¿Y quién es ese?*" "Oh, it's the television, *Má.*"

"That was a very bad day," Carmen remembers. Even now she doesn't want me to mention her real name out of fear that her mother might read this book. "I was lying, pretending to be something I wasn't. I felt dirty," she says. "Not because I was having sex with my boyfriend but because I had to lie about it."

> ## consejito
> ### Enlist an Elder Who Has Your Parents' *Respeto*
>
> Lee, who volunteers at a program that helps Latina high school seniors in the South Bronx attend college, tells me how challenging it can be to convince Latino parents of the importance of "going away" to college. Many parents just don't get the difference between a top-tier school far away and a community college where you can live at home.
>
> The solution? Get the help of an adult whom your parents trust and respect: a teacher, a guidance counselor, a nun, a priest, a minister, a *tia*—someone who can explain why going away to college is an opportunity that shouldn't be missed.

List all the reasons—academic reasons—why the college of your choice that is so far away really is the best. Erica, who wanted to be a reporter for as long as she could remember, talked about all the opportunities she would have attending a place that was renowned for its communications program. While learning to educate yourself about why a given school is indeed the best, you also have a responsibility to educate your parents. Though Erica assures me that it was no piece of cake convincing her police officer dad to let her go, because she had involved him in the decision-making process from the beginning—looking at brochures, reading the Barron's college evaluations—he ultimately had to agree with her decision.

Our eQucation

The proportion of Hispanics with a bachelor's degree was 11% in 1998, not significantly different from the 10% at this level of education a decade earlier.

Hispanics account for 11 percent of the general population, yet 14 percent of our nation's elementary and high school students are Hispanic.

So why do we lie? Why do we feel we have to live double lives? For Carmen, Erica, and the many of us who live secret lives, it's because we don't want to hurt, disappoint, or shame our mothers. We want our freedom, but we also don't want our parents to think less of us.

But even the best-intentioned lying carries a heavy price. While we know in our hearts that there is nothing wrong with our lifestyles, whatever these may be, we have grown up being taught just the opposite.

This is why it's so important to reiterate to yourself: "I'm not a bad daughter, or less of a daughter, for living a life that makes me happy." It is honorable to protect your mom's and dad's feelings; they *don't* need to know everything about your grown-up life. What you have to watch out for is that by protecting your mother or your family's sensibilities you don't feel what Carmen often does: that her feelings are being ignored and her self-respect diminished.

If you think the price of lying is too high, there is a simple enough solution: stop. Be sure you are comfortable with the lifestyle you have chosen for yourself—even when these choices have produced major mistakes and even when they provoke your parents' traditions and ways. It's very courageous to flip the script on your clan. Ours is not an individual-centered society; we do things with the family in mind. Sadly, Susana's story is too typical, even today, in the twenty-first century.

She is a thirty-three-year-old Dominicana raised in New York. She hasn't left her house because she is the only one of her seven sisters that is not married.

"It would be unacceptable for me to just move out and live on my own without leaving the same way they did," she says. All her sisters left their parents' home to live with a husband.

"When I meet guys now I don't even waste my time dating. If they are not interested in something serious, then I just move on. It's really sad, because the only reason I want to get married is to get out of Mamá's house." Despite being at her wit's end to get out and live in her own space, why doesn't Susana—who is financially independent—just move out? Why is she willing to risk marrying the wrong man and for the wrong reasons? "I don't want to disappoint Mamá."

For Susana, disappointing her traditional mother would be far worse than marrying the wrong man. And while at times she is saddened by her predicament, she's come to accept her choice. However, I strongly feel that if your sanity and well-being are at stake, you may not have a choice.

Yadira, the woman from "scenario 2" in the beginning of this chapter who gave up dorm life for her melodramatic mother, ultimately decided to buck convention, ignore her mother's tearful pleas, and move in with her boyfriend of four years.

Before she moved in, she explains, "Dad told me straight up that good, decent young women don't live with a man without being married." Now, she says, "My mother calls me crying all the time, telling me that she is afraid that I might be all used up and not marriage material. Both of them fear what *la familia* will say—the *el que dirán*—and that I will not live out my dream to be a writer but instead will lose myself in a sinful relationship."

Despite this intense pressure, and without her parents' *bendiciónes*, Yadira has stayed with her *novio*. And it isn't easy. She is the

consejito

Take Them on a Campus Visit

Take them on a tour of the campus. For my sister (and me) the tour made the biggest difference. For Rossana, now in her senior year at the University of Massachusetts at Amherst, a campus visit was the clincher. She had been accepted to a local premed program in New York City, as well as to the more prestigious program at UMass. Her dad, a taxi driver, was dead set against his daughter going away. *"De ninguna manera,"* he said. *"¡Mi hija se queda aquí!"* Rossana enlisted the help of her mother and guidance counselor and talked her dad—a first-generation Dominican—into visiting both campuses: one a run-down city campus, the other a beautiful secluded and modern facility. He changed his mind immediately when he got to see how many more resources were available to his daughter at the better school. He now proudly tells everyone that his daughter is becoming *una doctora.*

first woman in a family of strict Catholics to do so. Furthermore, the decision is still so complex and difficult for her that she can't bring herself to tell her grandmother. She fears that telling her *abuela* will be so guilt inducing that she might doubt herself and go back on this decision it took her so long to make.

When Yadira shares her story with me, I remind her of what she already knows: she has been blessed with courage. But she tells me that sometimes she is not so sure about that. What she does feel sure about is her conviction not to be unhappy, because some of her biggest life decisions were made to satisfy everyone but herself. She has already sacrificed a great deal by bowing to her family's will and staying home rather than going to college. She simply feels she can't make that mistake again.

Yadira's family is still making her pay for both her decision and her newfound autonomy–*las miradas, los chismes, las indirectas. . . .* Sometimes when she goes to family dinners she doesn't know whether to eat in the kitchen by herself or join the rest of the relatives in the dining room.

"I feel like an outcast, like I am shaming them, but moving out was something that I had to do for myself. At this point, I'm willing to live life without them because tradition and expectation are too stifling. It's come down to them or me."

consejito

Vete Pero No Los Olvides

Some of our parents really do fear that we'll go away and forget them or never come back. No matter how unfounded and ridiculous these fears may seem, it is our job to assuage them. So acknowledge their worries and reassure them. Promise, and make, frequent calls home; visit often; and let them know how responsible you're being in your new environment.

BREAKING UP WITH YOUR FAMILY

When you reach the point Yadira has, when you need your space, be it physical or emotional, you may need to temporarily "break up" with your family. Move forward with your decision without their blessings. Now, I know that this may sound like I am contradicting myself. How can you, on the one hand, respect your parents' *sacrificios*, and, on the other, completely disregard their wishes? Simple:

this is *your* life, and you owe yourself (and your *familia*) the responsibility of living it as *you* choose. The problem, in many cases, is that our mothers do not know how to mother adult *hijas*. As you are coming into your own womanhood, they are also growing into something else—mothers of *luchadoras* just like them! In addition, our parents, especially our mothers, are bound by "*el que dirá la familia, los vecinos, tu padre, tíos, y otros.*" You have to keep face for them.

Many times a "*mamá* divorce" is inevitable. The space that a "temporary divorce" from mom, dad, or the rest of the *familia* creates allows for healing to take place on both sides. It is scary and guilt-ridden, *pero* ask yourself this. Do you want to forgo your dreams for the sake of others? Do you want to be a *vieja* and say "I should have, I could have"? Do you want to rush into a marriage with the "wrong" man just to get out the house? Let go of your dreams because they may wreak havoc? Living for others may lead only to future resentment and disappointment and lost opportunities. *Mija,* as *difícil* as it may feel, as *complicado* as it may get for you, follow your heart's calling.

In the best of cases, this split is *only* temporary, and once your mom realizes you mean business, you can begin the process of negotiating *your* new rules and boundaries.

Adriana, who paid for an apartment while she lived with her *novio* in his place, behind her mother's back, stopped talking to her mother for several months after her mother found out about her secret living situation.

"Things had gotten really bad between the two of us," says Adriana of the relationship with her mother when she returned from college. "She was very involved in my life. There were no boundaries,

consejito

Se Me Va la Niña . . . the House (and Mom) Feel So Empty

Recognize that your departure may signal the beginning of empty-nest syndrome (the term doesn't exist in Spanish, but the feeling does). Dr. Belisa Lozano-Vranich, a New York City psychotherapist specializing in cross-cultural and women's issues, says that many parents experience feelings of loneliness when their children leave home. Mothers especially are susceptible to feelings of worthlessness, panic, and depression. While you're rejoicing over your newfound freedom, they're feeling just the opposite; it's no coincidence that many marriages fall apart when the kids leave. The departure of children can cause a vacuum that some couples feel incapable of filling.

One way to ease the pain is staying in touch. If you're the youngest, try to get your siblings involved. Take turns with older siblings visiting *Mami* during your first year away. You might even help her find a hobby. I have one friend who bought her mother a dog when she moved out. Believe it or not, it worked wonders. A little extra sensitivity might help your mother and father more than you know.

consejito

Te Quiero, Mom

Remind your mom that you love her. I know this sounds redundant, but your mom needs to hear it again and again from you. Find the words and the moment to convey that your choice to move away, while difficult, has nothing to do with your love for her or the family. Explain, with gentle compassion and no *escándalos*, that this has everything to do with you loving yourself and giving yourself an opportunity to live your dreams.

no sense of my private grown-up life. There were no discussions and conversations. We could not talk. I had to leave." Adriana says that she found an apartment with her best friend and told her mom she was out. However, instead of moving into the apartment with her buddy, she moved in with her boyfriend. Her mom found out about the secret arrangement when she called and a new roommate answered the telephone with "Adriana who?"

"We had a blowup and we split up," she remembers. For Adriana, who was figuring out many aspects of her life at the time, it helped that she was seeing a therapist during the mom-daughter turmoil. "I would have gone *loca* if I didn't have someone neutral who understood and helped me figure out what was going on," she said. Months later, her mother called, and they had lunch and talked. Their relationship is still getting stronger with each "*pleito*" and breakup and new conversation.

There are, however, stories that don't end as happily as Adriana's. There is always the risk that the separation can be permanent. This is a difficult decision, but one some women need to make to ensure the fulfillment of their dreams and their happiness.

HABLA CON TU MIMA: CROSSING THE CULTURAL GAP ON A BRIDGE OF WORDS

As much as we like to talk, I don't believe that Latinas talk enough about issues that trouble our souls, whether with our friends, our mothers, or our families. Despite our reputation for talking too much (and too loud) we don't communicate *deeply*—especially about family matters. Custom dictates that family drama stays at home. Counselors, therapists, teachers, professionals? They represent external intrusion and shame. And they are there for real *locos*, not for the rest of us. Many of us, when we have trouble with our families, we just kind of suck it in *o no los tragamos*—until we explode, and then no real *conversación* takes place.

One woman in her late thirties tells me that she is very open and assertive and "honest" outside of her home, yet when it comes to her mother, it's *otra cosa*. Just recently she learned she had a half brother a year younger than she, fathered by her dad with a *querida*. All those years, everyone knew except her. When she first heard she felt betrayed and wounded. How could she have lived in the dark so long when everyone around her knew the truth? It was at that moment that she understood the steep price one pays in a culture of *silencio*. How different her whole life would have been if half the family history weren't cloaked in secrets!

All of us have family *secretos*, family mistakes we're afraid to admit, *humillaciónes* our parents feel too angry or sad or proud to tell us, as if by talking about them, we might repeat them. Many more of us simply don't feel comfortable with an open and honest *conversación* with our mothers. But by not talking about things, we run the highest risk of repeating our mistakes. When we don't talk about our issues, we have no way of processing them and learning from the past.

SUAVECITO

When you find yourself making decisions that run counter to cultural expectations, my advice is to approach the situation as the Dalai Lama would—with gentle compassion. Gentle compassion, *chicas,* means to recognize and honor the path your parents have walked, the struggles they have survived, and the era they grew up in. Never forget where they have come from. Try on their shoes and empathize with the shock, the fear, and the emptiness they experience as they see their grown daughter live with strange and "foreign" values.

Wanting your own space does not mean you don't respect your culture. Breaking the Latina code of behavior *sin escándalos* and with lots of compassion and conviction is key. Remember, our parents want to feel useful and connected to us as parents and, most important, to know that we are safe.

The secret to bridging and surviving cultural and generational gaps with older family members is to show them *respeto* and make them feel like they're an important part of our lives. And *respeto* cuts both ways: we have to show respect for their lifestyles while being true to our own.

These days I often remind my mom that I need her as the mother of a grown woman with a child. And I give her what my son would call "mad props"—a lot of respect—for her dedication to the family. We both learned a great deal from our years of bickering; now I try not to judge her with my *gringa*-fied career eyes, and she tries not to judge me with her "traditional" eyes. I have also come to accept that while I don't always have to take her advice, I can welcome it and hear what she has to say.

Learning to honor our elders' *sacrificios,* respect their values, and treat them with gentle compassion sometimes may not be easy. But I promise you that the more we engage our older loved ones in honest communication, the more we model behavior that will help our children grow up in healthy, happy families.

SEVEN TIPS TO SOFTEN THE BLOW FOR THE LATINA WHO WANTS TO MOVE TO HER OWN APARTMENT, IN WITH HER *NOVIO,* OR ACROSS THE COUNTRY FOR A JOB:

1. Have a plan. By the time you are ready to move into your own place or across the country, you should have a firm hold on the place, the job, or, at the very least, the neighborhood you want to live in. You don't want to "explore" the idea of moving out, because your family will try to convince you otherwise. Yexenia, born in El Salvador and raised in Brooklyn, signed the lease to her new apartment and paid for two months in advance before she told her mother.

"I knew that Mami would try to talk me out of it. Having the apartment gave me a sense that there was no turning back. The decision was made," she said. Still, to ease the brunt of the pain, she told her mother in English, even though her mother speaks only Spanish. To Yexenia's surprise, her mother got it very clearly. And Yexenia learned that just because she had the apartment, it did not mean that her mother would not try to talk her out of it.

"Mami came up with all kinds of reasons why moving out was a terrible idea. '¡Ay, mija, yo queria que tu salieras de la casa vestida de blanco [in a white wedding gown]! Why are you going to spend that money when you could help out your *familia* . . . You could save to buy your own house. . . . What is the family going to say? . . . *Eres muy joven. . . . Estas liberal. . . .*'" The reasons continued until Yexernia held her mother's hands and repeated that she was moving out. Her mother cried and said, "*Pues, que se var hacer.*" All of Yexenia's mother's challenges echoed the voices of mothers of the dozens of Latinas I interviewed who moved out on their own.

2. Be financially independent. Jessie, who stopped relying on her parents when she moved out and in with a roommate, was especially adamant about this *consejo*. "Don't expect your parents to pay for your pad or buy your airline ticket to go job hunting on the East Coast if you live on the West Coast, and vice versa. By moving out you are saying, 'I am a grown-up,' and grown-ups are responsible." That is not to say that if you get into financial trouble you can't count on them. *Seria el colmo* if you move out without their *bendiciones* and approval and expect them to pay for your rent or move to another city!

3. Have a supportive boyfriend (if you are moving in with your man) and girlfriends who you can talk to. The best thing you can do for yourself is surround yourself with people who get your cultural "mother struggle" and who don't think your mother is an overprotective freak who needs to be institutionalized. Even in the heat of the battle, you know that the objections to your chosen lifestyle are all about her love for you and fear of *el que dirán la gente*. Adriana's Latino boyfriend—though he didn't agree with her mother's point of view—understood the Latina-mother syndrome and was able to support her during the worst of times. The worse thing that can happen when you are guilt-ridden is to have a roommate or *novio* tell you your mother is crazy—or more terrible, maybe, would be to have a friend who tells you that they would kill to have a mother beg her to stay so that she could cook, clean, and take care of her!

4. Be very sure and comfortable with your decision. You will be challenged about whys and why nots. And you should feel proud and happy that you are making the move and let her know this. This is not about being smug and arrogant ("I am grown and you need to get a life!")—rather it's a sense that you feel ready for *la vida–sola*–and are at peace with your decision, that this is something you want to do for you; it's not about them. You want to make sure they understand that is not your lack of love and commitment and *respeto* for them but something that will make you very happy, make them very proud, and ultimately help you move forward in life.

5. Use direct and clear language and don't beat around the bush. If you are moving out say, "*Me voy.*" I *am* moving out, and not "I want to move out." Direct language leaves little wiggle room for negotiation and says you mean business. This decision has been made. If you are direct, there is less bargaining. Many of us do come from countries with traditions of haggling in *el mercado,* even for basic necessities. So it is natural for our mothers (and dads) to want to "bargain" with us about our decision. When you explain yourself, do it slowly and clearly. And expect lots of tears, both yours and hers.

6. *No mientas*—don't lie. Women I spoke to who lied to their mothers and planned apartments, jobs, and futures by themselves or with their boyfriends in secret regret having lived double lives and leaving their most loved ones out of the picture. "It was painful not to share this happiness and excitement with Mom," said Yexenia. "If I had to do it again, I would have taken her with me to see the apartment, asked her for help decorating, and made her a part of this new adventure." Caution: this doesn't mean that you should tell her "everything" about the parties you will have, or the guys who can now, maybe, sleep over. Your mother does not want to know about your wild sex life or parties you plan to have! She does want to know that you are safe, happy, and acting responsibly. And if she "sees" you making these responsible decisions, she will see what a great daughter she has raised.

7. Tell Mamá first. Most of the women I spoke to say that Dad was the toughest to convince. That is why Mom is always the first and last woman in our lives.

A fierce Latina who made U.S. history . . .

 **Evelina Lopez Antonetty** has often been referred to as the "Hell Lady of the Bronx," a righteous title she surely earned. Frustrated by the public school system's lack of action, in 1965, in the midst of the civil rights and student movements, she joined forces with other parents to create an organization to advocate in their behalf, United Bronx Parents, Inc. As an activist, she spoke out about New York's citywide struggle for quality education. At first UBP focused on educational reform and educating public school parents, but it later expanded to include students, teachers, educational workers, and parochial school parents. In 1970, the organization expanded its program activities to related areas, establishing a bilingual and bicultural day-care center, an adult-education program targeting literacy and preparation for the GED, a youth-enrichment and -leadership program, and a citywide summer lunch program. Evelina, who was born in Salinas, Puerto Rico, on September 19, 1922, came to New York at age eleven. She died on November 19, 1984, which is Puerto Rican Discovery Day or el Día de La Raza, but the organization she founded continues to grow and address the problems that afflict minority families.

CHAPTER TWO

QUE BELLA SOY:
See the Pretty Girl in That Mirror There?

The first time I heard about *Yo Soy Betty la Fea,* then a hot new *novela* airing on Telemundo, I almost choked on my rice and beans. It was the story of a homely but ingenious young *colombiana* who rises to the top of a fashion-design company by winning over everyone, including her *príncipe azul,* with her brilliance and great managerial skills. The soap's producers "uglified" the character by giving the actress playing her a greasy, mousy hairstyle, tacky *vieja* clothes, horrific glasses, braces, and a *campesina* lisp. Despite these seemingly frightful looks, our "unattractive" heroine is able to triumph over the standard-issue glamorous, peroxide-blond-haired, designer-clothes-wearing, conventional beauties to earn the respect of her colleagues *and* her viewers. Every week, I watched this war between mind and body unfold with fascination. It was amazing television, particularly Spanish-language television. And its progressive message of brains over beauty gave me a glimmer of hope that times—even if just in prime-time *novela* fantasies—are changing.

Just as Betty Pinzón, our *"fea"* heroine, has to remind herself, as she's ridiculed by her vicious and superficial coworkers, that real beauty is found on the inside and never fades, we have to constantly remind *ourselves* of our worth in a culture dominated by Anglo standards of beauty. And while I hope we all get to a place in our lives where we truly embrace what it means to be beautiful *por dentro y por fuera*–for most of us that journey is long and painful.

FABULOUS SEÑORITAS

It is not an overstatement to say that Latinas, whether they live in the projects or on Rodeo Drive, always look put together. We have a style and a sense of beauty that is all our own. It's one of those wonderful things about *nosotras, las mujeres hispanas.*

Yet mainstream culture often refuses to represent us in our glory, and when they do show our style it's often been "borrowed" by a *blanquita. Barrio* trends make it to the "mainstream" and then are sported by white girls, though we never get the credit or make the money.

Statistics show that Hispanic females spend more money on lipstick, home hair-coloring products, makeup, and apparel than most other groups. And we certainly know how to coordinate colors: always match pocketbook with shoes; always apply the lip liner two shades darker than the lipstick–no matter what those beauty magazines say, thank you very much!

However, I often ask myself, when does this intense sense of beauty and style become a beauty trap? When does the pressure to always *hacerte tu máscara* become a metaphor for fears and insecurities we're trying to hide? Even as we set trends and embody a style that is globally imitated, many of us grow up feeling uncomfortable with our "ethnic" skin tones and features.

Too often young women tell me that they are too *flaca*, too *gorda*, too short, too *india*, too *negra*, or some combination of the above. When I look at our collective beauty, com-

---

mija, can we dress

According to a 1997 National Consumer Expenditure Survey, Latinos spent an annual average of $1,958 for apparel; their non-Latino counterparts spent $1,709.

Latina Spending Habits, Taking Pride in Our Appearance

Hispanic women spend a whopping $1.6 billion annually on cosmetics, fragrances, and personal-care products. We spend 27 percent more on cosmetics and 43 percent more on fragrance than our general-market counterparts.

Across all cosmetic categories, Hispanic women over-index the general market. For example, compared to the general market, 73 percent more Hispanic women are considered "heavy users" of foundation and 15 percent more are heavy users of lipstick.

plaints like these render me speechless. How have we been made to feel *fea* when we are so clearly *linda?!*

LOS CULPABLES

The images that we see around us—on billboards, in magazines, in movies, and on television—raise questions within us. "What do these images say about you? Do they affirm you, celebrate you? These women don't look like you and me, so what does that say about how pretty we are?

Since the birth of Hollywood, magazines and mainstream media have rendered us invisible or portrayed only those Latinas whose looks matched the Anglo ideal: long, straight dark hair, thin features, and a svelte body. Spanish-language media have all too often been complicit in perpetuating this oppressive trend. The fact is, it's hard to control media representations, though we *can* influence them by using or withholding our buying power. However, we have immediate and powerful control over the ways we affirm our beauty at home, and it starts with *nuestras familias.*

¿Y TU ABUELA, DÓNDE ESTÁ? THE CASE OF LATINO RACISM

Experts say that a woman's self-esteem, or *auto-estima*—the foundation for her ability to feel beautiful as an adult—is formed as early as the age of four or five. A girl is deeply connected to her mother when she's young, and through modeling her mother's behavior she forms her earliest notions of beauty and self-esteem.

Try answering these simple questions. Do you remember ways in which your mom manifested physical self-esteem when you were young? Did her walk have a swing? Did she admire herself in the mirror? Or was she always *quejandose* about her thighs, her *lonjitas,* or her *pelo malo*? How did she do your hair? Did she style it lovingly? Or did she tell you you'd be pretty if it just weren't for your frizzy hair? Did she affirm your beauty *and* your brains? Or did she tell you to stay out of the sun because you were already dark enough? How did she treat you generally? Were you affirmed when you completed a task successfully?

Think back further. When you and your *mami* stepped out, was she treated with respect in the barrio? Did she sport a 'fro and a broad *caderas*? When she walked into a bodega, did the attendant greet her with a "*Buenos dias, Señora, que hermosa se ve usted,*" or were you both invisible to shopkeepers in your suburban mall? And what about *Papi*? Were you his most beautiful *princesita*? Or was your *papi* simply not there?

Family definitions of beauty and early childhood experiences set the foundation for how we think about ourselves as we grow up. Seemingly innocent *comentarios*, as well as violent childhood experiences like sexual abuse and incest, teach us or rob from us the kind of self-esteem and sense of *belleza* that we're entitled to.

Our culture may seem to celebrate a healthy figure and Latina looks, but we have an insidious problem that we rarely discuss openly: internalized *racismo*. Although we're loath to admit it, Latinas and Latinos often feel prejudicial toward themselves and other Latina women who look ethnic, too *india*, too *negra,* or too *morena*. When was the last time a woman with Maya all over her face played the lead role in a *novela*? What about an Afro-Latina? How many dark Latinas have you *ever* seen play the lead?

The dreaded *patito feo* is usually the little girl with *azteca* or *africana* features. We have internalized so much the conquistador ideal of female (and male) beauty that we jump to claim the Spaniard *abuela* quicker than the Inca or African one.

When I was growing up, my racially diverse Puerto Rican family often teased me by threatening to pinch my nose with a clothespin to get rid of its African flatness and width. Naturally, I grew up with a major *complejo* about my nose. My sister Wandi was born with "*pelo malo*"—tight kinky curls—and was often told that she would be more "*linda*" if she could only run a hot iron through her hair and make her *pelo bueno*. Mari, the only one of us who was born blond and with European features, escaped these racist nicknames and family *críticas*.

A friend once told me the story of her fraternal twin nieces, one a light-skinned *guerita* and one a dark-skinned, kinky-haired *princesita*. Since the twins were born, family and friends continually affirmed the lighter one as *hermosa* and *preciosa*, but barely acknowledged the dark-skinned one. (Are you getting angry already? Good—but there's more.) My friend noticed with concern as the girls grew to be toddlers that the lighter, having received more compliments from the family, had a more outgoing personality. She loved to dance for adults and share her little girl *cuentos* while the other twin, who got substantially less public attention, was shy and withdrawn. While an argument could be made that twins seek to differentiate themselves from each other, my friend was convinced that the darker twin, who was rarely on the adults' radar screen, was suffering from low self-esteem. Her suspicion was confirmed, she says, the day the five-year-old darker twin was taken to a beauty salon to get her Afro-Latina curls chemically straightened. Now, for those of you who have never experienced a *desrizado*, it's up there on the pain scale with pulling out your nails. At a family gathering the next day, everyone commented on how *hermosa* the toddler looked with hair that, thanks to scalp-burning chemicals, now reached her tiny waist!

"You could see the little girl smiling in disbelief as she finally received the affirmation she had obviously been craving," my friend said. "It was a very painful and disturbing scene to watch." My friend confessed that most painful of all were the feelings from her own childhood this brought up, for she too had been the dark, skinny, kinky-haired one in her racially mixed Hispanic family.

Our families, often without consciously intending to, pass on a pattern of self-loathing and physical discomfort with regard to our indigenous looks. There are so many nasty names associated with *la india* or *la negra,* some still so disturbing to me that I refuse to even mention them. It's also saddening that our self-loathing has a complex hierarchy, with African on the bottom, Indian next to the bottom, and all the gradations approximating the European ideal ascending from that. I'm sure you remember some of the racist descriptions you heard growing up—it's the ugly Latino legacy of Spanish colonialism in the *Américas.* We as a *raza* have so internalized the racist attitudes of our European colonizers that many of us would rather wage a war against our own bodies and faces than question the prevailing standards of beauty. These psychologically crippling attitudes have stripped us of our ability to champion, or sometimes even *recognize,* the beautiful Indian or African women we are.

Growing up I was often lauded for my brains, but knocked for *mi nariz chata.* Since children tend to act out what adults expect of them, I excelled at school, but inside I always felt as is if I had the ugliest nose in the world. I often thought that if only I could change it, I'd be pretty. So by the age of twenty I had saved enough money to get a nose job. I didn't get a Debbie Debutante nose, but rather one that looked more like the noses in my clan. My decision, extreme as I understand it to be now, was born out of the desperation of not wanting to be teased anymore. I was a young woman who wanted to feel pretty, and I thought a less African nose was the way to achieve that. Of course, I soon realized that no operation in the world could make me *feel* attractive. What I really had to learn was that my self-esteem could not be increased from the outside in. No amount of surgery or affirmation will make you beautiful until *you* believe yourself to be beautiful.

Diosas de las Américas

Atabex is the symbol of Mother Earth for all peoples of the Caribbean and the descendants of the Taino Indians. In Taino lore, the Earth is feminine because only the female gives birth; and because only the feminine can create, so the Earth too must be female. Atabex has been known by five names: Atabey, Yermao, Guacar, Apita, and Zuimaco. It is believed that each of these names is connected to different stages in a woman's life, as expressed by her age and her ability to create life.

THOSE SEXIST AND RACIST IMAGES OF LATINAS

As we get older and step out of our homes, other cultural definitions of *belleza* begin to add color to our developing sense of beauty. I grew up watching two worlds that rendered me nonexistent: the imported Mexican and South American Spanish-language television, and English-language mainstream media. On Spanish TV, I don't ever remember seeing anyone of substance or value played by a *negra* or *india* actress. Those "ethnic" women were (and still are) usually relegated to playing *las criadas* or *las nanas;* they were illiterate and poor *campesinas;* or they depicted other subservient types.

English-language mainstream media is no better. When Latina characters are featured, we play prostitutes, welfare moms, maids, or the sexy spitfire. These certainly weren't the women I grew up with! And how can you have a show like NBC's top-rated sitcom *Friends,* based in New York, where one out of every four residents is Hispanic, and not have one Latino friend? According to a 1999 study by the California-based Tomás Rivera Policy Institute, an independent policy research organization, Latinos made up a mere 2 percent of characters during the 1999 television season. When you compare that number to our 11.7 percent of the population and the money we spend going to the movies ($500 million annually), the message from those who seek to entertain us is clear. We get no respect! Our invisibility continues in movies, TV programs, books, newspapers, and magazines, and with serious repercussions.

The *blanquito* factor: Hispanic "Whiteness"

The 2000 Census for the first time allowed people to choose racial categories. *Hispanic*, as we know, does not describe a race, but a nationality. Something quite fascinating happened in Texas. The closer to the border, the more likely Hispanics were to choose to identify their race as white—they were up to 80 percent more likely to identify themselves as racially white than those living in northern Texan cities like Houston, Dallas, and Austin, where they classified themselves as "some other race." Check it out:

Brownsville	80.9% white	16.0% other
Laredo	82% white	14.7% other
McAllen	76.7% white	19.6% other
El Paso	71.6% white	23.5% other
San Antonio	61.1% white	32.7% other
Houston	49.3% white	43.6% other
Austin	40.6% white	52.4% other
Dallas	45.7% white	48.1% other
United States	47.9% white	42.2% other

We just spend more...

According to a 1997 National Consumer Expenditure Survey, Latinos spent an annual average of $4,869 on food; their non-Latino counterparts spent $4,796.

THE LATINA TEEN

If our earliest notions of beauty start when we're toddlers, they become entrenched during adolescence. However you saw yourself during that crucial child-woman stage will stay with you forever. Dr. Lozano-Vranich tells me that most of her female clients who struggle with low self-esteem and body image issues have to go back and work through those difficult teen years.

Of course adolescence is tough for everyone, male and female, of any race or ethnic group, and minorities all the more. But added to the cultural invisibility and self-esteem issues faced by all minority teens, Latinas in the United States have a particular angst they share only with their African and Asian American sisters: representations of them are either nonexistent or caricatures. It's a double whammy for our developing sense of beauty.

Latina beauty is constantly under siege, either because of total omission, limited representations, outright misrepresentation, or stupid *comentarios*. And the lesson for young Latinas everywhere is crystal clear: we have to tell our own stories, make our own movies, publish our own magazines, support those who do right by us, put the pressure on those who don't—and stop looking for validation from mainstream media that are racist without even trying!

TOO *FLACA* UPTOWN, TOO *GORDA* DOWNTOWN

Beauty ideals are changing in the barrio. When I was growing up, *gordita* was a term of endearment, *un cariño*. But today it would be an *insulto* to call someone *gorda*!

During my girlhood, my mother made me drink all kinds of

ponches (liquid concoctions of raw eggs and grape juice) and *maltas* with lots of sugar to fatten me up. Her ideal woman was *llenita,* and I was dreadfully skinny. To be a *flaca* Latina was to grow up feeling *fea.* Women in my clan were healthy, with small waists and big *caderas* (or *nalgas,* depending on where you're from). They wore tight jeans and spandex to enhance their big butts, and the men loved it. I remember my pride at being complimented for having *piernas gordas* like my mother! I grew up desperate to have meat on my bones, and Mother Nature (and my genes) finally granted my wish when I hit eighteen and began to *hechar cuerpo.* But as the old saying goes, be careful what you wish for . . .

I got to college and discovered that *Mami*'s skinny *hija* was really a chunky *boricua* in a gringo world! That strange world outside of my barrio and family suddenly stripped my chunkiness and my rotund derriere of their attractiveness. Unfortunately, it was my first time away from home, and my desire to fit in was so intense that instead of questioning these new cultural standards, I adopted them as my own—I started a war against my "big" butt and thighs. And it made me feel schizophrenic; too *flaca* in the barrio and too *gorda* downtown. Where were Selena and J. Lo back then, when I needed them?

Some Latina sisters experience the other end of the *flaca* spectrum, developing bodies of grown women as young as twelve. The onset of early puberty is still being researched and remains a largely unexplained phenomenon, though statistics show that increasing numbers of Hispanic girls start developing as young as six or seven years old! Rosana, now twenty-eight, was one of those girls—at eleven years old she was going out with a nineteen-year-old man. Since she had the body of an adult, it was simply assumed that she had the maturity of one, too. It was a terrible assumption all around.

"I *felt* grown up. I *thought* I was a woman. I had this body, and everywhere I went men would just stare at me with lust and say things like '*¡que cuerpazo!*' My mother never talked to me about it other than to say, '*No dejes que nadie te toque.*' So I always dressed very sexy, and felt very desirable with so much attention. But now I look back and feel like I was cheated out of being a little girl—I got pregnant when I was thirteen years old."

EATING DISORDERS: THE NEW LATINA PROBLEM

Skewed notions of the "perfect" female body have begun a self-esteem crisis among young Latinas. It used to be that anorexia, bulimia, and binge eating were not part of life in the barrio; they were a *blanquita* problem. Our culture's celebration of food and more curvaceous bodies sheltered many of us from white middle-class women's food issues. But, as with many other issues in our lives, acculturation is quickly changing this. Experts note that as young Hispanic girls attempt to conform to the majority culture, they're increasingly placing an emphasis on thinness. Which, in turn, places us at a higher risk for bingeing, purging, and overly restrictive dieting. While studies on eating disorders typically do not include ethnically diverse populations, early research suggests that the problem in our community, while prevalent, goes continually underreported.

In one of the few integrated studies available, it was discovered that white women and Latinas have similar attitudes about dieting and weight control. In a study of more than nine hundred middle school girls between the ages of eleven and fourteen, Hispanic girls reported higher levels of body dissatisfaction than any other group, including white girls—even among the thinnest 25 percent! Clearly these statistics should be sending a wake-up call to all of us. If we allow these changing perceptions to go unchecked, we may find our young sisters and daughters in a vicious cycle of life-threatening behaviors.

I TRAFFICKED IN FANTASIES AND *MENTIRAS*

Mi culpa is what I have to say on this one. As the former editor in chief of a major magazine targeted at Hispanic women, I was part of an industry that put forth stereotypes about Latina beauty and women's bodies—essentially, about female perfection.

My first day on the job, I learned about the industry secret of air-brushing, or "perfecting," the picture. The art department folks (the people in charge of coordinating the images you see in magazines) showed me several selections of photographs for an upcoming fashion layout. Pointing to a pin head–size mole on the model's cheek and a slight discoloration on her skin, the designer said not to worry: "We can clean her up." A few days later, the already gorgeous model was beauty mark–free and sported a "perfect" complexion. And all this time I thought those pictures in magazines were real!

Because I knew the psychological danger of such practices, and because I came from a journalism background, where you report what you see, the idea of altering model's images made me uneasy. Magazine insiders would try to assuage my concerns by telling me that "women really don't want to see themselves in a magazine." As the magazine's editor, I was *supposed* to give readers something to aspire to! *Get with the program,* they said, gently nudging me. Somehow I just never could.

Celebrities concerned about their images also follow the script. The high-powered manager of one famous Latino entertainer called me and made me promise to "*limpiarle*" *un poquito* his client's acne-scarred cheeks for a cover shot. For one cover spread we were asked to erase another celebrity's scars from a childhood spiritual ritual. It is no overstatement to say that all of the images you have seen, and see, in magazines have been to some degree touched up by the magic of Photoshop.

In fact, some magazines (not *Latina* magazine, at least during my tenure) airbrush entire body parts on actresses and models. Through the wizardry of airbrushing, models and celebrities get to have perfect white teeth, bigger breasts, longer hair, and perfect complexions, among other features. In some cases, their waists and thighs are replaced with those of thinner or more curvaceous models.

The making of these magazine fantasy females may explain why so many girls and grown women report bouts of low self-image and depression after reading women's magazines. One study on how fashion magazines influence women's body-image satisfaction randomly selected college students to view magazines prior to completing a body-image-satisfaction survey. Half the participants looked at fashion magazines and the other half, newsmagazines. The women who read the fashion magazines reported being less satisfied with their bodies and more preoccupied with being thin than those who viewed the newsmagazines.

Latina magazine, however, was supposed to be different. It was supposed to celebrate our broad and beautiful diversity—in color, race, nationality, and size. It was a chance to redefine to mainstream America what "beautiful" really was. Although I did try to live up to that mission, with the help of some very committed editors, we found it challenging. And I left believing I had failed my readers. Though my commitment was, and continues to be, real, I could not change what I believe to be the established mentality (and trend) within the ranks of the magazine industry that considers a light-skinned, light-haired, tall, skinny woman the ideal of female beauty.

I remember demanding to see models that were *triguenas* and *gorditas*. I was tired of the incredibly thin, Anglo-featured Latina *modelos* we kept displaying issue after issue. And the readers were, too! The woman in charge of model scouting—a short, stocky woman with a beautiful Inca face—showed me hundreds of model cards that included photos of the models in different poses: close-up, glamour shot, full-body shots. The scout was frustrated because she just couldn't find what I wanted. She separated the cards into two sets, one that she referred to as the "dog" pile, and the other, the "good" pile. It might not surprise you to hear that almost all the women I thought were beautiful and visually interesting ended up in the "dog" pile. (I might also mention that the "dog" pile is industry-speak when comparing model's head shots. As I said, the fashion magazine world is a deeply problematic place!) I remember my blood boiling as I fought issue after issue to get these women on the cover and in the pages.

In addition to scouting the regular agencies for models who looked like real Latinas, I also decided to do a national casting call for gorgeous Hispanic women. In doing so, I wanted to send a message to the fashion and beauty industries. If they wouldn't broaden the image of Latina beauty, we would!

On one of these calls in Los Angeles, about a thousand women, from fourteen-year-old high school students to sixty-year-old *abuelas*, showed up. I was delighted—not only to see so many Latinas come to affirm their own beauty, but because we ended up being able to use dozens of them in the magazine to illustrate stories, articles, and beauty tips.

In the two years I presided over the magazine, I put only *one* Afro-Latina on the cover: actress Gina Ravera, whom you may have seen in the movies *Soul Food* and *Why Do Fools Fall in Love?* I remember being told by my higher-up that Mexican sisters on the West Coast would look at the issue and wonder what a "black" woman was doing on the cover of a "Latina" magazine. My response was that I did not think my Chicana sisters were that unsophisticated or ignorant about the Afro-Latina diaspora. I went with the cover, and it was one of the best newsstand sellers of the year. But the letters from readers were the real reward for me: "*Gracias,*" the letters cried out, "finally *una mujer trigueña.*" I didn't stay long enough to put a *gordita* on the cover, but I still have fantasies that *Latina* magazine, as well as other popular women's magazines, will get real about female beauty.

GETTING TO A STAGE WHERE YOU CAN SAY *A LA CHINGADA* OR *AL CARAJO*

A Latina in her early twenties tells me that she didn't think she was pretty until she got to college, and away from her family. She's skinny, dark, and smart, three traits that were not appreciated by her lighter-skinned family members. She never got any attention in the 'hood from Latino boys either. Even though she says wasn't looking for validation from men, their apparent indifference further eroded her fragile self-esteem. She remembers counting the number of times she was asked to dance at Dominican parties and surmising that the women who got to dance more, usually *las más llenitas,* were a lot more beautiful than her. But once she went away to college, everything changed—being skinny and dark was cool and exotic. And for a while she enjoyed her newfound status as the "only one." However, after three years, this too became tiresome. She was dating a man who, she believed, was more into her ethnic chic than who she was as a person. It was then that she finally came into her own. She realized that being exoticized by her peers was no less dehumanizing and painful than the unconscious racism of her family. With this painful realization came another less painful one: she was the master of her own aesthetic destiny. Her first act of liberation was to dump her new boyfriend. Her second act was cutting her relaxed hair. For years she'd yearned for the ease of a short haircut but felt too addicted to the affirmation her long, processed tresses gave her. Her transformation was a revelation. For the first time in her life, she was making decisions about her body and hair according to her own taste and comfort. She also noticed that although a few of her white liberal friends seemed less interested in her, the people she knew and liked best actually told her she looked more beautiful. The moral of the story? The ugly duckling can become a swan only after she stops trying to be a duckling.

LET THE MAKEOVER BEGIN!

Let's start with an excerpt from a beautiful poem:

> Don't give in *mi prietita*
> Tighten your belt, endure,
> Your lineage is ancient,
> Strong women reared you:
> My sister, your mom, my mother and I.

And yes, they have taken our lands.
Not even the cemetery is ours now
But they will never take that pride
of being *mexicana,* Chicana-*tejana*
nor our indian
woman's spirit.

—Gloria Anzaldúa,
"No se raje, Chicanita"/"*Don't Give In, Chicanita*"

Taking pride in our Latina beauty is a complex issue. When you feel like the "other" all the time, it is important to remind yourself with pride that you have a place in this culture and that *you* have the power to claim that space for yourself.

My beauty makeover is not the one you typically read about in magazines, in which your hair is streaked and your face done. This makeover involves beauty ingredients found deep in your soul: pride in your people's history, a positive frame of mind, positive friends and partners, a healthy diet and exercise, and a spiritual practice.

I also want to note that, unlike most other media mavens, I find age to be a crucial beauty ingredient—since maturity plays an important role in a woman's ability to be comfortable in her own skin. The older we are, the more likely we are to say, "*Que se joda* what others think!"

Here is my six-step plan.

BEAUTY LESSON NUMBER ONE:
GIVE YOURSELF DAILY *CARIÑITOS*

Get in touch with the inner goddess that is you! There is tremendous power in affirmations and positive thinking. More and more studies are demonstrating the healing effects of positive visualizations in *nuestras vidas.*

Negative words and thoughts have an impact! How you refer to or think about the body parts and features you don't like can have a lasting effect on how you view them. Replace *las quejas* with body-positive mantras. There is tremendous power in looking at yourself and saying, "Damn it, I'm hot, *soy bella, soy preciosa. Ser* Latina is beautiful!" Try looking in the mirror every morning for seven days and saying, "*Ay que linda,*" or, "What a beautiful face." See if you feel any differently about yourself at the end of the week.

Once you've mastered that, begin introducing daily *cariñitos.* Locate a favorite feature and remind yourself of how much you like it. "I like my legs because they are . . ."; "I love my toes because they are . . ."; "I love my *nalgas* because they are . . ." Lovingly describe each part of your body until you come to the feature you dislike most. Spend a week on that feature alone. In doing so you'll slowly teach yourself to love this feature. A good time to do this is before or after your shower or bath. Buy rich, scented body lotion and caress your body lovingly with it. You'll be surprised at how well you respond to a little loving care from yourself.

BEAUTY LESSON NUMBER TWO:
SAY *ADIÓS* TO NEGATIVE *GENTE* IN YOUR CIRCLE

I advocate for the removal, or as they say in the beauty industry, "deep exfoliation," of negative, competitive, or abusive people in your life. Take one of my *tías,* for example. Every time she sees me she makes a negative comment about my looks, such as "Your hair looks like a broom," or "Have you gained weight?" My response to her constant negativity has been to limit my exposure to her.

Another danger zone is nicknames. Our families and Latino friends come up with the darnedest (and sometimes painful) "*sobre-nombres.*" And they "lovingly" zone in on the one feature you may have an issue with. If you don't like the nickname given to you as a child because it calls attention to, say, your "*nalgas flacas,*" tell those doing the calling to stop. They might resist at first, *que estas muy seria,* or worse, say that you are turning into a *blanquita,* but if you hold your ground, sooner or later they'll realize that it's not fun for them *or* you.

While we don't necessarily choose family, we do choose our *amigas* and boyfriends. Sometimes we hang with people who simply aren't good for us. And as we try to achieve and grow, they seem to keep pulling us down. Often this dynamic is difficult to identify and stop. Take a moment to reflect on how many compliments your boyfriend or husband pays you. Do they outweigh his criticisms? If not, it's time to have a serious talk. Think about your girlfriends too. Do they support you when you have a problem? Are they genuinely happy for you when you get a promotion? Do they help you look your best when you have a hot date? Or do they tell you how overweight you are? Are weight and dieting the only things they talk about? You know the answers to these questions, and they can tell you if you need to reevaluate your criteria for friendship. (For more on this important subject, see chapter 4, "Talk Circles.")

Cities with the largest numbers of Latinos:

New York, N.Y.	2,160,554
Los Angeles, Cal.	1,719,073
Chicago, Ill.	753,644
Houston, Tex.	730,865
San Antonio, Tex.	671,394
Phoenix, Ariz.	449,972
El Paso, Tex.	431,875
Dallas, Tex.	422,587
San Diego, Cal.	310,752
San Jose, Cal.	269,989

BEAUTY LESSON NUMBER THREE: TAKE PRIDE IN YOUR LINEAGE

I often encounter Latinas with what I call a "*blanquita* complex." These women try to obscure their Latina roots by dying their hair, wearing blue contact lenses, or refusing to speak Spanish, for example. The sad thing about these women is that they're not fooling anyone, and the people they're hurting most are themselves. By rejecting their Latino roots, they are cutting off the possibility of feeling really good about themselves: let's face it, feeling good about yourself is feeling good about *where you come from.*

The first step is reading about our history. A friend once told me she didn't know she was living the effects of colonialism until she began reading books about Latin America in college. Feeling good about yourself in a culture where you're not the dominant group takes work. Put the work into getting to know the cultures that made you,

Easy Things You Can Do to Get in Touch with Your Heritage Now:

- **Have a Latin foodfest.** Prepare a Latin American meal from an old family recipe. The meal must include some kind of chile or *sofrito* as an ingredient, and nothing canned, please! Accompany the meal with any of the great Latin American wines and sodas or *aguas frescas*. Invite your best *amigas y amigos* over for a foodfest.

- **Invite fictional characters into your home.** Read anything by Julia Álvarez, Esmeralda Santiago, Ana Castillo, Sandra Cisneros, Denise Chávez, Liz Balmaseda, Cristina Garcia, or Junot Díaz; lose yourself in the poetry of Gloria Anzaldúa, Cherrie Moraga, Sor Juana Inez, Julia de Burgos, Eduardo Galeano, Piri Thomas, or Pablo Neruda.

- **Surf the Web and read the *noticias en Español*.** Cyber-travel to your family's home country and read the local newspaper. Some websites even have the local radio stations on-line so you can hear all the hit songs and shows.

- **Share family gossip.** Call your mother, your sisters, your cousins and tell each other family *chistes*, or discuss the most embarrassing, humorous, or favorite family moments.

- **Laugh with the Latin greats.** Rent comedies from yesteryear: Anything with Cantinflas (Mario Moreno), La India Maria, Chachita, or El Chavo del Ocho. Or find videos of the Puerto Rican comedic icon Popa en Nueva York.

and I promise you'll look at yourself with new and awe-filled eyes. So go out there and learn our history, and embrace your *merengue, ranchera, salsa, mestiza, india, africana,* Spanish, *conga* heritage.

BEAUTY LESSON NUMBER FOUR: YOU ARE WHAT YOU EAT

Be conscious about what you put in your mouth and *mueve el esqueleto!* Eating healthy foods—cutting back on junk food and fast

- **Play that funky music, Latin girl!** Put on anything by Los Tigeres del Norte, Marc Anthony, Selena, Maná, Ozomatli, Celia Cruz, Willie Colón, Mercedes Sosa, Los Terricolas, Hector Lavóe, Marco Antonio Muñiz, Juan Gabriel, Armando Mánzanero, Ruben Blades, Tito Rodríguez, Silvio Rodríguez, Lucesita, Milly Joselyn, Johnny Ventura, Trio Los Cóndes, Sandro, Trio Los Panchos, Fernandito Villalona, José Feliciano, Shakira, Carlos Gardel, Ismael "Maelo" Rivera, Carlos Vives, Gloria Estefan, Oscar de León, La Lupe, La India, or J. Lo. Pump up the volume and clean the house with bleach, King Pine, Pine-Sol, Mistolín, or whatever cleaning agent your mother and grandma used.

- **Dine out for under $10.** Go to the closest Latino barrio—if you don't already live there—and dine at a local greasy spoon. Take in the people, the kids, the waiters, and, yes, *la comida.*

- *Capicú.* Learn to play dominoes with three other *amigas o amigos.*

- **It's all in the mass.** Learn to cook *masa* from scratch for tamales or *pasteles.* Learn to make coconut flan, *pan dulce, habichuelas con dulce,* or anything that does not involve canned foods.

- **Get blown away.** Go to a Latina-owned beauty salon and get your hair washed and blow-dried Latina style.

- **Build an altar,** light a candle to your favorite *virgencita* or *santo,* or go to a Spanish mass on a Sunday morning.

foods and drinking more water—is a great way to increase your sense of well-being and your attractiveness.

Mira, you can tell yourself a million times a day what a babe you are, you can know the history of oppression and reclaim your roots, you can kick out *todos los negativos de tu vida*—but if you eat poorly and don't do any kind of exercise, you won't derive the most benefit you can on a physical level.

Some meDia that celebrate us:

Magazines:
• El Andar
• Latina
• People en Español
• Urban Latino Magazine
• Generation ñ

TV shows:
• Resurrection Blvd.
• Taina
• The Brothers Garcia
• ¿Qué Pasa USA?
  (reruns)

Eating poorly and not exercising will leave you feeling *sin ganas* (lethargic) and uncomfortable with your body. According to the American Council on Exercise, people who exercise regularly feel better. Scientists say that it's because chemicals called neurotransmitters, produced in the brain, are stimulated during exercise. Since it's believed that neurotransmitters mediate our moods and emotions, they can make us feel better and less stressed. Adopting both good eating habits and exercise will double your health and well-being.

BEAUTY LESSON NUMBER FIVE: WATCH THE MEDIA YOU WATCH

Think critically about the media you allow in your home and in your life. I realize how difficult it is to find media that celebrates us, but it is out there, so seek it actively. It's also important to surround yourself with uplifting images that celebrate you.

In my home, for example, I am surrounded by photographs and posters of strong and beautiful Mexican, indigenous, and Afro-Latina women, such as Jennifer Lopez, Frida Kahlo, Maria Felix, Rita Moreno, and dozens of pictures of family and friends. Their faces inspire and ground me, lift me and celebrate me, and remind me of how gorgeous we really are!

BEAUTY LESSON NUMBER SIX: CELEBRATE EACH OTHER'S LATINA BEAUTY

There is tremendous power when one Latina sister acknowledges that another is looking good. Support your *hermana* by encouraging and celebrating her special beauty!

Let me share with you one of my many hair stories: One day I decided go into the office with my hair curly. It was the first time that I'd gone to work without blow-drying my hair straight. The weather was hot and muggy, and I was running late. Erica, a colleague with an amazing sense of racial and national pride, screamed with joy when she saw my unruly mane, "Your hair looks *great* curly!" Later the same day my friend Ana, who has pin-straight hair, the hair I have always desired, told me, "What I wouldn't do to have curls like yours! Let those gorgeous *boricua* curls loose." Those two comments made me not blow-dry my hair for a month! I can't tell you how deeply their loving affirmation affected me.

Both Erica and Ana remind me of the power that friends have in championing one another. They remind me of that beautiful celebratory ode to *afro-boricuas* sung by Ismael Rivera, "*Las caras lindas de mi gente negra.*" I think we should all sing it to one another, for all the *caras lindas of nuestra gente bella.*

My son tells me that I love everything Latino, but there are some things I'm not so sure about. Our internalization of racism and ethnic prejudice and our blind acceptance of media images are a couple of those things. My friend Pati could not be more right when she said that the most important lesson of our lives is to love ourselves more deeply, especially because we are survivors of colonization. This is especially true when it comes to the issue of our beauty. I hope that as we come into our power as Latinas we will often challenge stereotypes as well as allow for greater recognized diversity in Latina beauty. I take tremendous pride in our racial diversity, and I want to see it reflected more often in all media.

As I see it, beauty is about self-respect, comfort in one's brown, *blanquita,* black, Afro-Latina, or indigenous skin, and satisfaction with one's *nalgas,* whether big or flat. Beauty is an attitude, a state of mind that shouts happily, *Que se joda*—What do you think about me?!

Being kind, fun, loving, charitable, strong, compassionate, open, and honest are some of the most admirable qualities I've seen in the women I consider beautiful. At the end of the day, you can match every shoe you have with your every pocketbook, you can dye your hair Shakira-blond and trim down to a Jennifer Lopez waist size, but if you don't feel *cómoda* in your own God- and parent-given skin and *curvas*, no mascara or designer dress or liposuction can diminish your discomfort.

Remember, true beauty is something that cannot be seen, only felt. It's a confidence that cannot be purchased at a makeup counter or a clothing store or fixed at a plastic surgeon's office. Beauty, lives *adentro*. It's the *confianza* you feel with yourself and the kindness and love with which you treat the sacred temple that is you. Your beauty is lodged deep inside, and only you can let it out. Once you do, *mujer,* it will emanate from your pores like light from the sun.

BEAUTY RECIPES AND *REMEDIOS* FROM THE KITCHENS OF OUR *ABUELAS, AMIGAS,* AND *VECINAS*

Belisa's Ginger-Honey Bath
A quick pick-me-up bath and skin moisturizer

Grate fresh ginger under hot running bathwater, then stir in lots of honey. Soak as long as you like.

A Mayan Skin Glorification
To smooth your face and neck

Mayan women were known for keeping themselves beautiful with the natural resources they had around them.

Scrape and crush fresh corn from the cob. Mix with warm water until you get a soft paste. Apply the paste to your face and neck. Let the mixture dry by sitting in the sun for half an hour, then rinse it off with fresh water. This should give you an incredible glow as well as make your skin smooth.

Maria's *Aguacate* Hair Potion
To strengthen hair and add shine

Take one overly ripe and browning avocado and mash it with olive oil and mayonnaise. Smear the concoction all over your hair. Put on a heavy plastic shower cap and sit underneath a hair dryer or a blow-dryer until the sauce forms a hard shell on your hair (don't use a superhot setting). Let it sit for fifteen minutes. Wash as usual. *Hint:* Before you get in the shower, you may want to rub shampoo through your hair to cut the grease.

Fragancia's *Café, Suela y Canela* Hair *Remedio*
(Fragancia's Coffee, Shoe Sole, and Cinnamon Hair Recipe)

This recipe is popular in the Dominican Republic. It strengthens hair and gives it incredible shine and growth.

2 cups unbrewed ground Spanish coffee (your favorite will do, but no decaf)
1 new leather shoe sole (from your local shoemaker)
3 sticks cinnamon
3 cups water

Place all ingredients in a large pot. The order of the ingredients does not matter as long as the water is always left for last. Cover and bring to a boil. Boil until the *remedio* becomes 1 cup, about twenty minutes or until the consistency is gooey. (Stir ingredients often, but keep covered the whole time it is boiling.) Once gooey, let cool. (The recipe will be brown or black depending on the color of the sole.) Apply to the scalp using a cotton ball. Massage into hair scalp only. Leave for twenty minutes, thirty if hair is in poor or, as Fragancia said, "critical" condition. Wash and condition hair as usual.

The secret of the recipe is to let the *remedio* boil longer, thirty minutes, if your hair is in critical condition. Apply once a week, or up to three times a week depending on condition of hair. Add more of everything except water for thicker consistency.

If you don't want to prepare the recipe at home, you can do what I do, buy it ready-made. Dominican Republic–based companies, Shekmar Industria and Industrias de Productos Quimicos, C por A sell them under the names Yoriel and Lafier at beauty-supply stores in United States cities with large Dominican populations, such as New York, Boston, Miami, and Union City.

Titi Mercedes and the Miraculous Aloe Plant
An all-purpose cure!

According to my *tía* Mercedes, every one of us should have an aloe vera or *sábila* plant in our homes for good luck. I can't swear to how lucky it is, but the ancients used it to cure almost everything, and it really does work. Cut a sliver open and rub the fresh gel on sunburned skin, burns, or even acne scars. Mix a sliver of aloe vera gel with eight ounces of fresh water; drink this mixture every morning to alleviate constipation.

Fresh Oat Mask
Fresh avena or oatmeal makes a great mask that deep cleanses and fights acne.

Mix three tablespoons of fresh uncooked oats with the same amount of water, adding more water or oats as necessary to make a firm paste. Apply to your face, and leave it on for fifteen minutes. Wash well with a warm, wet cloth. Finish with witch hazel or homemade natural astringent (see below).

Egg-White Mask
Egg whites make a great cleanser.

Whip one egg white and pat it onto clean skin. Leave it on for twenty minutes, then wash with warm, wet cloth.

Natural Astringent
Refreshes and cleanses.

Mix half a cup of each: witch hazel and orange-blossom water (*agua de azahar*) with a dab of *agua de rosas* added for a sweet scent. Use in the morning or at night after washing your face and before applying moisturizer.

Relaxing *Remedios* to Sniff or Drink
Fresh chamomile—brewed as tea or just to inhale.
Orange-blossom water or té de azahar
Aguas de colonias, *lavender baby cologne, will remind you of your* bebé *days; sprinkle it on clean sheets and you'll sleep like a baby.*

The Magical Jericho plant
Comadronas (midwives) place a Jericho plant (found in most botanicas here) in a bowl full of cool water just as the labor pains begin. As the dry and brittle plant begins to open and blooms in the water, the mom-to-be begins to dilate. Some midwives believe that the plant actually helps speed up the birthing process.
Titi Mercedes's Home Good-Luck Talisman: Place a Jericho plant in a bowl with water, add seven pennies, and pray for the job or the money you seek. Have faith.

Home Potpourri

In a large pot, boil cloves, anise seeds, and cinnamon. Turn off the heat and let the vapor fill your home with a sweet and delicious scent.

Lydia's Post-Childbirth Healing
For relief after childbirth

Piedra de alumbre (*sold at* botanicas)

Place the *piedra de alumbre* plant in a sitz bath with warm water. Sit with your genital area resting on water. Great for easing pain and healing vaginal wounds from episiotomies or other operations.

Titi Mercedes's *Buena Suerte* Bath:
To make your wish come true

Try to find eight-ounce glasses of each of the waters listed—if you can't get all of them, get as many as you can find.

Ocean, river, spring, lake, and rain water; holy water; coconut water; and Agua de Florida
seven tablespoons of honey
a bunch of white flower petals (any flower will do, as long as it's not from a plant with thorns)

Fill a pot with all the ingredients, and bring to a boil. Turn off the heat and let it cool. After your regular bath or shower, pour mixture over yourself from head to toe while praying for your wish. (I find that the start of the week, particularly Monday mornings, work best.)

A fierce Latina who made U.S. history . . .

 In 1989, **Ileana Ros-Lehtinen** became the first Latina to be elected to the United States House of Representatives. Born on July 15, 1952, in Havana, Cuba, she and her family fled the country when she was seven years old. After earning her bachelor's and master's degrees from Florida International University, Ileana became an educator, founding a private elementary school in south Florida before getting involved in politics. The Republican member of Congress currently serves on the International Relations and Government Reform Committees and, as chair of the Subcommittee on International Operations and Human Rights, is the first Hispanic woman to chair a House subcommittee. Through her political initiatives, she quickly became a leading figure shaping foreign policy, especially toward Latin America—she played a key role in the passage of the Cuban Democracy Act and the Helms-Burton Law. This fierce Latina is widely regarded as an international defender of human rights and democracy, and is active as well on the domestic front on such issues as education and child welfare. If her proposed constitutional amendment to protect the rights of crime victims goes through, her impact will be felt nationally.

CHAPTER THREE

THE HEALTHY LATINA:
¡Cuidate muchacha!

*W*henever my mom or the *viejitas* in my block wanted to warn me against the kind of *amiga* they didn't particularly care for, they'd call me over and whisper in my ear, "*Mira, mi'jita, las malas costumbres se pegan, ten cuidado.*" Little did any of us know that the "baddest" American habits revolve around health! For Latinas, the American diet and lifestyle have begun to spell a health crisis. As *malas costumbres* increasingly often include behaviors that are potentially deadly—consumption of fast foods, rampant alcohol abuse, smoking, narcotic drug use, and high-risk sexual behaviors—and compromise our collective health in the United States.

In recent years, researchers studying Latina health have been baffled by a phenomenon called "the Latino Paradox," an index showing that recent immigrants—*los recien llegados*—arrive healthier and with longer life expectancy rates than those of us who've spent many years here. Studies have shown that among the less acculturated women—typically those inhabiting a lower socioeconomic status than their more long-term American counterparts—the rate of heart disease and breast cancer is lower.

This paradox is intriguing. Despite economic poverty and, for many, the stresses of political repression, we arrive in America healthy. But as soon as we begin ordering Whoppers in English, *se jode la cosa.* We see a precipitous drop in our well-being and mortality rates. One study found that Hispanic females who patronize fast-food restaurants will make twelve visits there in a thirty-day period.Is it really so surprising that our rates of obesity, heart disease, and diabetes are going through the roof?

One major factor in the deterioration of Latina health in America is stress. Unlike back in the homeland (or for that matter in the *barrios* we grew up in), where, despite economic or political hardships, the buffer of extended family and community helped alleviate the burdens of child rearing and familial responsibilities, in the United States we Latinas find ourselves having to negotiate the stress of competing values and identities (Latin versus American). We are also increasingly often living alone or far from our families and loved ones—without a safety net of relatives and friends to support us as we negotiate the emotional stresses of single motherhood, dead-end or high-stress jobs, lack of education, few opportunities, language barriers, sexism, and racism. Add that to unhealthy eating habits, lack of exercise, substance abuse, die-hard *costumbres* like "*aguantar*" (ignore it until it bleeds), doing for *la familia* and others before we do for ourselves, and the lack of affordable, preventative health care in this country, and we are staring into the abyss of a cultural health crisis.

Dime con quien andas, y te diré quien eres.

—POPULAR *DICHO*

THE WAYS OF OUR HEALTHY *ABUELITAS*

I don't know if *your* grandmother was fond of Big Macs, but my *abuelita* never asked me to supersize anything for her. Mami Angelica was an emblem of strength and good health. I suspect that this had a lot had to do with her nutritional habits, faith, family, and social networks. Well, guess what: those are all the things that health-care experts see as protecting our recently arrived *hermanas*

Diosas de las Américas

Temazcalteci is an Aztec goddess; her name means "Grandmother of the Sweet Bath." She teaches us how to use medicinal herbs in order to maintain our health or to banish illness as summer turns to autumn (perhaps with the use of teas, as her name implies). Symbols associated with this *diosa* are medicinal herbs, healing amulets, and water.

from the health-care traps that acculturated U.S. Latinas walk right into every day.

My *abuela* lived in New Jersey for most of her adult life, yet she stuck to very *boricua* foods: rice, beans, meats, fish, fruits, vegetables (even starchy ones like yucca, plantains, potatoes, and the like). She preferred water to soda, and cooked the heartiest *caldos*—they could resurrect a *borracho* or the dead! Though she smoked cigarettes, I never ever saw my grandma hanging out on a corner lighting up or drinking alcohol. The only women in the old country who smoked and drank *en la calle* were "*cualquieras.*" She frowned on promiscuous sex but was very sexually active within her marriage. (She told me that the man she married at age seventy-two was the love of her life, and I heard that during the honeymoon years, the neighbors next door couldn't sleep at night for all the racket! They say good sex keeps you young . . .) She was always surrounded by her nine children, fifty grandchildren, more great-grandkids and dozens of church sisters and neighbors. For all the years she lived and worked in America, Mami Angelica led the life of a *recien llegada*!

Today's typical *recien llegada* is still much like grandma. Although she has to negotiate the stress of a new country, a new language, putting food on the table, if she is undocumented *la migra* and new ways, she's decided not to engage the values of her new homeland. Instead, she buffers her stress by reproducing a solid network of family and community, to help ground and support her.

However, most of the acculturated Latinas don't live our lives this way. We live American lives and we assimilate American ways; in many cases we simply *are* Americans. This is why it's crucial that we become aware of the new health risks our new ways of life carry.

THE HEALTH OF THE ACCULTURATED LATINA

Acculturation is the process of incorporating aspects of the mainstream culture—in this country, the ways of the gringo—into our repertoire of behaviors, lifestyle, and beliefs. Taking on the tools to survive in America. As years and generations pass, we replace some customs from the "old country" with those of the new. It's both natural and inevitable that we incorporate *americano* habits into our lifestyles, but this process alters everything in our lives, from our language to what we eat, the way we cook our food, our family structure, the role of family in our lives, and the adjustment to previously taboo behaviors. However, it doesn't seem to alter our identity as Hispanics.

Food and nutrition together make a good example of how acculturation can affect our health. The more we assimilate in this area, for instance, the more we begin consuming processed foods and fast foods.

My working mother was the "made-from-scratch meal" kind of mom. I don't ever remember eating take-out hamburgers or Chef Boyardee for dinner. *Nunca!* But while Mom would soak *habichuelas* or *frijoles* for hours, I use canned beans. And what are some of the ingredients found in the canned beans I use? Monosodium glutamate, dehydrated onions and garlic, disodium calcium EDTA to promote color, propylene glucol, and acetic acid. See what I mean? I could list dozens of other examples of the different nutritional habits of the three generations of women in my family—my *abuela*, mother, and me—but in a nutshell, their meals could be described as gourmet

Salud-at a Glance

Here is a quick checklist of the "Latina health rules" I discuss in greater detail throughout the chapter. Copy it and keep it handy—it will help you focus on your biggest priority: you!

❑ Become *numero uno* on your "to do" list.

❑ Bring a few old-school *abuela* customs into your "*agringada*" and modern *vida*—wholesome foods, spiritual faith, *musica*, and laughter; cut back or eliminate smoking and drinking.

❑ *Deja de aguantar* the pain. Don't ignore physical symptoms! See a doctor if you're not feeling well. Your health is a number one priority, *amiga*.

❑ Have a yearly gynecological checkup and a routine annual physical.

❑ Explore yourself down there: get to know your vagina and your entire body *de pies a cabeza*. Leave no beauty mark, scar, or square inch of your body unexplored.

❑ Investigate your family medical history. Tell your doctor *todo*! There should be no shame in a physician's office.

Latino, while mine are more like drive-through special-value meals. Sure, I could argue that I have no time to hover in the kitchen, and that making meals from scratch takes up too much time. But I know that's just a cop-out, since my mother raised five children and always worked outside the home.

And this is just the beginning. There is a long list of other habits that we more acculturated *hermanas* have embraced, some of which are, frankly, not so healthy. Social drinking and recreational drugs are two of them. That's why Latino health professionals, such as Harvard-educated doctor and researcher J. Emilio Carrillo,

❑ If doctors are scary or taboo, declare a "family health day" so you don't have to face the doctor on your own. Go get a mammogram and cholesterol test with all the women in your clan.

❑ Get your blood pressure checked regularly! The number one leading cause of death among Latinas is heart disease.

❑ Turn that TV off and do something! Exercise, dance, *mueve el esqueleto*. Walk, run, move your *pompis, chica!* Exercise doesn't just keep the weight off; it makes you healthy.

❑ Eat balanced meals. Strike out the Big Mac, Whopper, Doritos, and soda and replace with real food: *arroz, caldos, frijoles, tortillas,* fruits, fish, veggies, meats, and lots of water—eight glasses a day will keep you young!

❑ Declare a "me day" once a month. Take one Saturday or Sunday each month and spend all day on yourself. Go to the hairdresser, get a massage, use a sauna, work out, take yourself to a movie, read a book, or take a bubble bath—whatever will give you quality time with yourself.

❑ Claim your sexual power. Don't agree to anything that makes you sexually uncomfortable, and learn to express your needs. Your *mami* may not have told you this, but I will—good orgasms are part of good health!

❑ Be aware of your stress level. Make a boundary between you and your *problemas.* Create an end-of-the-day ritual and let go of your problems until tomorrow. You owe it to yourself to sleep peacefully every night.

are cautioning us to think hard before we drop the old-school *abuela* habits. Dr. Carrillo says that, as far as health and nutrition habits are concerned, "The children of second-, third-, and fourth-generation Hispanics—you, me, our kids and grandkids—will have to figure out what *costumbres* we are going to keep, which ones to drop, and how we are going to preserve the customs that we decide to maintain."

So if poor, recently arrived Latina sisters are healthier and live longer than the rest of us do, it's certainly worth looking at their lifestyles.

making progress

In the past twenty years the number of Hispanics earning bachelor's and master's degrees has increased 235 percent.

PAINTING THE PICTURE OF LATINA HEALTH

National health statistics show that we are in bad shape. Take cancer rates, for instance. Last year, breast cancer was the most commonly diagnosed cancer among Hispanic women—with more than eight thousand cases. It's also the leading cause of cancer deaths among our sisters; 1,800 died of the disease in 2000. Colon, lung, and cervical cancer, respectively, were the second, third, and fourth most commonly diagnosed forms of cancers among our women. In fact, the death rate from cervical cancer is 40 percent higher among Hispanic women than non-Hispanic women. Large percentages of minority women report not having had a Pap test within the past year. Among Latinas, the percentage of those who have never had a Pap smear was 43 percent.

The picture with AIDS is just as alarming. Statistics show that of all women living with the disease in the United States, more than 75 percent are Hispanic and African American. Among Hispanic women ages twenty-five to forty-four, AIDS is the third leading cause of death. Obesity has risen to 36 percent for all American women, but among Mexican-American women (not to single out *mejicanas*—they were the group surveyed and tested in this particular study) it's an astonishing 50 percent. On top of this, heart disease and diabetes are among the top ten diseases killing Latinas in the U.S.A. (By the way, Hispanic men are in worse shape when it comes to health, including cancer deaths. More Latinos suffer cancer deaths than Latinas. For more information on cancer, call the bilingual hotline 1-800-ACS-2345 or visit the bilingual website *www.cancer.org.*)

I don't mean to alarm or depress you. The fact is that all of these diseases are preventable. While you may not be able to save the Latino masses, you can take a hard look at your own health and that of your loved ones and determine if anything needs revising.

Assimilation vs. Acculturation

Okay, so you have heard these words thrown around and maybe one of them was used to describe you. Still, you are not sure what they mean or if there is really a difference between the two. Without getting too technical, let me break it down.

There is huge difference between being acculturated and being assimilated, especially as it relates to what happens to identity, traditions, and values in the process of living, procreating, and dying in the United States.

According to the dictionary, *acculturation* is the cultural modification of an individual, group, or people by adopting or borrowing traits from another culture. The acculturated Latina takes some "gringo" customs, habits, and values and incorporates them into her life without shedding the ones that she carries. She holds on to some of the values of her culture and combines them with some tools of the new dominant culture for survival and progress. The acculturated Latina becomes a hyphenated something that describes her new American identity combined with her parents' heritage. She is a hybrid of sorts; her identity is now Chicana, Cuban American, Nuyorican, Salvadoran American, Colombian American, and so on.

Assimilation, on the other hand, is described as a process; to absorb into the culture or mores of a population or group; to take in and appropriate. Used as nourishment, assimilating is being absorbed into the system. The assimilated Latina replaces the culture and values of her ancestors with that of the dominant culture. She has been absorbed by the gringo world, save her Spanish surname and, perhaps but not always, "Latino" looks. In the life of the assimilated Latina, very little Latino heritage is found in her customs, rituals, mores, and beliefs. She has digested mainstream American traits and taken them as hers.

Studies have shown that unlike the immigrants of earlier centuries, the Norwegians, Germans, Polish, and Irish, for instance, Hispanics in America are not assimilating, but are acculturating. That is, we are taking on the tools necessary to compete and thrive in this country, without completely loosing our identity and traditions. One of these studies was the Yankelovich Hispanic Monitor 1998, which found that "there is no real erosion of our Hispanic identity across generations."

Okay, so now that you know the difference, are you acculturated or assimilated?

The Latino politician

In 2000, there were no Latino senators and no Latino governors.

Puerto Rico, a commonwealth of the United States, broke new ground in 2000: island residents elected its first female governor, Sila Calderón.

According to a 1999 Substance Abuse and Mental Health Services Administration Household Survey on Drug Abuse—which includes marijuana, cocaine, inhalants, hallucinogens, heroin, or any prescription type psychotherapeutic used nonmedically—nearly 30 percent of Latinas between the ages of twelve and seventeen reported having used an illicit drug over their lifetime, while 20.1 percent reported use over the past year, and 10.5 percent reported use over the past month. Nearly 42 percent of those from eighteen to twenty-five reported having used illicit drugs over their lifetime while nearly 22 percent reported having used drugs over the past year and 14.2 reported use over the past month. Twenty-eight percent of Latinas twenty-six years and older reported illicit drug use over their lifetime, 6.6 percent reported use over the past year, and 3.8 percent reported use over the last month. (Please see sidebar on Latinas and alcohol.)

REVISING THE FUTURE— SI, SE PUEDE

These statistics are terrible—let's not kid ourselves—but despite these disturbing numbers and trends, all is not lost. Almost all the diseases for which we are at risk are lifestyle related. Early detection, a change in diet, and a cigarette- and drug-free life can help reverse the trend, medical experts say. Good health starts and ends with you; you have the power to protect yourself. As daunting as it is even to *think* about changing gears, each one of us has the power to make health a priority. The bottom line is that we have to believe "*si, se puede*"—yes, we can.

SELF-CARE

Self-care is the most empowering and important habit I've ever introduced to my life. It's *the* first step to a healthier Latina.

Self-care starts with the simple and subtle recognition that you are the top priority in your own life. Latinas, like most women, are socialized to take care of others, often at the expense of our own needs. If you think this is an *abuela* trait that we no longer have, think again. It's still revolutionary for many of us to go to the doctor when we are feeling fine. It's even more radical to find Latinas who openly embrace the attitude that says "*Yo soy primero que nadie*"—My physical, mental, and spiritual needs come before anyone else's.

STOP *AGUANTANDO*—LET IT GO

I can't tell you how many *amigas* I know who let colds turn into respiratory infections, or minor conditions into bigger problems. I know one woman who passed a gallstone before she went to the doctor, and another who waited until the lump in her breast doubled in size before getting a mammogram. (The practice of having mammograms among Latinas age forty or over was 54 percent.) It seems that we wait and wait, letting all kinds of things stand in the way of taking care of the real business: ourselves.

Latinas are all about *aguantar*. *Nosotras aguantamos a los maridos cabrones, a un* bitchy boss, or a rela-

Latinas and Alcohol

Nearly 19 percent of Latinas between twelve and seventeen years of age reported having consumed alcohol, while 9 percent reported "binge" alcohol use and 1.5 percent reported heavy alcohol use. Almost 50 percent of Latinas between eighteen and twenty-five reported having consumed alcohol, while 32.4 percent reported "binge" alcohol use and 9.8 percent reported heavy alcohol use. Of Latinas twenty-six and older, 41.6 percent reported consumption of alcohol in their lifetime, almost 21 percent reported "binge" alcohol use, and 4.7 percent reported heavy alcohol use.

tionship that hasn't worked for years. We take a deep breath and hold it together—for the family, for the sake of the kids or for *el que dirán*. Pain management has been drilled into us from an early age. It's what we saw growing up, what our *cultura* and families reinforce, and what far too many of us continue to do today. But it's one of those unhealthy traditions that is particularly dangerous: by putting our basic needs on the back burner, we sacrifice our mental and physical health.

Self-care throws out the concept of *aguantar* and embraces the concept of *yo*. I know it's a hard word to change, but I promise your life will bear more fruit for the effort.

YO BEFORE OTHERS

During a routine visit to my doctor last year, I told her an anecdote about myself that speaks volumes about how we Latinas deprioritize our health. The healthiest I've ever been was when I was pregnant with my first child. I remember going to great lengths to care for myself in mind, body, and spirit. During the nine months of pregnancy, I exercised, ate balanced meals, took vitamins, rested, and visited the doctor regularly. It was hard work, but I didn't mind it at all.

Only my diligence wasn't exactly for me—it was for the little being I had growing inside. While being responsible for the unborn baby's good health and taking precautions to give him a great start on life is commendable, I was following in that classic Latina tradition of taking care of someone else's needs before mine. And sure enough, as soon as I delivered and finished breast-feeding, I was back to my old ways.

Laura Jimenez of the National Latina Health Organization, a group formed to raise Latina consciousness about our health and health problems, echoed my concerns. "Latinas are socialized to be caretakers. [A Latina] takes care of everyone else and ends up neglecting herself. Latinas don't come in on their own for Pap smears or

Life rules from an Aztec goddess: Protect your uterus. Conceptions, immaculate and otherwise, happen. . . . Be selective about what you swallow.

CHICANA POET PAT MORA

pelvic exams, but if they get pregnant, [health] becomes a priority. Once they give birth, their attendance drops. Taking care of themselves is second priority." The truth of her words struck a deep chord in me.

How often do you realize that your annual physical exam is three years past due? How many times do you feel sad but avoid even asking yourself *qué me pasa?* let alone answering truthfully? How many hours a week do you have to yourself? And do you fill those hours organizing messy closets or doing the family laundry instead of relaxing and being good to yourself?

The tasks, people, reasons, and the stuff we place before ourselves are endless. Yet these forms of self-avoidance carry a steep price. The less we take care of ourselves, the less well we are mentally and physically. Just think, *Señorita Sacrificada*: your seeming selflessness is actually depriving the people you love of the happiest, healthiest you there can be!

DECLARE A "ME DAY" ONCE A MONTH!

As incredible as it may sound, a bubble bath was what got me started on a regimen of self-care. My son was five years old at the time. I was a single mom, working as a producer at a morning television show on the graveyard shift, from four A.M. to two P.M. As soon as I got home from work, my second shift would start, *en la casa*. Between the stress of work and the responsibilities of motherhood, I was running myself into the ground. One day, I just broke down. The loneliness of being single, the exhaustion and *burra* schedule of work had finally caught up with me. I called my mother, crying, and pleaded with her to take my son for the weekend. I needed to exhale!

That weekend I stayed home and slept until I could sleep no more. When I woke up, I prepared myself a warm, sweet, delicious bubble bath, throwing rose petals, milk, and honey into the tub. I ordered takeout and rented a bunch of movies. In fact, I didn't leave

Health Organizations Advocating for Our Health

American Cancer Society (ACS)
www.cancer.org

COSSMHO (The National Coalition of Hispanic Health and Human Services Organization)
1030 15th Street, N.W., Suite 1053
Washington, DC 20005
202-387-5000
www.cossmho.org

Hispanic Dental Association
188 West Randolph Street, Suite 1811
Chicago, IL 60601
800-852-7921
312-577-4013
e-mail: hdassoc@aol.com
www.hdassoc.org

Hispanic Salud
www.hispanicsalud.com

La Casa de las Madres
www.lacasa.org

Latina Rights Initiative (LRI)
Puerto Rican Legal Defense and Education Fund

99 Hudson Street, 14th floor
New York, NY 10013
212-219-3360

Latina Roundtable on Health and Reproductive Rights
116 East 16th Street, 7th floor
New York, NY 10003
212-533-9055
e-mail: latinarights@mindspring.com

Latino Health Institute
95 Berkeley Street
Boston, MA 02116
617-350-6900
Fax: 617-350-6901
TTY: 617-350-6914
e-mail: info@lhi.org
www.lhi.org

MANA, A National Latina Organization
1725 K Street, N.W., Suite 501
Washington, DC 20006
202-833-0060
www.hermana.org

Mujeres Latinas en Acción
www.uci.edu/orgs/mujeres

National Alliance for Hispanic Health
1501 16th Street, N.W.
Washington, DC 20036
202-387-5000

National Association of Hispanic Nurses
1501 Sixteenth Street, N.W.
Washington, DC 20036
202-387-2477
Fax: 202-483-7183
www.thehispanicnurses.org

National Center for Farmworker Health
1770 FM 967
Buda, TX 78610
512-312-2700
www.ncfh.org

National Hispanic Council on Aging (NHCOA)
2713 Ontario Road, N.W.
Washington, DC 20009
202-265-1288
Fax: 202-745-2522
www.nhcoa.org

National Hispanic Medical Association
1411 K Street, N.W., Suite 200
Washington, DC 20005
202-628-5895
www.nhma.org

National Latina Health Organization (NLHO)
PO Box 7567
Oakland, CA 94601

800-971-5358
www.clnet.ucr.edu

National Latina Institute for Reproductive Health (NLIRH)
1200 New York Ave., Suite 206
Washington, DC 20036
202-326-8970
www.nlirh.org

National Latino Alliance for the Elimination of Domestic Violence
PO Box 623
Dunn Loring, VA 22027
703-205-9040
800-342-9908
www.dvalianza.org

National Latino Fatherhood and Family Institute
5252 East Beverly Blvd.
Los Angeles, CA 90022
323-728-7770
www.nlff.org

Prevención, Inc.
www.prevencion.org

Society for Advancement of Chicanos and Native Americans in Science (SACNAS)
PO Box 8526
Santa Cruz, CA 95061-8526
333 Front Street, Suite 104
Santa Cruz, CA 95060
831-459-0170
www.sacnas.org

the apartment all weekend—I spent forty-eight hours thinking about no one but me!

I've come to call these bubble-bath time-outs "me days," and they are now a monthly gift I give to myself. "Me days" center me and get me back on track. At first it may seem selfish to put your job, children, *novio, familia,* and *amigas* on hold. But I promise you that the serenity you give yourself will transform every aspect of your life. After my "me days," I'm eager to spend time with my son, more relaxed at work, and a more sensual and tolerant girlfriend. One day a month, *chicas,* is all it takes to make you a happier woman.

Start by introducing "me days" slowly. One woman I know started with ten minutes a day. Each morning, the first thing she does when she wakes up is give herself a big hug, look out the window at the sky, and say thanks for all of her blessings. It's her way of loving and keeping herself centered. You can work these ten-minute prayers into a Sunday-afternoon walk in the park (*sola*) and eventually expand them into a full day of celebrating you.

The whole point of a "me day" is to take care of your soul—it's the first step in putting yourself on the "to do" list. With "me days," you give yourself the gift of solitude, of taking the time and space to have your own thoughts and feelings. And you'll find that something profound happens deep inside when you lovingly take care of *you.*

One of the things I had to deal with when I first began to think more about myself was guilt. I experienced tremendous amounts of guilt as I became more selfish with my time. Even though I was supposed to be relaxing, I felt anxious about errands waiting to be run and chores I could be doing. Crazy as it now sounds to me, doing for myself actually felt like a waste of time!

Time and practice have helped me understand that guilt is a useless emotion and a wasteful mental exercise. Guilt drains you. Unfortunately, guilt is also a big part of Latina psychology. There's no sense in trying to ignore it; it'll simply creep up on you when you begin to behave in ways that break with your family traditions. Yet if you start now, the uneasiness you feel with this newfound *egoísmo* will ease over the years—and just like cooking, sex, wine, and womanhood, it'll only get better with time.

HABLA CON TUS COMADRES

Of course, you don't have to be alone *all* the time. One of the tools I find most effective in processing stress is talking about what's stressing me with my sisters, my mom, and my extended network of girlfriends. As I'm always saying, we Latinas don't talk enough about the things that trouble us most. By discussing the stresses and pressure in your life, you'll realize that to some degree all the women in your circle are in the same boat. By talking openly about your life's hardships, you can also explore ways you might change your current patterns. Putting oppressive cultural and personal assumptions on the table lets you see how damaging and ridiculous they can be. Also, trying to subvert your cultural training alone can be hard, but with a good group of girlfriends you might find that you have the support and understanding you need to stick up for yourself.

If you're in a committed relationship, I encourage you to begin finding time during the week to check in and share with your partner. Too frequently we see living together as de facto intimacy when, in fact, intimacy is about time you take out of your busy schedule to share. This same rule goes for your children. Find a few hours a week to spend with each of them alone. Cultivating and nurturing your individual relationships with family members is a great way to be connected so that it doesn't feel forced or leave anyone taken for granted. In fact, as you start demanding more quality time from the special people in your life, you may notice that they begin to understand your need for quality "alone" time, and may even start demanding some alone time as well.

ES MEJOR PRECAVER QUE LAMENTAR

Have you ever heard the popular saying "It's better to prevent than lament"? That *dicho* speaks volumes about the most important aspect of health care. Preventive care is self-care. Self-care is preventive care.

Why do so many of us wait until it bleeds or we can't take the pain before we go see a doctor? I can't even tell you how many smart, amazing, fierce modern Latinas I know who exhibit this kind of careless behavior. While many of the women in my close circle have health insurance, I realize that for many members of our community access to health care is limited by economics. In 1999, one out of three people without health insurance in this country was Hispanic.

It's hard to access health care when you don't have insurance or the money to visit the doctor. Even when you can afford it, it's tough to get *adequate* care when you don't speak fluent English or when the information you get is culturally irrelevant. But the fact remains that many of us who *do* have the means don't go to the doctor, either. *¿Porqué?* The first reason is probably fear. "People in power can be intimidating," says Laura Jimenez. One of my doctor friends adds that people also fear bad news and see doctors as potential messengers of *malas noticias*!

It can also be incredibly frustrating to deal with the bureaucracies that manage medical care in this country. With HMOs, doctors have to see more patients to make the same amount of money they made ten years ago; this means that the sheer volume of people seen by HMO primary-care physicians strips the doctor's visit of any individual specificity. Often your doctor changes without warning, or the overloaded doctor assigned you as a primary physician can barely remember your name, let alone your medical history.

One way to diminish fear when dealing with doctors and hospitals is to remember that you are *not* helpless *or* powerless. You have the right to demand that your doctor explain your condition to you in detail. You have the right to ask as many questions as you want to ask. You have the right to have things explained to you in greater detail if you don't understand something. And in the event that there is a language barrier, you also have the right to demand a translator. Most hospitals have translators on staff; if not, one should be on call in the area. So remember, *you have medical rights*. Doctors are there to *serve* you (after all, *you* are paying *them!*), and you have the right to demand the best care available to you.

Notwithstanding all the barriers, the good news is that there are many Latino health professionals trying to change our invisibility within health care and the downward spiral of our health. Hundreds of Hispanic medical professionals and organizations are working overtime to help empower us in the area of health. Many organizations are pushing for a more holistic approach to medicine, such as treating the entire family, as opposed to just one person. If you have access to the Web, type the words "Latina health" into any search engine to find both Latino doctors and health organizations.

"WASH REAL GOOD, *PERO NO TE TOQUES* DOWN THERE!"

Sadly, our *cultura* is still riddled with taboos about our "private parts" and our sexuality as women. This is one of the reasons we continually top the sexually transmitted disease charts. Experts are calling these "*panocha*" problems a silent epidemic. According to a Centers for Disease Control and Prevention study, the prevalence of chlamydia in Mexican Americans (the group of Latinas studied) in June 2000 was 5 percent in women versus 2 percent in men. Gonorrhea rates among Hispanics increased from 67.4 cases per 100,000 people in 1998 to 75.3 in 1999. And Latinas are the largest group between the ages of fifteen and twenty-four currently infected.

The AIDS numbers are even more dramatic. When it comes to HIV and AIDS, minority women are also leading the way. Out of all women who were infected with the virus in 1999, 77 percent were either Hispanic or black.

Even now, when there seems to be so much information about sex and sexually transmitted diseases, sex and sex education continue to be taboo issues in the Latino community. We remain mired in a culture of *silencio*.

"On top of not talking about sex," says Laura Jimenez, "there is also tremendous reluctance to examine our own genitalia. You need to know your body so that you can see when things are off." Sadly, the church, the family, and the notion of *santa/puta* makes us shameful about confronting gynecological conditions head-on.

ELIMINATING SHAME

Getting to the gynecologist is one victory, but once we are there, another hurdle comes up: shame and guilt about our sexual histories and vaginas. Many of us feel ashamed about our sexual past because we fear being judged. But honesty with your gynecologist is crucial. Your doctor couldn't care less if you've had one or fifty sexual partners, one or ten abortions. Hear me, sister: *no le importa!* Your doctor is neither a priest nor your mother. Please be as honest as you can be, since the more your gynecologist knows about your sexual history and health, the better able he or she will be to scan you for potential diseases and interpret present symptoms. In many cases HIV is discovered by its secondary symptoms, such as chronic yeast infections or virulent bouts of herpes.

GO AHEAD, *TÓCATE* . . .

Do you know what a healthy vagina looks like? What a healthy clitoris looks like? Are you aware of what a normal menstruation cycle is? What normal vaginal fluid looks and smells like? Do you know how to give yourself a breast exam? Do you know what a Pap smear is? Do you know what a yeast infection is? Have you ever had a bladder infection? These are all very basic but important gynecological questions, and each of us should have a good idea of how to answer them. Ignoring your gynecological health can lead to early and unwanted pregnancy, infertility, disease, and, for a growing number of Latinas, premature death.

With young Hispanic women today, educators point out, there is still a real emphasis on being a virgin, so the family assumes—often incorrectly—that sex is not happening. This denial about sexual activity among our youth in the family and community results in a health crisis. Young Latin men and women are simply not getting or seeking information on ways to protect themselves sexually, until they get pregnant or sick—if then.

When sex is shrouded in secrecy, the chances of engaging in risky behavior quadruple. Without an open cultural dialogue it is very difficult for women to feel empowered to say to their *novios*, "Let's protect each other, *papi*, let's talk about safe sex." When your community and family are telling you you're bad for having sex in the first place, the pattern of secrecy is simply reinforced. It's up to us to break that pattern. (Stay tuned for more on this in chapter 7.)

VIRGINS NEED GYNECOLOGISTS, TOO!

I was not taken to a gynecologist throughout my teen years because it was assumed that I was a virgin. (And I was—but that wasn't the point.) Whether or not you are a virgin, women's health experts agree that *all* women eighteen and over should have a yearly gynecological exam. There is much more to women's reproductive health than having or not having sex.

WRITE DOWN YOUR FAMILY'S
MEDICAL HISTORY

One of the best things we can do for our own health and that of our families is to create a medical history, by interviewing our relatives and keeping a log of our family's medical facts. Not only can it save lives during an emergency (like whether or not Tia Rita is allergic to penicillin) but it can also tell us many things about our future health.

My grandfather died of diabetes, and my mother and three *tías* are living with the disease. That means I run a higher risk than those who have no family history of the disease. Knowing this important fact tells me that I have to eat a balanced diet, watch my weight, and incorporate lots of exercise into my life. It's simple: the more you know about what can happen, the more you can do proactively to ensure that you remain healthy.

And don't forget that part of a thorough family history is daring to reveal the secrets too. Mental illness and addictions to alcohol and drugs are as much part of a family medical history as diabetes or hypertension. And don't succumb to shame about any of it—it's not as if these things are anybody's fault!

Shame makes us avoid things that could potentially be fixed. For example, my friend's moody uncle Jesus turned out to be manic-depressive. Six months after being diagnosed and put on the proper medication, he was more vital and functional than ever before in his life. So when you're trying not to think about a family "secret" because you want to avoid feelings of shame, just remember this handy *dicho: No secrets, no shame.*

I'M OFF FOR A CHECKUP . . .

Doing your homework not only means knowing your family history, it also means paying attention to the latest health information. *Para que no te cojan de pendeja.* Medical breakthroughs are made every day, so keep abreast of what's going on, and see if it can help you or someone in your family.

Are you ready for the checkup? Has a physical made it to the top of your busy "to do" list? To help you along, I consulted a friend who happens to be a doctor and asked him to prepare a list of questions that you should have answered *prior* to your doctor's visit. He also helped with a list of items that you need to share with your doctor so that he or she can assess your needs better.

Before the Visit
Questions to Ask Your Primary-Care Doctor (Internal Medicine, Family Medicine, or Obstetrics-Gynecology)

1. Ask where your doctor attended medical school and did his or her residency training. Does he or she have board certification?
2. A woman doctor may help you feel more comfortable. Is there one in the practice available to you?
3. How are after-hours calls handled?
4. What other doctors in the practice are available to you, and who are the covering physicians?
5. What's the average waiting time to get an appointment?
6. What insurance does the office accept?

During the Visit
Things to Share with Your Doctor or Gynecologist

1. The date of your last menstrual cycle
2. The number of sexual partners you've had and whether you had protected or unprotected sex
3. Your own medical history and your family's medical history, if you know it
4. Your allergies, if any
5. Any medical symptoms

6. Medicines: prescribed; *borrowed;* over the counter; *remedios* from a *tia, curandera,* or *espiritista;* or home remedies.

MEDICAL TESTS AT EVERY AGE

I have included a chart that lists the tests you should have at every age, and a resource list at the end of the chapter to help you access Latino health organizations, hot lines, and books. You can give the women of different generations in your family a powerful gift by sharing this information with them. Break the silence and involve your *abuelita* in your new health regimen.

My approach to health mirrors my approach to life: holism. If someone in my family is ailing, I am too. So as I've learned to take better care of myself, I've also become more conscious of the well-being of my loved ones. By empowering yourself through preventive health care, you empower the women you love.

SALUD—TO YOUR HEALTH!

To embrace a healthy attitude that says "me, myself and I" will take an extraordinary amount of courage on your part. You'll definitely be breaking a legacy of Hispanic female behavior. But I assure you that it will not be to the detriment of you or your family. To be proactive about our health is one of the most courageous things any one of us can do.

If at first I felt queasy about this *"egoísta"* attitude of placing my needs first, I've come to realize that—bizarre as this may sound—it has benefited those I love and who love me. I am a better mom, a better *hija,* sister, and friend when my physical, mental, and spiritual needs are being met. At the end of the day, my child needs a healthy mother. My mother wants a healthy daughter. And as my brother Alex told me when I shared with him that I'd finally got a much-needed and past-due physical, "When you're well, I'm happy."

I have learned too that I cannot give what I do not have, and if I am running myself into the ground doing for others, I will have nothing but grief and angst to share with those I love.

The bottom line about your health is that you and no one else is responsible for it. Nothing should come between you and your health. Yes, it takes guts, time, patience, *cojones,* stamina, and unwavering conviction to make health a priority in your life. But it can be done, and you can do it. Start small, *mujer,* but do start and remember that other *abuela*-ism: *no dejes para mañana, lo que puedes hacer hoy!*

Elba's Wanting Bath

Baños in our culture are for more than just scrubbing dirt off your skin. They are healing and medicinal rituals for the mind, body, and soul, and many of these *bañitos* have been with our families for dozens of generations. There is probably a bath to take away every kind of pain or bring about any kind of joy. One of the most common "healing" baths is the one I have titled Elba's Wanting Bath. I have heard different variations of this *baño,* but this one is my favorite.

My wise-beyond-her-seventy-years *amiga* Elba tells me that the most important part of doing any bath is having faith. She has been doing this particular *baño* for most of her life, the one kind of ritual she feels has the most positive effects. Elba's Wanting Bath is, indeed, a "want bath." Whatever you may want at the time you are taking the bath will come to you as long as you have faith and you do the ritual with self-love. This bath is great because you can do it for different things, depending on what you are going through or need at the time. So whether it be love, good health, or tranquillity, this bath will work wonders as long as you stay focused and keep in mind what it is that you want. Remember: the most important ingredient is faith.

Annual Health Tests

I said it before, but it's worth repeating: self-care is preventive care and preventive care is being pro-active about your health and going for the annual physical. Not sure what tests to request? To get you started, I consulted with Dr. Yvette Martas, Assistant Professor, Department of Obstetrics and Gynecology, New York University School of Medicine. In between seeing patients and delivering babies, she produced this table for us. It spans the ages—from thirteen through sixty-five and older, three or four generations in your *familia*. Share it with your *amigas*, *comadres, tias,* and the rest of *la familia.*

Please keep in mind that the chart below is basic. Everyone's health history is different, so please consult with your physician about your unique medical needs.

Annual Health Tests for Women Ages 13 and Older

AGES	ROUTINE	HIGH RISK
13–18	Pap smear	hemoglobin (Hgb), bacteriuria, STD, HIV, rubella titer, tuberculosis (TB) skin test, lipid profile
19–39	Pap smear, cholesterol	hemoglobin (Hgb), bacteriuria, mammography (every 5 years), fasting blood sugar, STD, HIV, rubella titer, tuberculosis (TB) skin test, lipid profile, thyroid stimulating hormone (TSH)
40–64	Pap smear, mammography, cholesterol, fecal occult blood test, colonoscopy (every 5 years after age 50), bone density scan (at least one during perimenopause and then a follow-up)	Hemoglobin (Hgb), bacteriuria, fasting blood sugar, STD, HIV, tuberculosis (TB) skin test, lipid profile, thyroid stimulating hormone (TSH)

| 65 and older | Pap smear, urinalysis, mammography, cholesterol (every 3–5 years), fecal occult blood test, colonoscopy (every 5 years), thyroid stimulating hormone (TSH) | Hemoglobin (Hgb), fasting blood sugar, STD, HIV, tuberculosis (TB) test, lipid profile |

Pap smear: This test evaluates the health of the cervix by screening for abnormal cells. Cells are removed by a gynecologist or other health care provider by brushing or scraping the cervix during a pelvic examination, and are then evenly spread on one or more glass slides. Each slide typically contains hundreds of thousands of cells. All Pap smears should be sent to an accredited laboratory to be stained, examined under a microscope, and interpreted. All sexually active women should have a Pap smear every year. Women who have never been sexually active should have a Pap smear by 18 years of age and then every other year.

Hemoglobin (Hgb): This is a blood test that can reveal whether or not a woman is anemic. Hemoglobin is the protein that carries oxygen to our tissues using the red blood cells.

Bacteriuria: This is a simple test to check for bacteria in the urine or to diagnose a urinary tract infection. A specially treated paper is dipped in a urine sample during an office visit. A person may have no symptoms and still have bacteria in the urine. Sometimes further analysis is suggested based on this simple test.

STD: This stands for sexually transmitted disease. Herpes, gonorrhea, and chlamydia are three common STDs. A health care provider can check for STDs at the same time that a Pap smear is performed. Women may have these diseases and not exhibit any symptoms. Some STDs can cause infertility if left untreated.

Rubella: This is also known as German measles. Young women in their childbearing years should make sure they are immune to this. (Immunity is established through a series of vaccinations as a child.) This will prevent moms-to-be from transmitting this disease through the placenta (in utero) if they are exposed to rubella during their pregnancy. Rubella can cause fetal abnormalities.

Tuberculosis (TB): This is an infectious disease that can infect any organ, but most commonly infects the lungs. Tuberculosis affects approximately one-third of the world population. It can be spread through the air. Social factors influencing TB include poverty, overcrowding, and inadequate health services. Medical factors include HIV infection and immunosuppression. To test for TB, a small needle is used to inject a minute quantity of tuberculin beneath the skin. A health professional will check the skin in 48–72 hours for signs of induration (a change in the skin which is indicative of exposure to tuberculosis.)

Lipid profile: This is a cholesterol check of a blood sample in a laboratory. It gives you information on your total cholesterol, or "good" and "bad" cholesterol. If your cholesterol is high, medication may be needed. The best way to prevent "bad" cholesterol, which causes heart disease, is by eating a nutritious diet and getting regular exercise.

Mammography: This is the evaluation of the breast through a screening of the tissue. Low doses of radiation are used to x-ray the tissue. The breasts are gently placed between two plates before being x-rayed. This test can help find calcifications in the breast, which could indicate breast cancer if the calcifications are in a particular pattern. A biopsy would be ordered to further examine any irregular lumps and tissue found during the mammogram.

Fasting blood sugar: Diabetes is a significant problem for Latinos and Latinas. A simple random blood test can determine if your glucose level is too high and further testing is required. Remember, having a high level of glucose in the blood has nothing to do with the amount of sugar you eat. It is affected by your overall diet.

White flowers (roses, carnations, or any white-petaled flower will do)
Agua de florida, *available in botanicas, bodegas, or on-line
    botanicas. (I buy mine at a mainstream chain drugstore; see
    what yours carries.)*
Your favorite perfume
Sugar or honey

You can do this bath at any time of the day, but Elba recommends nighttime, since that's when you're ready to be re-

Thyroid stimulating hormone (TSH): This is a blood test also. The thyroid is the "main gland." If it is underactive, women are prone to miss their periods, suffer from depression, and gain weight, among other health concerns. An overactive gland can make women feel jittery, cause difficulty concentrating, and cause heart palpitations, among other side effects.

Fecal occult blood test: This is an evaluation that checks the stool for blood. The test can be taken in the privacy of your home or in a lab. A stool sample is collected and tested using guiaic cards. Blood in your stool could be an early sign of colon cancer.

Colonoscopy: This is an extensive evaluation of the colon (the large intestine) that requires the expertise of a gastroenterologist. Light sedation (drugs to help you sleep) of the patient is also required. It is performed using a probe with video capability, which allows the physician to check for polyps in the colon. Polyps may be present even if you do not show any symptoms.

Bone density scan: For this test, a woman lies down on a table for 15 minutes while a small computer reads the density of her bones. The scan helps doctors determine if a patient has Osteopenia or reduced bone mass. Commonly known as osteoporosis, this is an indication of low bone mass and small architectural deterioration of the bone tissue. Osteoporosis makes the bone extremely fragile and prone to fractures. You don't have to fall to fracture a bone with this progressive disease. In fact, you can fracture a bone just getting out of bed. There are medicines, including but not limited to, hormone replacement therapy, which can help slow this process. However, early prevention through nutrition is key.

laxed and can really focus your energy on what you are asking for.

Put the ingredients in a pot with plenty of water and bring the mix to a boil. As you are putting all the ingredients in, remember to think or say out loud why you are doing it. So, for example, if you want good health, keep repeating "Good health for me and my family."

Once the ingredients have all come to a boil, turn the heat off and let it cool to lukewarm. Take your usual bath or shower, then bathe yourself with the concoction. It is better if you do your whole body, including your hair, and do *not* rinse it off with water. As you let the water and all its contents slide over your body, remember to visualize what you want. Repeat the bath as often as you feel it is necessary.

Fragancia's Cold-Remedy

Been coughing so much you're about due for a chest replacement? Don't take any more of those over-the-counter cold medicines. Most of them repress the symptoms, rather than help you get over the illness. According to my friend Fragancia, you should boil a quart of water, an aloe leaf that has been opened and peeled (you can get an aloe plant from any plant store or botanica), some orange peel, and a cinnamon stick for ten minutes; when the tea is ready, sweeten it with honey to taste. Instead of drinking orange juice from a container, buy oranges and make *real* orange juice (sweeten it with a little honey if the oranges are tart). Drink plenty of water, double the eight-glass a day rule, and let your body do the rest.

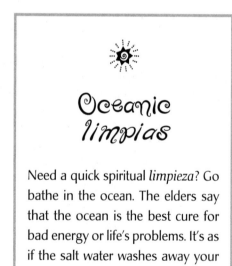

Oceanic limpias

Need a quick spiritual *limpieza*? Go bathe in the ocean. The elders say that the ocean is the best cure for bad energy or life's problems. It's as if the salt water washes away your *complicaciones*.

I've heard that the cleansing power of the ocean is so profound that even crossing by car or plane will do the trick.

Mami's Ginger-Honey Tea

Whenever I got a cold, Mom would simmer a chunk of fresh ginger for about forty minutes. Then she'd strain the liquid into a cup, squeeze in the juice of half a lemon, and sweeten it with honey.

10 Questions to Ask Your Gynecologist:

Make the most of your annual appointment with your gynecologist and be prepared to ask and listen. Don't be shy, embarrassed, or worse, rushed. Remember that it's your health and you are paying for the visit. Assistant Professor at the New York University School of Medicine and obstetrician and gynecologist Dr. Yvette Martas urges all women to bring a list of their questions and concerns to the appointment. Not sure what to ask? Here is a basic starter list. You know your own medical history, so tailor the list to your health needs.

1. How important is it to have my period once a month? What role do diet and exercise play in getting my period regularly?

2. How can I avoid sexually transmitted diseases? How can I be tested for sexually transmitted diseases?

3. What types of behavior or genetic factors increase my risk of having breast cancer? How can I decrease that risk?

4. Can I get a cholesterol check?

5. How can I get Pap smear? (if sexually active or over 18 years of age)

6. What types of behavior or genetic factors increase my risk of having cervical cancer? How can I decrease that risk?

7. What are my options for contraceptives? What are the pros and cons of taking oral contraceptives ("the pill") or any other method discussed?

8. If I am in a same-sex relationship, do I still need to visit my gynecologist regularly?

9. When should I have my first mammogram?

10. How often should I visit you? Should I see any other type of doctor for preventive care?

Some healing books I love:

The Four Agreements: A Practical Guide to Personal Freedom, by Don Miguel Ruiz (San Rafael, Cal.: Amber-Allen Publishing, 1997).

Healing with Plants in the American and Mexican West, by Margarita Artschwager Kay, et al. (Tucson: University of Arizona Press, 1996).

Herbal Secrets of the Rainforest: Over Fifty Powerful Herbs and Their Medicinal Uses, by Leslie Taylor (Indianapolis: Prima Publishing, 1998).

Homegrown Healing: Traditional Home Remedies from Mexico, by Annette Sandoval (New York: Berkley Publishing Group, 1998).

Infusions of Healing: A Treasury of Mexican-American Herbal Medicine, by Joie Davidow (New York: Fireside Books, 1999).

Nuestros Cuerpos, Nuestras Vidas: La Guía Definitiva Para la Salud de la Mujer Latina, by La Collectiva del Libro de Salud de Las Mujeres de Boston (New York: Siete Cuentos Editorial, 2000).

Our Bodies, Ourselves, by the Boston Women's Health Book Collective (New York: Simon & Schuster, 1976).

Taking Charge of Your Fertility: The Definitive Guide to Natural Birth Control and Pregnancy Achievement, by Toni Weschler, MPH (New York: HarperPerennial Library, 1995).

Latina Realities: Essay on Healing, Migration, and Sexuality, by Oliva M. Espin (Boulder, Colo.: Westview Press, 1997).

¡Salud!: A Latina's Guide to Total Health—Body, Mind, and Spirit, by Jane L. Delgado, Antonia Novello, Ph.D. (New York: HarperPerennial Library, 1997).

Curas de la Cocina Latina: Desde El Aguacate Hasta la Yuca: La Guía Maxima Al Poder Curativo de la Nutrición, by Abel Delgado, editor, *Prevention Magazine* (Emmaus, Penn.: Rodale Press, 1999).

Homejae a nuestras curanderas: Honoring our healers, by Luz Alvarez (Oakland, Cal.: Latina Press, 1997).

Where Women Have No Doctors: A Health Guide for Women, by August Burns et. al. (Berkeley, Cal.: The Hesperian Foundation, 1997).

Latino Families in Therapy, by Celia Jaes Falicov (New York: Guilford Press, 1998).

Finding Our Way: The Teen Girls' Survivor Guide, by Linda Villarosa and Allison Abner (New York: HarperCollins, 1995).

Health Issues in the Latino Community, by Marilyn Aguirre-Molina, Carlos Molina, editor, et. al. (San Francisco: Jossey-Bass, 2001).

Hispanic Voices: Hispanic Health Educators Speak Out, by Sara Torres (Sudbury, Mass.: Jones and Bartlett Publishers, 1999).

Sisters of the Yam: Black Women and Self-Recovery, by bell hooks (Boston: South End Press, 1993).

Alcohol Use—Abuse Among Latinos, *Issues and Examples of Culturally Competent Services,* edited by Melvin Delgado (Binghamton, N.Y.: Haworth Press, 1998).

Mimi's *Té de Tilo:*

If you're so stressed out that you toss and turn in your bed instead of falling asleep, stop thinking about what happened during the day and go make yourself a *té de tilo*. According to Mimi, you can just boil fresh or dried *tilo* leaves and then drink the tea—*without* adding sugar or honey. (You don't want a stimulant!) *Tilo* leaves are very relaxing and help you get a good night's sleep.

Vicks VapoRub

When Mom found out that there was actually a lip balm that smelled like her Vicks VapoRub ointment, she was thrilled.

This ointment was a staple in our medicine cabinet growing up. Rub the Vicks over your chest, cover it with a piece of brown paper bag, and put on a T-shirt or pajamas. Get under the covers, sip the ginger-honey tea, and your cold will be gone!

A fierce Latina who made U.S. history . . .

Emma Tenayuca was born in San Antonio, Texas, on December 21, 1916. Her mother's parents were from Spain, and her father was a Texan Indian. Her pride in her culture and her sense of justice led her to dedicate her life to the struggle for justice for all people, especially farmworkers. A labor organizer and a strike leader, she was jailed more times than Cesar Chavez and Dolores Huerta. She joined the Workers Alliance in 1936, an organization of the unemployed founded by socialists and Communists, 90 percent of whom were pecan shellers and agricultural workers, and the Communist Party in 1937. She is responsible for organizing the first successful strike of pecan shellers in San Antonio in the 1930s. The strike, which lasted for several months, was ultimately joined by some six to eight thousand workers, most of them women, and forced the pecan industry to raise its wages to prestrike levels. Emma earned a master's degree in education from Our Lady of the Lake University in 1974; she died on July 23, 1999.

CHAPTER FOUR

TALK CIRCLES:
The Power of Latina Friendship

A friend, a *comadre,* an *amiga,* can help you get through a rainy day, making you feel beautiful, smart, special, and loved. She can also hook you up on a blind date, even help you land that dream job, or put you in your place when you need it.

Friends play different roles in our lives as they help us mark life's stages and allow us to define ourselves better. They help lift us up when we're down, and they bring us back to earth with periodic reality checks. Latina friends in particular can go a long way to helping us nurture self-esteem, pride, and a sense of connectedness that says, "I get you, *mi hermana.*"

There is something very special and different in the ways we Latinas interact with one another, look out for one another, and care for one another. For starters, we never shake hands when we greet each other: we kiss and hug without reserve, not really thinking about that so-called personal space that non-Latinos hold dear. We hold hands in public, and anytime there's dancing going on (whether it's in a club or an apartment), you'll find straight Latina girlfriends dancing the night away, *en grupo,* in twos or threes. But that's just the beginning—a true *amiga,* a true *comadre,* becomes blood, part of your extended family.

Congress and the state legislatures

20 Latinos serve in the House of Representatives; 5 of them are Latinas.

There are 51 Latino state senators and 135 Latinos in the state legislatures.

Growing up, Mom always told me that my *hermanas* and *hermanos* and cousins were my friends, that blood came first. That's the first thing I was taught about friendship. But since I was a middle child sandwiched between two older sisters and two younger brothers, my place in the birth order forced me early on to seek out buddies outside of my family. I always found myself connecting outside of the family circle and embracing friendships with people I wasn't related to. Despite my mother's preference that friendships stay within the blood clan, once an *amiga* entered my life, she became part of my family.

My friendships with other Latinas have been special to me throughout my life; more than once they've even been crucial to my survival. But I wasn't always this conscious about the importance of Latina friendship. What brought it home to me was working in journalism, a fiercely competitive and white-male-dominated profession—that's where I first understood my need to bond with other women on the same trip, coming from the same place.

THE *COMADRE* CONNECTION

One of the best things we can do for ourselves in the new century is bring back the tradition of Mayan and Aztec talk circles, or the secret societies of *damas africanas*. Circles and *sociedades* like these let us make cultural and spiritual connections, not to mention provide professional pick-me-ups.

We have a long and strong ancestral history of *hermandad* and *comadrismo* that stretches into our lives today. Our African sisters in the New World, for example, got together in secret groups that nurtured them and their families like fresh water from a spring. These underground groups kept cultural and religious traditions alive, even under the worst circumstances we can only imagine. They met daily, weekly, monthly, annually, or whenever they could in makeshift temples or homes, where they would commune, pay homage to their gods, and pass on sacred rituals in the secrecy of the group. In these groups, women found comfort, safety, and support. My great-grandma Mamá Lucia (whom I never knew) continued a tradition passed on to her by her mother and her mother's mother. She hosted a weekly "*centro*" in a small shack behind her house in Ponce. As a child, my mother was able to experience some of these meetings. She remembers that the little shack was small on the outside but "huge on the inside." Its centerpiece was a very elaborate altar adorned with tropical flowers, plants, and statues of different saints. Mami recalls lots of women of color, native Taino and of African descent, chanting, praying, and worshiping the dead spirits. Many of these groups, like my great-grandma's group, came and went without historians taking notice. But because of our oral traditions, the stories remain alive within our families. Ask the elders in your family if there were any such meetings or rituals among womenfolk in their community when they were growing up. For instance, Puerto Rican women of African descent have long had *sociedades* where they would attend socials, have cooking contests, and mostly be among their own in a cultural comfort zone.

Then there is the tradition of talk circles, which still exists in many parts of the Southwest in native communities. For centuries, Aztec and Mayan and other Native American women had talk circles, a private space to be, to share stories and community *secretos,* and to decide on the next male leader. Yes, it was the female elders that decided in secret who the next leader of a tribe would be (many still do). Scholars have pointed out that those female talk circles are today's version of *comadrismo.*

It's hard to replicate these practices of communing and "helping each other out" in the dizzying pace of today's world. You might even

Loan-rejection blues

- Latinos were 176% more likely to be rejected for conventional loans than whites.

- Latinos were 172% more likely to be rejected for government loans than whites.

- Latinos make up to 10% of the population vying for loans but received only 5% of all loans.

- In Los Angeles, where Latinos make up half of the population, they received only 14% of the loans.

wonder if they're really necessary, since we're not enslaved and our lives aren't usually in danger. But no matter how well we live compared to earlier generations, most of us lack two major luxuries that our ancestors, even our mothers or *abuelas,* had in forming communal kinships with *vecinas,* church sisters, and *comadres:* energy and time. Our jobs and family obligations constantly vie for our attention, leaving us little for "extras." But we must forge a strong circle of Latina friends for our survival and the survival of our children, our culture, and our traditions. We may think we know very little of what our foremothers knew, but between us we carry *la tradición, las recetas,* and the family secrets.

Every Latina needs to surround herself with a tight-knit *grupo* of like-minded women who can nurture, support, and remind her that she is not *loca.* The fact that we have been and still are marginalized in mainstream America makes the case for this kind of Latina friendship even stronger. We are portrayed as one-dimensional women, either sex objects or baby-making machines. Professionally, Latinas continue to be chronically undervalued, underemployed, and underpaid.

There will always be times when you find yourself the odd one out: the only Latina in an office, the only one in your family who went to college, the only one who refuses to marry and have kids, or the only victim of an insidious form of abuse or sexism or discrimination. . . . Those are the times when you need a sounding board—a fellow Latina who gets you, and reminds you that you are not alone. This is why I nurture and forge friendships with like-minded professional Latinas, women who share similar racial, national, cultural, political, and economic backgrounds.

THE FABULOUS LIPS

One of my favorite authors, African American sister Iyanla Vanzant, says that one of the most important things women of color should do for themselves in the twenty-first century is bring ritual and ceremony back into their lives. This involves gathering, celebrating, and revering one another. By doing this, she says, we nourish one another's souls and gain the strength to live our daily lives.

The ritual power of Latina friends gathering and revering each other is immense. I have witnessed it in my life for the past ten years, rarely giving a second thought to how much strength I get from each of these "ceremonies" with my fellow *mujeres*. But deep inside I know that, with every meeting, my soul leaves nourished.

For years, I have been part of a monthly gathering of more than thirty Latina professionals. We call ourselves LIPS—short for Latinas in Power, Sort of—and we're an informal organization made up of an assortment of personalities, professions, religions, marital status, sexual orientations, colors, nationalities, and political inclinations. All of

---

Diosas de las Américas

Oyá is a Yoruban goddess who rules the winds, the whirlwind, and the gates of the cemetery. Her number is nine, and she rules over the *egun,* or dead. She is also known for the colors of maroon, flowery patterns, and nine other colors. She is a fierce warrior who rides to war with Shangó, sharing lightning and fire with him. Legend has it that she wears pants under her skirt—always ready for war. In fact, she is said to be the only female Orisha to go to war with the male Orishas. (*Orishas* are divinities of the Yoruban pantheon that represent the forces of nature [*The Altar of My Soul: The Living Traditions of Santería,* by Marta Moreno Vega].)

us speak English, though not all of us speak Spanish. And we hail from different parts of Latin America and the United States. Most of us were born and raised in this country, or have lived here for most of our lives. We all have demanding careers outside the home. And most important, we share a desire to connect at a different level with fellow professionals and a wondrous pride in our distinct Latin backgrounds.

My close friend and mentor Rossana, publisher and CEO of a major Spanish-language daily newspaper in New York City, started the group with a modest goal: to organize the then-growing number of Latina journalists in the New York tristate area so that they could get to know one another behind the bylines and press conferences where we often met.

LIPS the idea, she says, began right around the time of the slaying of her friend and mentor Manuel De Dios Unanue. At the time, several Latina reporters from the local newspapers, current Lipsters as we call ourselves, were attempting to interview Rossana about the crusading slain journalist. "It would have been such a different story had they [Evelyn and Elaine] known me," she recalls. She also remembers that many of her male journalism colleagues seemed to have a natural bond probably initiated at the best watering holes in the City—something the female journalists didn't have.

"We didn't get that kind of opportunity," she said. Eventually she hoped that LIPS would emulate the powerful New York–based group 100 Black Men, a national alliance of African American men of business, industry, public affairs, and government devoted to mentoring and empowering black youth. That inspiration came when she went to an event in the Bronx where the organization was adopting a school. She hoped LIPS would one day do that, among other things. That next level she says will come with time. For now, it is a space to unwind with the girls.

Rossana turned to two other Latina sisters, television correspondent Maria Hinojosa and editor Aileen Gelpi; between them they mapped out a list of women they wanted to invite. They borrowed a conference room in the Caribbean Cultural Center, an organization that researches and keeps records of the Afro-Latino diaspora, in the heart of midtown Manhattan. Rossana catered the meeting with rice, beans, *tostones*, and baked chicken. In hindsight, the choice of where to hold the first meeting was magnificent, as this center is one of the most recognized research institutions for Africans of the Americas. LIPS was blessed by the spirits of our ancestors, and thus destined to blossom.

Eight out of the twenty women invited went to that first meeting, and LIPS was born. I actually skipped the first meeting—I was surprised to be included in the list in the first place and suspicious about the whole thing. ("'In *power*'? *Me?!* I don't *think* so!") But when I got a second invite I became curious about where this was going; I went to the meeting, and I was hooked. After spending an evening with women I really didn't know but who seemed to share culturally and professionally many of the frustrations and concerns that I was going through as a television journalist, I decided that this group felt right. It felt great.

We quickly decided on several rules. First of all, men—Latino or otherwise—were not invited. But children (including boys) were. It's not a man-hating group (far from it; we love our men and recognize their importance in our lives), but this is about us, *las chicas*. It's a girl group that allows quiet time *para las mujeres*. Rossana pointed out how our society champions all kinds of "boy time," like sports watering holes, but not female time. When is "girl time" supposed to happen? In the kitchen? In the mall? No. These get-togethers are occasionally about recipes and *ropa*, but also about so much more.

My son, BJ, has grown up with all these fantabulous Latinas. I sometimes secretly wonder how my fourteen-year-old boy, who many times sits quietly, listening to all these *mujeres* exchange war stories about love, husbands, recipes, politics, career, and even sex, will be

Homeownership: casita, dog, and purple picket fence

The national average for homeownership is 66%.

Whites: 73%
Blacks: 47%
Latinos: 46%

affected by this neat exchange of *nueva latinas.*

The last LIPS rule was about membership. To become a Lipster, you had to be invited by one. Once you were on the list and had been to a meeting, you were on the mailing list forever. We each take turns hosting a meeting in our homes. That's it! We have no president, no vice president, and no agenda—except to eat, drink, and gossip. It's our private space to exhale.

I always host the Christmas and Tres Reyes meeting. We have a gift exchange and my mother makes *pasteles* (Puerto Rican tamales). Some of the women bring their *coquito* (Puerto Rican nutmeg) or Colombian *ponche,* others flan or *pan dulce,* and we reflect on the year that has passed. Every year I try to bring a musical surprise. For several years, in keeping with the female theme, I invited Retumba, a group of female *congueras,* to play and celebrate with us. Last year, I invited a traditional *parranda* (Puerto Rican carolers)—three old *viejos* and a *vieja,* like the great Trio los Panchos— who sang traditional songs from all of the Spanish Americas.

My Anglo neighbor saw the group tuning their guitars and *guiros* in the hallway prior to the *asalto,* the surprise musical attack, and asked if I'd invited the Buena Vista Social Club to my apartment!

Ten years and many new moons later, the original eight has blossomed to more than thirty. It has expanded to include various successful media professionals—TV producers and journalists, magazine editors, Internet journalists, publishers, criminal attorneys and public defenders, public relations experts, a poet, a playwright, and a college professor. It is a group of strong, powerful beautiful *mujeres* who dance to the beat of their own *congas.*

CELEBRATING ME

The monthly get-togethers in our living rooms are different every time. As I said, there's no set agenda, for the most part; it's just that special time. These wonderful women, each possessing a unique inner and outer beauty, have taught me much about life: trust, honesty, envy, ambition, motherhood, loyalty, patience, *locura,* self-doubt, and love. I've seen up close and personal what it means to be a professional Latina working and living and trying to keep it real in all areas of our lives. We have survived divorces, breakups, and firings; we've celebrated new jobs, promotions, new careers, births, and many birthdays; we've given referrals, gotten each other jobs, and thrown baby showers. And with each new meeting we forge another intimate link. It's Latina friendship with a consciousness at its best.

CELEBRATING *LAS MADRES*

About five years ago, one of us suggested that we host a Mother's Day brunch with *our* mothers. We celebrated the first LIPS "mom brunch" the Saturday before Mother's Day. Everybody chipped in and cooked or brought something. Maite's mom flew in from Puerto Rico, Maria's flew in from Chicago, mine took the train from New Jersey, and the women whose mothers were too far away or had passed on brought their *madrinas, comadres,* or sisters. On that special Saturday, we celebrated our mothers. There was poetry, food, music, funny skits, dancing, and oral history. My mother caught everything on a new video camera she had just gotten. The ritual with our moms showed me new sides of my fellow Lipsters, and it showed my mom another side of me. Through the easy exchange between *hija y madre,* I watched us learn about our mothers and ourselves. Five years later, those special mamá brunches are still going strong, full of poetry, sometimes live musical serenades, *cuentos, chistes,* and delicious food. And my mother always looks forward to this annual ritual, having forged friendships and camaraderie with several of the mothers she sees once a year.

About a year ago, as more and more Latina professionals in New York learned about LIPS, we reluctantly realized that we had to limit the number of women we could have in the group. We had grown, thanks to our open-door policy, but by the seventh year we'd reached a comfort level with one another that we felt could be broken if we kept growing; it's hard to have intimacy in a group of more than twenty people! Then there was the reality that few of us have homes that can accommodate such a big group. But could we just close out these great sisters who were coming out of the woodwork? That's when Lee and Elaine came up with the idea of starting a younger version of LIPS. We put together a list of young Latina professionals who had wanted to come to our meetings, as well as others who we thought might like the idea of a talk circle, and hosted the first meeting of LIPS Jr. I don't know if the group will thrive as ours has, but it seemed like the magic was everywhere. A comment I overheard one junior Lipster make to another on the elevator was typical: "It was great—I feel like I've known these women forever!"

GRUPO DE CAFÉ

We weren't the only ones with this great idea. Several thousand miles away and unbeknownst to us, another group of remarkable Latina professionals was also blossoming. Based in Denver, Colorado, they call themselves Grupo de Café, and I learned about them through a reporter who had profiled the group. Unlike LIPS, these women have a website and have made their talk circle an agent of change, both within the group and outside it. They use the site to post news about themselves and their successes, and to celebrate the success of other Latinas they've never even met—they picked up a small story about the book you're holding in your hands, and gave kudos to me and my editor, fellow Latina Becky Cabaza.

Grupo de Café has been meeting at a local coffee shop at 7:30 A.M. every Friday morning for the past ten years. They formed *el grupo* for reasons similar to ours for forming LIPS: a need for *apoyo* and connectedness on a professional level. The two founders, Rosemary and Denise, were two of only four Latinas working at a big law firm of one hundred lawyers.

"We just wanted time together away from the office, where we could talk about office politics and share things in common," says Rosemary. "An environment where we knew we could always trust the people there and could speak freely." The group expanded through referrals, friends dropping by, interested family members, and people in the coffee shop who were curious about what those women were doing every Friday!

As was the case with LIPS, a group like this starts with the need to have someone deconstruct the office agenda and then it morphs into something that feeds other parts of your life.

Rosemary told me that the friendships she has formed through the *grupo* are an important part of her life. "You have to make time for each other and then stick to it. In the reality of our busy lives, this has to be a constant."

STARTING YOUR OWN TALK CIRCLE

LIPS's and Grupo de Café's stories of *comadrismo* with a cause can be replicated—by you. And it's not just about professional support, though that can be the starting point. It's about something much more profound—a safe place to feel connected and supported.

FOLLOW THE LEADER

While LIPS has thrived without a formal leader, for some women the leader can be one of the most important parts of forming and sustaining a successful group. You need to decide for yourselves what works best for you.

All the Grupo de Café women tell me that Rosemary is the driving force behind the group. They describe her as "amazing" and "always doing great things for the community"—such as going to schools, talking to our people about the issues they face every day, and inviting students to visit her at work and observe her on the job.

Denise from the Grupo de Café says that a leader should be someone who is motivated and visible in the community. But she should also motivate the other members of the group. "Rosemary has gotten us on more boards and political campaigns than we would have by ourselves," one of them said. The group as a whole has become an agent for change, carrying its spirit far beyond the coffee shop where they meet.

SET THE AGENDA

What do you want your *grupo* to be? Whether it's a book club, a professional group, a girls-night-out group, a workout-buddy group, a spirituality group, or just a hang-in-the-living-room *grupo,* you have to have a theme that connects all of you. And start small—ten at the most. If you can, include several women you don't already know intimately.

When you are trying to set an agenda for the talk circle, make sure that you are being realistic. As Rosemary says, "Don't set too many goals. Don't expect too much. Make the commitment to spend the time together. Treat [the members] with the respect that you give your coworkers."

In other words, don't push it; let it blossom.

Other women in the group offered similar advice. "People will fall in and out. Get to the point of comfort, where you want to do things. Be realistic. Get together for lunch or coffee or a drink, start small with things you're each able to do. And let it grow from there. If other Latinas want to get together, it'll progress."

DECIDE HOW THE GROUP WILL GROW

Have a clear membership policy, but be flexible. For LIPS, fluidity worked like magic—until we reached the saturation point. Since you can't just keep inviting everyone, be selective. It's about protecting the trust and comfort level of those who are invested in the group.

SET THE GROUND RULES

Once you've formed the group and you're meeting on a regular basis, it's important to set the ground rules that will give the group its shape. Grupo de Café had to grapple with a breach of privacy when a new member of the group carried the conversation that they'd been having outside of the group. As group member Michelle, an attorney, says, "It was hard on the sanctity of the group. This was always a safe place for us to give our opinions. When the incident happened and our trust was violated, it was a challenge getting over it. We meet in a coffeehouse every Friday. This is an open area and you can be overheard, but we also know that if I am sharing a concern about our community [in Denver] and it's shared beyond the group, it is very hard to get back into speaking your mind. It made us take a step back. This was a challenge that we had to overcome. And we did."

As Rosemary put it, "If you can't find a place where you can be yourself, it's really easy to lose yourself."

Don't be surprised if the group has a profound impact on you. LIPS and Grupo de Café have both evolved from a group of women getting together to share ideas, opinions, and concerns at a professional level to a collective of amazingly intelligent and motivated women who truly care for one another and their community. Their members have helped one another do everything from keeping jobs to raising families. Grupo de Café, for example, mentored a formerly homeless young woman through college, made gift baskets five years in a row to benefit a cancer charity, helped a young Latino campaign

Comadre Wisdom for Starting a Circle in Your City

- Choose a day and stick to it.

- Pick a day that will work for everybody. Make a commitment, put it in your calendars, and be sure you make it.

- Choose a leader or leaders, and rotate responsibility.

for a local judgeship, and become generally more active in politics and community issues.

According to Denise, "Professionally, there's no question that this group has helped me a great deal. I've become politically concerned with being a voice for our community. Personally, I feel that if I fell behind somebody would wait for me, and that person would most likely be someone in this group. I like myself better when I am around these people."

For another woman, the collective is all about *comadrismo*. "The first word that comes to mind when I think of what this group has done for me personally is friendship. I have a huge family and I would match every one of these women with any of my five sisters. You can't even describe how wonderful it feels to go in any morning with a concern or a problem, be it professional or personal, and know that you have people who will listen and talk it over. I would be missing a piece of myself without my *hermanas*."

Sylvia, another *comadre* in the talk circle, told me that she joined the group seven years ago, drawn by the chance to have professional role models who she could relate to. As a result, she says, she feels better about herself.

"When you're the only Latina in your workplace, you stand out. This is the place that I call home. Some of these women know me in a way that my siblings don't. These women are home."

For all the members of these groups, the circle of Latinas can be deeper in its effects and richer in its rewards than therapy. "We are all in the same position. We are ourselves. No pretensions."

DEFINING *AMIGAS* AND *COMADRES*

I cannot define what a friend is to you; only you can do that for yourself. To me, a friend is someone who covers your back no matter what, who, when called for, will put aside personal interests to back you up. In my friendships, loyalty and discretion reign. Envy, jealousy, and competitiveness don't. For a very long time, I thought every woman I called *amiga* embodied my definition. Thinking that way, the trust and openness I brought to my friendships allowed me to live extraordinary moments. I have felt cared for and loved; I've been guided and supported by *amigas del alma.* But I also discovered the hard way that definitions of "friend" vary from person to person. As a result, I have also lived tearful disappointments, feeling disrespected, used, and even betrayed by women I considered *amigas.*

I learned that there are different roles friends can play in your life. Learning to divide friends into categories will help you sort out those roles. Because friendship is a magical thing and no single definition can do it justice, the categories of *amistades* that you establish in your heart must be flexible. At first, I worried that doing this made me a *mentirosa* or a user. I don't come from the tradition of categorizing friends. Besides, I asked myself, isn't friendship all about trust?

But then the reality of *la vida* hit me. Not all the women with whom you forge relationships are *comadres* worthy of an honest exchange about intimate life details. Learning to figure out what *kind* of friends your friends are can save you from disappointment, humiliation, and heartache.

DIFFERENT *AMIGAS* FOR DIFFERENT REASONS

An old adage says there are three kinds of friends: those who come for a reason, those who come for a season, and those who stay a lifetime. When I shared this notion with my friend Nina, she told me that she also has three kinds of friends: A friends, B friends, and C friends. A friends are the most intimate, B friends are close but not intimate, and C friends are . . . friends, but not close.

Friendship is something that also has agendas. You can be that mom with the only pool on the block or the Latina on campus with the best taste in clothes. What you bring to the "friendship"— *cualquier cosa,* fame, fortune, or the only large flat-screen TV in the neighborhood—may be something *la otra* wants. Agendas come in all colors, and you need to protect yourself from these "friends." *Amigas* like that—Latinas and not—come by the dozen.

Chances are, you already have categories of friendships, even if you haven't thought about it consciously until now. What are your categories? Do they work for you? I have five different kinds of *amigas,* as I'll explain.

AMIGA SOULMATE OR AMIGA COMADRE

Ana is my girl soulmate. We've known each other since college, but we didn't connect then, even though I was keenly aware of her. In fact, I stayed away from her because I thought she was arrogant and loose. (She later confessed that she'd had a similar view of me!) It wasn't until we were well into our careers that our souls connected; since then, we've developed a strong, sisterly bond. I can be weak and vulnerable, strong and fastidious, forgetful and loud—and she still loves me. With every success we have in our lives, there is an unselfish celebration, as if her successes and failures are mine to celebrate and weep over, and vice versa. Through Ana's devoted friendship, I learned many of life's lessons: about charity, honesty, integrity, loyalty, and the meaning of *familia.* You take a family's love as a given, but you cherish those bonds built outside of that natural structure.

The foundation of what is really special about Ana is our shared cultural experience. She's also a first-generation Latina of Puerto Rican descent, she's my age, and she shares my love of music, food, and politics. I can spend a lazy Sunday afternoon reading the papers with Ana or a crazy night dancing salsa. We can share a poem or a song, a good meal or a joke. She says she likes me because I laugh at her corny jokes. I think she likes me because deep inside she knows that I recognize her real comedic timing, among so many other exceptional talents. Ana gets it when I talk about family issues, career concerns, or man problems, and her advice is always straight up, often blunt and practical.

We've taken life-altering vacations to Cuba, France, Puerto Rico, and Mexico, among other places. We are so intuitively connected that even our taste in clothing has melded to one. We're constantly laughing as we discover that we're wearing the same article of clothing in the same color, bought and put on with no knowledge that the other had done the same. I feel honored that I can count on *una amiga* like Ana.

It's an easy friendship that is joyous and spiritual, trusting and extraordinary. It was built with time. A friendship like hers is truly priceless.

How can you tell if *you* have an *amiga* soulmate? Actions speak louder than words; the recipe for this kind of friendship is honesty, loyalty, consistency, care, laughter, support, and time.

OTHER KINDS OF AMIGAS

Besides the soulmate or *comadre,* I believe there are four other kinds of *amigas,* each valuable in her own way:

- the *amiga colega,* with whom you can share deep professional questions, issues, and concerns;
- the *amiga consejera,* whom you seek out for spiritual advice;
- the *amiga del hangueo,* someone you know who can take you to the parties; and
- the *amiga* acquaintance, a woman with whom you might share general talk about the job or celebrity gossip, but never any of the really personal stuff.

Each of these friendships provides something very different for you, and none of these is more or less important than the other. If all your friends were soulmates, the intensity of the friendships would probably burn you out. If all your *amigas* were acquaintances, you would feel a profound lack of intimacy in your life. The ideal we can strive for is a balance of all five types of friends, and the awareness of who our friends are to us—as well as who we are to them.

I have tremendous faith in the power of friendship between women, and not just Latinas. When I screen the wonderful footage of my friendships in my memory, I am reminded of how wonderful it was to know that I wasn't the only one not feeling popular with the boys or stressing needlessly over a test or dating a man who (as my girl would remind me) was no good for me. I remember being assured that I would get that job I really wanted, that my health would be okay, and how much better I felt for the assurance. And I remember the bittersweet joy of sharing sorrow.

That goes for all my friendships—with Latinas, Anglos, Asians, and African American women. But I also see how unique and important Latina friends in particular have been for my personal growth. They have allowed me to discover in small and giant ways that I am not alone. They've shown me that a sisterhood of women shares my experiences and peculiarities as a bicultural and bilingual woman living in two worlds. And I've learned to draw from the tremendous energy that comes from sharing with women who look like me and share similar traditions and common concerns. Sharing with the familiar.

Through all the pleasures and the disappointments that the many female friends have engraved in my soul, I witnessed the awesome power in my life of friendships with women. And with each wonderful new friendship that I welcome, I relearn the importance of female relationships in helping me sort out the myriad questions, issues, and frustrations I face daily as a woman, a Latina professional, and a single mother.

Some friends whom I thought I'd have in my life forever lasted a season; others I thought would be gone after the new moon have been with me a lifetime. But all of these friendships, however short or long, however sweet or bitter, have been important in shaping the woman I am today. Just as your friendships have shaped you, and will continue to shape you for as long as you live.

A fierce Latina who made U.S. history . . .

 **Ellen Ochoa**'s achievements are out of this world, literally and metaphorically. In 1990, NASA selected her to train as an astronaut, and three years later she became the first Latina to travel into space when she participated in a nine-day mission to study the earth's ozone layer. She has logged more than 480 hours out in space. Born in La Mesa, California, in 1958, Ellen soon became an extraordinary scholar. She earned a bachelor's degree in physics from San Diego State University and a master's and a doctorate in electrical engineering from Stanford University—*and* she's happily married with two sons. NASA has honored Ochoa with seven awards for outstanding achievement, including the Exceptional Service Medal (1997), Outstanding Leadership Medal (1995), Space Flight Medals (1999, 1994, 1993), and two Space Act Tech Brief Awards (1992). Think of it—astronaut, wife, mother, *and* Latina. In 1999, Ellen, who is one of five kids, was chosen by former president Bill Clinton to serve on the presidential commission on the celebration of Women in American History. This was crucial to the validation not only of women as an inherent part of America but of Latinas who have played a significant part in this country's history!

CHAPTER FIVE

CENTERING YOUR SOUL:
Spirituality Latina Style

I consider myself a deeply spiritual woman, yet I don't follow any organized religion. Instead, I have a spiritual practice that borrows from Santería, *curanderismo, espiritismo,* Latin folk Catholicism, Christianity, and even Buddhism. I call it a spiritual fricassee. And while my deeply religious, daily-churchgoing mother is very uneasy with the way I praise God, I have found solace in the new "spiritual home" I have made for myself. Every day, I celebrate my spirituality and honor the sacred soul that I am. Do you?

Religion has always been central to my life—I'm sure it started in my momma's womb—but I didn't always accept that *God* was at the heart of it. After a long hiatus from things spiritual, though, I realized that I wasn't fighting the higher power in the universe; I was rejecting someone else's interpretation of it. Even so, my faith—though tested time and again—was always grounded. And in times of trouble or joy, I always reserved a secret prayer and a holy thank-you to *Papa Dios* and the *santos* and *virgencitas* that I grew up with.

Even if religion is not central to your life, I'll bet some form of spirituality remains deeply rooted in your soul. Our faith in a higher power is, I believe, ancestral. And no matter how many generations we have been here or how acculturated we've become, Latin folk are deeply *religiosos*. For many of us, however, religion and spirituality remind us of a dark and sometimes scary alley we'd rather walk past than through. For those of us who emigrated here and those of us born here to immigrant or even second- and third-generation Latino parents, finding a spiritual practice that feels right can be especially challenging.

The recent exodus from the Catholic Church tells part of the story of Latino faith in the twenty-first century. In a 1997 survey conducted by the National Opinion Research Center, just under 70 percent of U.S. Latinos identified themselves as Catholic. That figure was down 11 percent from the 1970s. Moreover, the more we acculturate, the more we are likely to change faiths. A 2001 study on Hispanic faith by the California-based Tomás Rivera Policy Institute found that as we acculturate, there is a clear linear conversion toward other religions, mainly Protestantism. That is, as we get farther from the first generation, we also tend to convert to other Christian and non-Christian religions, or become agnostics, atheists, or drop religion altogether. For example, whereas 74 percent of first-generation Hispanics were Catholic, only 59 percent of third-generation Hispanics were.

Patrisia calls herself a *Guadalupana-Budista*. She grew up a Catholic in a strict Mexican American family in Texas. Her mother said three rosaries a day, her grandma, eight. Patrisia says none, but that does not mean she doesn't respect the power of their prayers.

"My mother and *abuelita*'s prayers kept me alive, saved me, and guided me, and I want to honor them." So today while Patrisia, who left the Catholic Church in her late teens, does not recite rosaries, she does pray—in the form of Buddhist chants—throughout the day.

Patrisia also prays to *La Morena, La Virgen de Guadalupe,* but not in the traditional form of the Catholic Church. She prays to *La Virgencita*'s indigenous representation, that of Tonantzin, or Mother

Jefecita. I am still faithful to you, who represents the Nation, even though I now may be a Pentecostal, Jehovah's Witness, Adventist, Baptist or Mormon.

—CARLOS MANSIVAÍS

Where Did we come from?

In 1997, one in two of the nation's foreign-born residents were born in Latin America.

There were four Latin American countries among the top ten countries of birth of the nation's foreign-born: Mexico, Cuba, the Dominican Republic, and El Salvador.

Three out of four U.S. residents born in the Caribbean lived either in the New York or the Miami metropolitan areas.

More than half of the Mexican-born population lived in the Los Angeles and Chicago metropolitan areas.

Earth. For her, *La Señora de Guadalupe* represents a connection to her ancestral roots. "The female energy of the *Virgencita*," Patrisia says, "gives me comfort." In addition, she also practices Buddhism, with daily chants, mediation, and yoga. Buddhism, she says, represents to her the ability to have a choice.

Luz Maria, also born and raised a strict Mexican Catholic, in California, calls herself an atheist (though her dad doesn't know; it would devastate him). And yet despite her avowed atheism, every year she erects an altar for her dead ancestors on the Day of the Dead. "It's not about Catholicism or religion," she says. "It's about a rite that honors my Azteca ancestry, *mi abuelita* and my *perrita* Tasha."

She left the church in her teens, more than a decade ago. Feeling guilty after she lost her virginity, she says she "was ready to repent and never have sex again till I got married. When I confessed, instead of a shoulder to cry on, the priest lashed out at me. He made me feel so bad, like I was a prostitute." Her rituals today all are about ancestors.

By contrast, another Latina I know, Betty, who grew up an Evangelist, is part of a growing number of so-called born-again Catholics. At forty years old, she completed her first communion by going through the year-long Rites of Catholic Initiation for Adults.

Most of us don't choose a religion; we are born into one. But as adults we are making choices that are counter to the "traditional" religious practices of our parents, grandparents, and great-grandparents. And just as many other things have morphed in our lives, so has religion.

My religious journey, which I believe resembles that of many Latinas at the crossroads of their mothers' or family's religious values, has taken me through moments when I have even questioned whether or not God really existed. I lived moments of anger, too, with God. I was cynical about the Church. The institutional church simply did not celebrate the free spirit and woman that I was becoming. Have you ever felt that way? Did you have a beef with God? The institutional church?

Faith in Our Community

Seventy percent of Latinos are Catholic. Twenty-two percent are Protestant (covers non-Catholic, and includes Jehovah's Witnesses and Mormons). Eight percent are other—Jewish, Buddhist, Santero, Agnostic, Atheist, or no religion.

Latinos are becoming Protestant as they acculturate.

CATHOLIC	PROTESTANT
First generation: 74%	First generation: 18%
Second generation: 66%	Second generation: 25%
Third generation: 59%	Third generation: 32%

It took me a while to understand that spirituality is not religion and that faith planted a long, long time ago by my mother is a source of strength. Whether you're Catholic, Pentecostal, Buddhist, Baptist, Jewish, Muslim, or a Jehovah's Witness, or, like me, a freelance believer of all practices, understanding and embracing the power of spirituality in your life is an extraordinary thing. But spirituality doesn't end with the mind and soul—it also extends to the body, which is why the second part of this chapter will deal with the spiritual power of herbs, a long-time Latina tradition.

No matter what your faith is today, no matter what combination you practice and what you call it, the most important thing is that you find a way to honor yourself as the sacred soul that you are.

MY SPIRITUAL JOURNEY

I was born into and raised by a family of devout Catholics and Pentecostals. When I was growing up, the only books we had in my home were several copies of the Bible—in Spanish and later in English. Right before I hit puberty, my mother converted to the Pentecostal faith, taking us with her (and no, we didn't have a choice!). Around my fifteenth birthday, the Pentecostal church's teachings started feeling oppressive to me. I had no use for the particular "God" that my church was selling, especially because it seemed like he thought *everything* was a sin: listening to music, dancing, wearing makeup or pants, even letting your hair loose—let alone taking contraceptives or having premarital sex. I hated feeling like a sinner all the time. The God of my fundamentalist church was so tyrannical and so judgmental that I didn't want him in my life. For many Catholic Latinas, the feeling of being "left" out of church rituals gave them a bitter taste in their hearts. One woman I spoke with tells me she left the Church as an adult because she had never understood why she could not be an "altar girl" while her brother could be an altar boy.

Diosas de las Américas

Chasca is an Incan goddess who created the dawn and twilight, the gentlest aspects of the sun. Her consort is the sun god, Inti. Chasca uses light to draw sprouts from the ground and inspire blossoms. She is also the special protectress of virgins and young girls. Her rapport with Inti and her tender nature give Chasca associations with love. According to lore, she communicates with people through clouds and dew in a type of geomantic omen observation. She was the Incas' personification of the planet Venus.

When I went away to college I left behind my mother's God-fearing, church-loving lifestyle and found a new sense of freedom. But in times of trouble or good fortune, my Christian grounding would unexpectedly surface. Before I took a test I would say a silent prayer, "*Ay Dios mio que todo me salga bien.*" Every time I applied for a job, I secretly had a shout-out to the Almighty.

My reconciliation with God came in my late twenties. Fresh from a broken marriage, with a two-year-old son and looking for a full-time job, I was spiritually lost. Emotionally sad and broken, as well as on the rocks financially, I yearned for help. And help came, in the form of prayer: every time things seemed to get out of hand, I would stop and pray. Then one day, on a trip to Texas, I happened to find the most beautiful tiny wooden Jesus. It was sweet and simple and carved by an unknown artist, and I felt an overwhelming urge to give it a place in my home. That was the beginning of what today is one of my *altares*. It was also the beginning of my reconnecting with my spiritual side.

Where we Don't live

According to the U.S. Census, the two states with the lowest Hispanic population are Vermont and Maine.

DIOS APRIETA, PERO NO AHORCA

My emerging faith also brought me back to the African roots of my early childhood religion, Santería and *espiritismo*. When I was a little girl my *abuela* Angelica had an altar with a beautiful Indian *santo* in the corner of her living room. He was bronze, like the color of tropical tamarind, and had a full head of jet-black hair and a colorful feather headdress. This *indio* looked fierce. I remember the fresh carnations, red apples, bananas, and red wine that adorned the altar. It was a powerful image that lay dormant in my mind. Later, as I began celebrating my faith through the building of my own altars, an *indio* like my grandmother's found its way into my hands—and onto my altar.

What I have come to understand is that, while no one single organized religion speaks to my faith, I have learned to carve out my own spiritual space. Along the way, I've created my own rules for moral conduct based on the beliefs held dear in my Judeo-Christian, *espiritista* home: a strong love of family and community, and a sense of charity and kindness to myself, my neighbors, and the larger community. I try to resist the negative power of envy and jealousy and lying, and I'm a practicing believer in the power of love. I like to think that I practice those very beautiful Christian teachings that made Jesus Christ one of the most powerful teachers of all time.

My belief isn't airtight, and that feels fine. When I told a priest I know and love that I wasn't sure I believed in his God, he told me he wasn't sure either. "I practice God," he said, "I don't just believe in him." On the other hand, he said, there are people who go to church and say they believe in God but don't practice him. And there are those, the priest told me, who say they are atheists, who don't go to church and who reject the God they were taught in childhood, but practice God in their everyday lives. He told me that I'm one of those people.

My eclectic brand of spirituality is manifested everywhere in my life. In my home there are little altars everywhere, for the *santos*, the *orishas* (gods), my living relatives, and my ancestors. They embody my fervent belief that I am protected by paying tribute to the *orishas*, and to the people that I love. These *altares* also serve as a place for me to meditate, to reconnect with my intuitive self, to be myself. Altars were the way of the Aztecs, the way of my African ancestors, the way of my family, and in all likelihood the way of your family.

At one end of my apartment I have an altar to Santa Barbara, the patron saint of powerful women. This *santa* represents duality, since in the Yoruban religion this *orisha*, a god in Santería, is Changó, the male god of lightning and thunder. Since the syncretism allows for both male and female characteristics, Santa Barbara reminds me that duality is a source of strength. At the other end of my apartment is *la virgen de Regla*, known as Yemayá to Santería practitioners. The mother of the sea, she is mysterious and nurturing and deep. Regla helps me go deep into my soul. Whenever I get too stressed out I return to the beaches, her domain of power, and nurture my soul.

At the entrance of my apartment stands an *indio,* my grandma's reminder of the strength, courage, and perseverance of our *raza.* An Oyá painting protects my dining room. She is the *orisha* goddess of the wind, the only female *orisha* to go to battle with the men. She lets me connect with my warrior spirit when I have to fight for something I believe in.

My fricassee religion gives me strength and *tranquilidad* to understand that *todo lo que pasa tiene razon ser*–everything that happens happens for a reason, a higher and sometimes mysterious reason. This coming full circle and calmness was not something that happened overnight or because I read a book. It has taken dedication for me to learn the history–familial, cultural, and spiritual–of my family and my ancestors. My spiritual journey has been and continues to be a slow, lifelong walk. And I know that yours is too.

LEARNING TO WORSHIP
A TU MANERA

Worshiping is one of the most personal things we do. It doesn't matter whether you are a Jew, a Muslim, a Jehovah's Witness, a born-again Christian, a Pentecostalist, a Mormon, a Catholic, an agnostic, or an atheist–how and what you worship should be *your* choice, and based on *your* life's needs.

Color of candle	Meaning
White	Clarity, peace, purity
Green	Money, luck
Red or pink	Passion, love, romance
Blue	Peace
Black	Takes away negativity
Yellow	Love, happiness

No matter what your faith, or even if you feel you don't have one at all, I encourage you to make a sacred space for meditating, praying, asking for help, and giving thanks. All the religions of the world have erected *altares* of one kind or another. You may already have an altar in your living room and not even know it– a vase with fresh flowers, favorite souvenirs, and pictures of loved ones on a wall are all symbols of the sacred in our lives.

Creating Your Altar

To the Aztecs, the Mayans, the Incas, and many African ancestors, altars were a way to pay homage to the deities, the deceased. They were also a place where life was affirmed.

In your home an altar can be a quiet place where you ask for help, give thanks, and contemplate your day ahead or your life.

Altares are also places that allow you to become one with your self.

Getting Started

In setting up your altar, realize that you have the power to decide what it is and what it will mean. You should not adhere to any particular rule or mandate. Your altar can be as simple as setting up a candle, a picture, water, and fresh flowers.

Space

Choose a place in your living space where your altar will not be disturbed, perhaps a corner in your bedroom or your living room. *Los Mayas* considered the eastern corner the best place to set up an altar; that is where the sun rises.

Earth Elements

Flowers and living elements are important. To the Mayans, red and white flowers helped purify and clarify *el ambiente*. Adorn your altar with anything from mother earth. A plant, a seashell, a

FIND YOUR *SANTA* OR *SANTO*

Finding your *santo* can be a powerful experience. Most Christians and pretty much all *santeros* believe that every person is born with a guide, a guardian angel, *un protector*. Ask your parents if you were named after one, or decide on your *santo* by picking the one that matches your birth date. Look at a Catholic calendar, and you'll see feather, or a rock from your garden or from your local park are all good things. It's a very personal choice, and it should reflect you.

Water
Water cleanses; it also purifies. It nourishes and deflects bad *energía*. A fresh glass of water should always accompany your altar.

A Candle
Why is fire important? It gives us light and direction. It's symbolic of life. Please don't leave a candle flickering all night or when no one is home, as that can be dangerous.

Personal Talismans
If you want, you can have pictures of your family members. (You may want to make a separate altar for your deceased loved ones.) Or of yourself as a child, if it is the child spirit you want to celebrate. A *virgencita* or a *santo* can also be used. Place things of personal empowerment—anything from your childhood, an old toy, a crystal, or a family heirloom. Or use a *milagrito*, an amulet—anything that is special to you.

Maintenance
Keep it clean and dust free. Never leave dried and wilted flowers with cloudy water. A friend and *santera* priestess, Marta, recommends that you clean the *bóveda*, or altar, on Mondays. Mondays are holy days, the beginning of the week.

a *santo* and an angel for every day of the year. There is also a patron saint for every country and city in the Americas.

Some people believe that the *santos* or angels choose you. For example, I know many Latinas who feel chosen by Guadalupe, the fierce brown *virgen* who represents and protects *la raza*. She teaches perseverance and kindness, and her brownness—her *mestizoness* and fierceness—is an important symbol to many of us *mestizos* in a spiri-

Praying to the Santos and the Virgencitas

THE SAINTS AND THEIR COLORS	THEIR MAIN PURPOSE
San Alejo, purple	To ward off envy
San Elias, red, black	
Santa Anaisa, yellow	To help you find a man; sex
Santa Bárbara, red and white	Wealth, ambition
San Antonio, brown, white, and green	To help with work, school, or career; to help you get a man
San Lázaro, yellow	Health
San Gregorio, white	
Caridad del Cobre, yellow	Fertility; children and family
Saint Jude, yellow	Matters that seem impossible
San Miguel, red, green	Protection
Virgen de Guadalupe, red, yellow, and green	Anything and everything; she is the protector of *la raza mejicana*
Santa Clara, white	For peace and sense of clarity

tual world whose imagery is Anglo. She is an indian *virgen*. The first brown *virgen* for the *mestizos* of the *Ámericas*. She appeared to Juan Diego and in Tepeyec, the sacred mountain of the Aztec fertility goddess, Tonantzin.

To find your *Santo*, let your own character traits guide you. Maybe the name of a saint rings a bell inside you, or you take a liking to a special *virgencita*. Listen to what your intuition is telling you. Finding your saint and finding out about your saint's religious and cultural significance will not only bring you spiritual joy but can actually enhance and deepen your connection to your homeland, or the homeland of your parents or *abuelos*. Maybe you'll realize, as I did, where your affinity for Santería and *curanderismo* comes from, or get a yearning to make a pilgrimage to the old country. Faith leads you in many directions and can bring many blessings into your life. You deserve to spend time exploring yourself through the symbols of your faith.

OUR SPIRITUAL LEGACY LIVES ON

SANTERÍA

Much has been said and written about Santería, a lot of it disparaging (voodoo zombies, gruesome animal sacrifices . . .) but most of these stereotypes are based on ignorance, and completely miss the beauty, depth, and history of this vibrant religion.

Santería has been surviving and thriving in the Americas for five hundred years, despite brutal attempts to exterminate it. Born in Ile Ife, Nigeria, and spread throughout West Africa, Santería, or *la Regla Lucumi*, was brought here by enslaved Africans. Denied religious freedom, slaves continued paying homage to their beloved *orishas*, or saints, covertly by matching Catholic saints with their own deities. In this way it's a lot like the folk Catholicism practiced all over the Americas, which is peppered with the Santería, Aztec, and Mayan *diosas*, as well as shamans and seers.

The basic belief in Santería is that a supreme being named Olorún, or Olodumare, is the source of the *ashé,* who represents the spiritual energy of the universe, or our concept of God. This supreme being reigns over a group of *orishas,* each of which has specific characteristics and myths. Just as ministers of Protestant churches and the pope of the Catholic Church believe they have special access to God, *santeros* and *santeras* (Santería priests and priestesses) believe that they have direct contact with their *orishas,* who in turn share their followers' wants with Olorún. This communication is accomplished through ritual, prayer, divination, and *ebo* (offering), which can include sacrifice.

Santería is a religion rooted in a complex system of initiation, so knowing someone within the religion is extremely important. To be initiated at each level of practice, you must be aided by both a *padrino*

> The name Guadalupe is a corruption of Arabic meaning *río de amor, río de luz,* river of love, river of light.
>
> —ANA CASTILLO, GODDESS OF THE AMERICAS

> One of the most powerful and beautiful aspects of Santería is that from the moment you enter as an initiate, you are never alone. You have a family of guides and teachers. It is truly a community religion.
>
> —*SANTERÍA* PRIESTESS AND SCHOLAR MARTA MORENO VEGA

Many of the old wisdom keepers died without passing on what they knew because my generation and my parents' generation were being pressured to assimilate, to turn our backs on the old beliefs.

—CURANDERA ELENA AVILA

or *madrina* and an *ayugbona* (assistant) who are themselves initiated. In fact, one of the most powerful aspects of Santería is that from the moment you enter you are never alone. Your journey in Santería is always guided by a complex network of initiates along the way. If this sounds appealing to you, I strongly encourage you to look into it more deeply.

CURANDERISMO

The word *curandero* comes from the verb *curar,* which in Spanish means to heal. *Curanderas* are healers who heal with prayers and *hierbas.* They are our doctors. They believe in the concept of mind, body, and soul working together in divine universal harmony. They use elements from Mother Earth to heal.

"They never harm, they are not *brujas.* Real *curanderas* are here to heal, to *proteger,*" my tía Mercedes, who inherited the "gift" from my dead great-grandmother, a respected *espiritista,* in Puerto Rico, gently reminds me.

In her extraordinary book *Woman Who Glows in the Dark: A Curandera Reveals Traditional Aztec Secrets of Physical and Spiritual Health,* Elena Avila explains that "*curanderismo* is an earthy, natural, grounded health-care system that seeks to keep all of the elements of our being in balance. *Curanderos* believe that human beings—along with animals, plants, minerals, water, earth, air and fire—are a part of the living earth system. Illness, they believe, occurs when all aspects of self and nature are not in harmony."

It has always been puzzling to me how the *curanderos'* knowledge, recorded in the mind and not on paper or the Internet, has survived for hundreds of years despite all the attempts to vilify and erase it.

There are about five different types of *curanderas,* just as there are different types of specialists among doctors, therapists, chiropractors, and pharmacists.

The *hierbera,* or *yerbera,* is a herbalist; she uses plants as her medical tool to cure ill people and can unleash the medicinal power of plants to heal almost anything. The *sobadora* is a *curandera* who specializes in *sobos,* or massages. Her healing tools are her hands. Some *sobadoras* never touch you but instead work with your "energy" to heal. My deceased grandma Mami Angelica, a *curandera* who specialized in *partos* and *sobos,* worked with both her hands and the expectant mom's energy to help deliver babies. A *comadrona* to some, or *partera* to others, is our native midwife. Her specialty is, one could say, obstetrics and gynecology. *Parteras* (the word derives from the verb *parto,* or birth) help the expectant mother throughout her pregnancy and birthing process. *Comadrona* is what these women are called in my native Puerto Rico and other parts of the Spanish Caribbean; *parteras* is what they are called in Mexico and South and Central America. My grandmother was a *comadrona* who helped deliver hundreds of babies, including my first child. A *consejera* is a *curandera* who heals by talking. She is a therapist, of sorts. However, unlike the modern-day shrink, who is limited in the interaction with the client, a *consejera* is a *curandera* who heals with the power of *pláticas.*

Elena Avila explains that *consejeras* allow you to *desahaogarte, de corazón a corazón,* "to speak until everything is released from the body, soul and heart." This type of *curandera* allows you to "undrown" yourself. Avila explains that this *consejería* is one of the "gold nuggets" that she found in the *curanderismo* tradition. As a woman is "*platicando*" or *desahogandose* with me, I rub rosemary oil on her third eye (found between your eyes above the bridge of your nose) and I spread incense, usually copal, and sage. It becomes a sacred place to release the dramas and *sustos* (a post-traumatic syndrome of sorts) lodged deep in the soul. With the simple act of faith and conversation, the healing process begins.

Espiritistas channel the spirits and energies of those who have passed. They guide and heal through the divine power of their channeling the sacred, visions, and dreams. My great-grandmother Mamá Lucia was a revered *espiritista* in her day, and my *mamá* still remembers with awe and mystery cleaning the altars of the *centro,* the place where

Curandera Power

So, you have decided to visit a *curandera* and have no idea what to pay her. Elena Avila, *curandera*, teacher, and author of *Woman Who Glows in the Dark: A Curandera Reveals Traditional Aztec Secrets of Physical and Spiritual Health*, congratulates you but cautions to be on the lookout for charlatans.

She advises you to run the other way if a *curandera* tells you that for several thousand dollars she can give you a *mojo* that can cure *"el trabajo"* or a hex placed on you by your ex. And, if she promises to cure your cancer or rid you of your *grasita* and make you skinny for a pretty penny, I say report her to the local authorities.

The New Mexico–based *curandera* says, "The biggest healing that you can receive from a *curandera* is acceptance of what is."

In her twenty years healing through *"curanderismo,"* Avila has seen her share of "magic," but says that "it has been only when the other person is completely committed to healing herself."

"The biggest myth surrounding *curanderismo* is that there is magic involved, that you go see this woman or man with these great mysterious powers and she or he can make a problem go away like magic. No," she says, "that is not the case. While many of today's *curanderos* are wise in the world of plants, herbs, the soul, the human body, the spirit, and the earth, there is no such thing as magic.

"You are your own medicine," she advises. "Don't give that healing power to anyone; use it to heal yourself."

Another myth is that *curanderas* never charge.

It used to be that the "old school" *curanderas* never charged. Well technically, she points out, they may not have taken payment for services but they did accept donations, "offerings," or used the barter system. And those were different times, too, she says. "Most *curanderas* were supported by their husband, family, or the extended community." For instance, she explained if Don Pepe went to chop wood, he would set aside a portion for Doña María, *la curandera*. While this is still the case in many parts of Mexico, the Spanish Caribbean, and Latin America, it is not the case in the United States. The reality is that United States–based *curanderas* need income to survive. Many are poor, single mothers or simply don't have the extended community common in the old days and the old country.

The costs of services vary from region to region and specialty and, of course, what you are looking to heal. Use your intuition and common sense to tell the fake from the real thing. She says that a good barometer could be the cost of a current doctor visit. For example, if a chiropractor charges about $70 per visit, that's about what you should expect to pay at *huesera's* practice.

they met to worship and heal. True *espiritistas* have the gift of "reading" you on the spot or telling you things about yourself that only you know. And, as my tía Mercedes cautions, good ones never charge.

Hueseras are *curanderas* who, like chiropractors, work with readjusting your spinal cord. These are the most rare of all in the United States, according to Avila.

Most *curanderas* do embody all specialties—healing with the power of touch, plants, prayers, words, dreams, the spirit world, and the energies of the divine universe. How do you become one? You are born with a gift, you are trained by a *maestra,* a *maestro,* or an elder, or you are "claimed" as one. There are no official *curandera* schools; it is strictly an oral tradition that is passed on. Unfortunately, these wise women are very rare. My aunt and I talk about how the gift is passed on and how to her, so many of the modern *hijas*—you and me—are refusing to heed the call of the ancient voices that may lead us to *la tradición.* "*No tengan miedo,*" I hear her say. Don't question it with external and Western philosophies that make us doubt or corrupt what we were born knowing.

Do you have a *curandera* or a *santera* in your ancestry? I never knew I did until recently. I thought that my family was strictly Catholic or Pentecostal, but by asking questions, sometimes to the chagrin of my mother and other "nonbelieving" relatives, I have learned so much about my rich heritage. I have found a native legacy that I never knew about. And each day I remember more. What is your native spiritual legacy?

Leading a spiritual life doesn't mean you have to belong to an organized religion or even choose a *santo* if that is not what you want in your heart. For me, being closer to God ultimately means being closer to other people—and being more in tune with myself. Living a spiritual life is about being gentle with your soul, with the earth and all of its inhabitants. It's about recognizing that, above everything else, you are a special and a sacred creature of the universe.

I have learned many ways to practice my faith without the help of religious institutions. Each day I try to see myself as a sacred temple, and in the comfort of my private space and daily life I honor my living relatives and my ancestors. As challenging as it gets sometimes, I try to see God in every human being, even the envious, the greedy, and those who try to hurt me—not to mention the racists, the sexists, the homophobes, and the prejudiced. I also have learned to stay away from bad energy; I find it contagious. In learning to take care of myself, I've come to understand the second important dimension of caring for the soul: caring for the body. Latinas have used herbal cures for centuries as the physical manifestation of divinity. By using cures and healers you are engaging in an age-old ritual of purification and healing. Although these approaches have sometimes been coopted by the New Age non-Latino/na gurus of the West, we must remember that these are *our* traditions, with deep roots in our spiritual beliefs and lives.

LAS HIERBAS, THE NATURAL HEALING REMEDIES OF OUR ANCESTORS

The use of herbs and oils to alleviate pain and discomfort has been part of our culture for hundreds of years. Given a chic name—aromatherapy—the practice has recently become trendy and popular.

Las hierbas can help reduce stress and *ansiedad,* enliven the spirit, heal a medical condition, and even help *aliviar* some emotionally related disorders.

Genuine treatments use highly concentrated essential oils extracted from various healing herbs. As of now there's no regulation on this form of treatment, so you have several options. Above all, though, it's important to go to a place with experts who know what they're doing. If you don't have the money to get your herbs this way, or can't find a botánica in your barrio, you can buy oils and try them out at home; but do your homework first. There is some disagreement on such issues as the amount of oil necessary to achieve a desired effect, the most effective method of administration, and the length of time necessary to continue treatment. Use your discretion, and make sure to read the directions on the package, because natural products can be very dangerous if you use them improperly.

NUESTRA AROMATHERAPY

Worried about something? *Prende una velita,* have faith, recite a silent prayer, and get ready to see spirituality at work. If you put your mind to it and decide to cleanse yourself of whatever it is that is troubling you, the bath oils, candles, and affirmations in this section can soothe your soul. Below are a few recipes to get you started.

SPECIAL BATHS

Buena Suerte Bath
The things you'll need:

a gallon of water
a small bunch of albahaca *(basil)*
a small bunch of hierbabuena *(mint)*
9 tablespoons honey (optional)

Boil the water in a big pot. Cut the basil and mint into small pieces. When the water boils, place all the ingredients into the boiling water and simmer for twenty minutes; then turn the heat off, and cover the pot. Let the water cool to lukewarm and drink a cup of it (you can add sugar or honey to sweeten it).

Now bring the pot to the bathroom, set it aside, and take a shower as you normally would. When you're done, do a *despojo* or *limpia* (cleansing): use a strainer to gather the herbs and peels from the bottom of the pot and scrub them all over your body. Then use the remaining water to rinse off. Do not rinse the herbal water off.

Get That Man Bath

The things you'll need:

a dozen fresh rose petals (pinks and reds)
a teaspoon of honey
half a cup of milk
a spoon of powdered cinnamon
three perfumes of your choice*

First shower, then fill your bathtub with warm water. Crush all the petals with your hands and sprinkle them into the water, along with the honey, the milk, and the powdered cinnamon. Lastly, spray your perfume into the water, as much as you like. Stay in the bathtub for about half an hour, and relax while visualizing the qualities of the man you want to attract. (See also the Love Recipe in chapter 6.)

I also hear that San Antonio works magic. Take a small statue of Saint Anthony; dunk him in a cup of water upside down; light a brown, pink, or red candle, and pray for that partner. Leave the statue of el Santo in that uncomfortable position until he grants you your wish. And offer an offering, such as flowers, fruit, or a daily rosary.

---

*If you only want to use one perfume, that's fine too; just make sure it's the one you use when you socialize.

Caution: Be specific about the kind of man for whom you wish. An *espiritista* told me of a young woman who got a boyfriend—but not the one she wanted. She had a hard time getting rid of the "loser."

Peace in My Home
What you'll need:

incense (any kind you like; I like sage or copal best)

Light the incense and put it in a metal container you can easily carry around your home. Close all the windows and go through your entire home, making sure the aroma of the incense permeates the whole space while you chant your peace prayer.

This is one used by a local *consejera* I know:

Inciensio bendito de Jerusalem	Blessed incense of Jerusalem
Que saque todo el mal	Take out all the bad
Y entre todo el bien.	And bring in all the best.

When you've done this throughout your home, open the door and leave it open for five minutes. The cleansing of your house, combined with the incense, will take out all the bad energy (or spirits) and bring in the good.

It might be a good idea to take a *buena suerte* bath (page 145) as well.

FINDING A REAL *SANTERO* OR *CURANDERO*

The best way to put together a good network of spiritual advisers is to look through your own network of friends and family. You'd be surprised how many of your close friends might have a *santera* or *curandera* to recommend! The guides will come; all you have to do is ask and be open.

Visit a *botánica* in your area, or in cyberspace (a great tool if you live in the suburbs). The people who work in these small shops are usually very knowledgeable about herbs, oils, candles, and the spiritual network available in the neighborhood. Also, most *botánicas* have a spiritual adviser on the premises.

A couple of cautionary notes. First, there are a lot of charlatans out there, stealing people's money in exchange for promises of fame, fortune, health, and men. *Cuidado.* Never get an on-the-spot *consulta* or *limpia.* Trust is crucial for healing. Observe and examine the place. Your ability to "feel" the energy is your best asset. Ask yourself if you feel comfortable in the *botánica.* Is there something there or with the person's energy that does not feel right? A friend tells me to always go with my head covered, because bad *energía* enters through the head. In the best possible cases, you may want to go several times before asking for a *consulta.*

Second, these bath "recipes" were given to me by trustworthy *curanderas* and *santeras.* They will bring you your wants *only* when they're coupled with hard work toward getting what you want and honest faith. As my *mami* always says, *ayudate que Dios te ayudará.*

A *Limpia* for Your *Casa*
Cleaning your home with a coconut

Mamá Lucia did this once a week in her small house. With your covered feet, roll a fresh coconut from the innermost areas of your home, toward the outside. Start with your bedroom, praying for peace and *tranquilidad* and anything else you wish for your household. When you have finished rolling the coconut all over your home (don't pick it up inside), use your feet to roll it outside. Once outside, take the coconut to an intersection and crack it open. It's best to choose an intersection that you rarely use. Don't look back; the negativity that may have been in your *casa* is carried out and crushed by the passing cars.

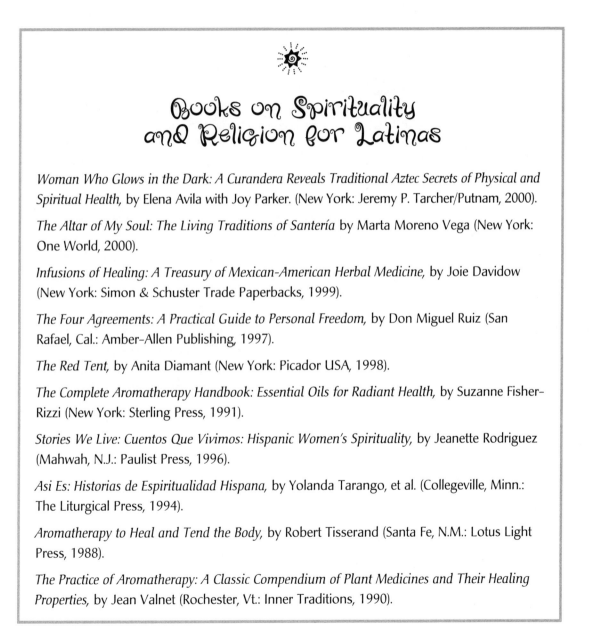

Books on Spirituality and Religion for Latinas

Woman Who Glows in the Dark: A Curandera Reveals Traditional Aztec Secrets of Physical and Spiritual Health, by Elena Avila with Joy Parker. (New York: Jeremy P. Tarcher/Putnam, 2000).

The Altar of My Soul: The Living Traditions of Santería by Marta Moreno Vega (New York: One World, 2000).

Infusions of Healing: A Treasury of Mexican-American Herbal Medicine, by Joie Davidow (New York: Simon & Schuster Trade Paperbacks, 1999).

The Four Agreements: A Practical Guide to Personal Freedom, by Don Miguel Ruiz (San Rafael, Cal.: Amber-Allen Publishing, 1997).

The Red Tent, by Anita Diamant (New York: Picador USA, 1998).

The Complete Aromatherapy Handbook: Essential Oils for Radiant Health, by Suzanne Fisher-Rizzi (New York: Sterling Press, 1991).

Stories We Live: Cuentos Que Vivimos: Hispanic Women's Spirituality, by Jeanette Rodriguez (Mahwah, N.J.: Paulist Press, 1996).

Asi Es: Historias de Espiritualidad Hispana, by Yolanda Tarango, et al. (Collegeville, Minn.: The Liturgical Press, 1994).

Aromatherapy to Heal and Tend the Body, by Robert Tisserand (Santa Fe, N.M.: Lotus Light Press, 1988).

The Practice of Aromatherapy: A Classic Compendium of Plant Medicines and Their Healing Properties, by Jean Valnet (Rochester, Vt.: Inner Traditions, 1990).

A fierce Latina who made U.S. history . . .

 There are very few people out there who have not heard the story of **Selena Quintanilla Perez.** Born on April 16, 1971, in Lake Jackson, Texas, to Mexican American parents, Selena was tragically murdered by an employee of hers on March 31, 1995. This untimely death cut off what most think would have been a successful crossover career into mainstream American pop music. By the time she died, at age twenty-three, she had already crossed cultural and generational boundaries among Hispanics, being popular among both young and old. This talented performer was a strong, family-oriented Latina, and very active in antidrug campaigns and AIDS-awareness programs. Selena's first language was English. Because she learned Spanish only after her singing career had taken off, she learned her first Spanish songs phonetically, but she ultimately became a fluent Spanish speaker. In 1987 she was named Female Vocalist of the Year and Performer of the Year at the Tejano Music Awards. Two years later she signed with EMI Latin, and in 1990, she and her band, Los Dinos, released what became a multimillion-selling debut album. She won her first Grammy in 1993 for Best Mexican American Performance for her album *Selena Live,* and her second Grammy in 1994 for *Amor Prohibido,* which also went gold. Less than a month after her death, then–governor of Texas George W. Bush declared April 16 "Selena Day" in her honor.

CHAPTER SIX

SECRETS OF LATINA DATING—
the Barrio Girls' Rules Revealed!

*W*ho needs rules to catch a man? Is there really a formula for finding and catching a good Latino? In the last few years we've been bombarded with books promising to teach "loveless" women how to get a man and live happily ever after. Often these books paint a pathetic picture of a lonely woman who feels incomplete without a ring on her finger or a man holding her hand. After reading these books and debating them with my *amigas,* I have decided that there is really only *one* rule: Finding a healthy relationship—one that's spiritually *and* physically fulfilling—takes knowing yourself, your needs and wants and wishes, and making no excuses for them.

A short book published in 1995 titled *The Rules: Time-Tested Secrets for Capturing the Heart of Mr. Right,* by Ellen Fein and Sherrie Schneider, started the dating drama. It broke down the mysteries of dating and courting into a simple set of dos and don'ts for women to follow when trying to snare a mate. Even though these rules were based on antiquated notions about dating, they opened a can of worms because they encouraged women to "fool" men into commitment. A couple of years later, Denene Millner came out with a version for black women, *The Sistahs' Rules: Secrets for Meeting, Getting, and*

Keeping a Good Black Man. Millner smartly challenged Fein and Schneider's ideas, arguing that rules which *might* apply to white men won't fly well with black men. I read both books with curiosity, but my Latina girlfriends laughed off most of the advice. We agreed that while all men—no matter what race—share similar pathologies (obsession with their *pipis* being the most common), Latin men are very different from Anglo and black men. Dating, in particular, is a completely different animal in our culture. In this chapter I pick up where those two books left off, not because I think we need a set of dating dos and don'ts but because until now no one has talked about the uniqueness of dating in Latino America.

When I was in the fifth grade, my best friend was an "older woman," a sixth grader named Rosita. Rosita was much more experienced in the ways of men than I was. She was in a relationship with an older boy, Pablo, a seventh grader. They mostly held hands and walked to and from school. To my thinking, Rosita had Pablo eating from the palm of her hand. In fact, Rosita had almost every sixth-, seventh-, and eighth-grade boy dying to have the honor of walking her to class, carrying her books, doing her homework, even marrying her. And what, pray tell, did Rosita possess? She was *bajita, gordita*—not at all the usual tall, skinny blond type we constantly saw promoted as the ideal in magazines and on TV. But Rosita had sky-high self-esteem and the right attitude. She had an uncanny way of carrying herself, an awesome confidence that silently told all the little dudes in our elementary school in Jersey City, New Jersey, "*Soy una diosa,* and you will kiss the ground I walk on!" *Coño,* even at eleven, Rosita understood the workings of the male mind! Rosita taught me my first lesson about dating: when it comes to men (and everything else in life, for that matter), it's all in your attitude. But attitude aside, what is it about dating that's so baffling to us?

For starters, the word "dating" doesn't even exist in regular Spanish speech—I looked it up in a Spanish-English dictionary, and it wasn't there! That tells us something already. In most traditional Latino homes (and mine was no exception), dating is a negative subject, if it's discussed at all: Latina teens do not date. "*Esas son cosas para las gringas,*" my mom would say. Latina girls are jewels protected by their fathers, *tíos,* and *hermanos* until they are ready to leave the house, first for college, then for a husband. They can't be going out into the world exploring the ways of men.

My own attitudes about romance have changed (along with many other things) in the process of acculturation. I've picked up new *costumbres,* like dating, and incorporated them into my life. But even so, dating—especially between a Latina and a Latino, and even in second- and third-generation Latino homes—is one of the topics we are still learning how to negotiate.

Here's why: Latinas date a future husband; we date to marry. We do not go out with a man for self-discovery or to gain experience. We don't date for fun as a rule, and we don't date casually. We do it *para casarnos.* In our *cultura,* the leap between a date and *noviazgo—*his becoming your man, you his lady—happens in a flash, usually after the first kiss. Even the most liberated of us find casual and serial dating uncomfortable. In the innermost corner of our minds and hearts, we shun that kind of dating—even if we think we shouldn't! Many of us dated on the "sneak." Even when our parents welcome dating, it is always with *pero*s, "buts" that are stricter than those in Anglo culture. For example: a guy never goes into your room to "hang out" with you; you always see him *en la sala.*

On the other hand, there's a different attitude toward the Latino on the same issue: as soon as he's out of the womb, a Latino boy is praised for his imagined virility, judged by the number of women he will one day have. As soon as *el niño* can crawl and talk, curious family members—mostly the men in the family—start asking him, "*Y cuantas novias tienes?*" That preschooler had better say he has at least three girlfriends or his male relatives will worry out loud that he's going to grow up to be a little "*maricón.*" (I hate this kind of prejudice, but even though many of us have learned to throw it in the garbage, where it belongs, it's unfortunately still very real.)

The notions of gender politics and dating I was raised with were as skewed as anyone's raised in a traditional Latino home. As the youngest daughter in a family of five, I would never be given the chance to follow my oldest sister's lead and get pregnant at fourteen (before she could even figure out where her G-spot was!). Instead I was encouraged to follow my second-oldest sister's lead: she was eighteen, everywhere she went with her fiancé of three years, she was chaperoned by me or one of my little brothers.

The result was that I went on one date in all of high school—one! His name was Phillip, and even that date was on the sneak. Phillip was in my junior year biology class, and I told my mom we had to study for a midterm, but instead of studying, we went to a movie. Sorry, Mom!

My brothers, however, dated lots of young women; yes, some were Latinas, but in the eyes of many they were the "loose" ones—*callejeras,* as my mom and our nosy *vecinos* would say under their breath. It was made very clear to us from day one that a good Latina girl has ONE *novio,* and one day she will marry him. These kinds of double standards placed me at a real psychological disadvantage when it came to dating. How about you?

One of my favorite shows growing up was *The Brady Bunch.* I always yearned to have a mom like Mrs. Brady. I remember how Marcia's first date—a rite of proud passage for white girls, it seemed—was a cause of celebration in the Brady home. Mom Brady and Marcia even went shopping for the perfect "first-date dress."

Can you imagine? What was your first date experience like? Was it on the sneak? Did you get a "special first-date dress and makeup lesson" from your mother? Or did your father and brothers "male block" the young man trying to hit on you? Or were you one of the lucky ones whose date was welcomed à la Mr. Brady, with "Welcome, *mijo,* make sure you bring my *hijita* back before midnight"?

Then there was the college dating scene. I saw my *gringa* roommates so easily and happily date a variety of guys that it freaked me out. They had no problem going out with John on Wednesday, Peter on Friday, and Harry on Sunday, and juggling them like that for months *como si nada.* That was so alien to my sensibilities that I found myself thinking like those *chismosas* on the block: *estas son unas cualquieras.* I talked to them, trying to understand how they could date several guys at a time and have nothing "*serio*" happen. "Oh, I'm just dating," they'd say. They weren't even thinking about having *un novio.*

I eventually did my share of dating in college, but whenever I dated more than two guys at the same time, I found myself feeling *incómoda,* as if a pair of tight panties were giving me a high wedgie. Have you ever dated more than one man at a time? How was it for you? If you never did it, do you wish you had, or are you glad you dated one at a time?

A month after I graduated college and returned home, I met my future husband. He became my *novio* by about the second date, and I married him a year later. It wasn't until after my divorce four years later—and with a two-year-old son in my life—that I truly learned to date. *Gracias a Dios.*

Since then I've learned that dating, in many ways, teaches you about *you.* In the process of being sweethearts, you learn to set the

Diosas de las Américas

Oshún is a goddess who rules over the sweet waters of the world, the brooks, streams, and rivers, embodying love and fertility. She also is the one we most often approach to aid us in money matters. Oshún is the youngest of the female *orishas* but retains the title of "Great Queen." She heals with her sweet waters and with honey, which she also owns. She is the femme fatale of the *orishas* and once saved the world by luring Ogún, the god of iron, out of the forests using her feminine wiles. In her path, or manifestation, to goddess, she saved the world from drought by flying up to heaven, turning into a vulture in the process.

La música

In the recording industry, Latin music sales jumped 25 percent last year while the overall U.S. music market shrank by 2.4 percent, according to the Recording Industry Association of America.

rules you want to have in your life with a man. Dating can make you strong and wise about your womanhood, and you can test (and taste!) all kinds of men in the process. While many Anglo women seem to understand this a lot better than Latina, Asian, and black sisters do, we're slowly learning some of the lessons our own cultures didn't teach us.

Years of dating trials and errors have taught me *muchas cositas* about our men. Let me share with you some things that I learned.

CATCHING A GOOD LATINO

Nuestros hombres son especiales, and to capture their *corazonsitos,* ladies, we must celebrate how special they are. They are not Anglos or African Americans or Asian men . . . *son hombres latinos.* We don't have to take crap from them or forgive the inexcusable, but the road to a Hispanic man's heart is different than that for other males of the species. For example, Latin children grow up knowing that courtship is a serious thing, and men are expected to play a traditional, chivalrous role. Even the most modern Latino knows he has to treat a woman "like a lady." And our men are definitely not from Mars—they are from Mother Earth, and, like you and me, they are lovely sensual specimens who were socialized with different romantic values from those of their non-Latino contemporaries.

But in America in this new millennium, even the most modern Latino still has deep issues about his role in the dating game. If his father didn't teach him how to treat a lady, the *viejos* in the 'hood did, or his mother did. And one thing he doesn't appreciate—I don't care how much he tells you otherwise—is for the woman he's sweet on to be a serial dater. Your dating *muchos hombres,* frankly, turns him off. It brings back those *puta–mala mujer* stories he grew up listening to (see chapter 7, "Latina Sexual Mystique"). To his way of thinking, *he* can date many others, but his "lady" can't. (Obviously, I didn't invent this "rule"—I'm just telling you what I know.) Your Latino lovely will be wondering, What does she think, that I am *cabrón*? In his eyes another man is not competition but a *falta de respeto* to his manhood. See, in his eyes, he is supposed to be "*el único*," your *macho*, your *rey*, the one and only. Yes, *mujer*, even if you are just dating. Thing is, above anything else, *respeto* is the one thing we need to understand about our men; their maleness is to be always honored, especially in front of other men.

Mamá, give me my televisión

74.5% of Latino homes receive cable or satellite television service

84.7% of Latino homes have VCRs

For me, if dating were a board game, it would have only two players: the *papi* I'm sweet on and me. There's no finish line or "prize" at the end; it's not a game that necessarily leads to marriage. The object of the game is getting to know one *papi chulo* at a time and his getting to know me, both of us having fun and being open to growth. It's not about gaining a husband but making a male friend—*es una cita*, a meeting (or meetings) of two people, two minds, aside from the sexual sparks that might fly between them. But that's my board game, not yours; in *your* game, *you* establish the ground rules, including how many can play.

Feeling comfortable dating—however many players your game holds—is the most important dating rule for the *nueva latina*. But there are others.

THE SECRETS

So just how *do* you successfully catch a good Latin man and keep him, if that's your goal? I have figured out ten golden rules for getting and holding *un buen hombre*, and I'm going to share them with you.

But first, *chica,* you need a bath! No, I'm not saying you smell bad—if we believe the numbers, Latinas smell better than just about anyone. This is a magical bath for love, and it starts with a recipe.

You know by now that I'm a big fan of special *baños,* but this one is my all-out favorite. It's an attitude booster for goddesses, one I use whenever I'm ready to date. I should really name it after my worldly friend Rosita from grammar school, since she was the inspiration; one day I asked her what it was like to kiss a boy, and she said, as if everyone already knew this, "It's like sucking on an orange, *nena!*"

1. CHARM CON SINCERIDAD; DON'T MANIPULATE

The Rules says that to get a man, you have to pretend to be interested in everything he does, because men *love* to hear all about themselves. While it may be true that most guys love to hear themselves talk, Latin men generally don't like *sorpresas,* and they hate liars. Just listen to the lyrics of popular Latin songs—they're mostly about *mujeres mentirosas!*

So don't pretend you like soccer when you really love baseball. Don't pretend you like cars, knives, or whatever that honey you have your eye on is into. Be real—*no pretendas nunca.* How would you like it if you found out that a guy you'd been talking to for months was pretending to like poetry because you do? Or if later on he confesses—as you break up—that your dental assistant job didn't fascinate him but really grossed him out?

Charm him with your true self, your loves and hates, your quirks and, yes, even your warts. Dating is about getting to know each other, not fooling him into spending time with you, then committing to you. That is why you should never pretend to like everything he says. And *por favor,* don't let him go on forever. Tell him your story, and ask him to share his, but don't pretend to like *esto* or *lo otro* because you think it pleases him. If you do, it will blow up in your face. The dating process is not all about him and his likes; it's about you, too, and that won't be lost on Señor Right.

That doesn't mean you should go to the other extreme and ignore

Love Recipe

A clean bathtub

A dozen ripe and juicy tropical oranges (Latin American oranges work best, but
Florida, Texas, or California oranges will do), washed but left whole

A bunch of fresh mint leaves

Your favorite perfume or essential oil (patchouli, lavender, ylang-ylang–essential
oils have sexy properties in them)

Your favorite candle and mood music (optional, but recommended!)

As you're filling the tub with warm water, drop the oranges into the running water, throw in the mint leaves, and add a few drops of that favorite oil or perfume. Then light the candle and play music that makes you say, *Ahhhh, I am a goddess . . .*

This fun bath includes eating and exfoliating with both the oranges and the mint leaves, so take the time to enjoy it–twenty minutes at least. Suck on some of the fruit, and rub the other ones all over: elbows, thighs, tummy, legs, and face. Alternate between the eating and the exfoliating with the mint and the oranges. Rinse with the bathwater; don't soap off the sweet juice from your skin. (And don't worry about feeling sticky; the mint leaves and the acidity of the orange juice counter the stickiness.)

I do this when a relationship has ended, when I meet a new man, or when I'm just in the mood for a boost! And as good as it makes you feel, it really is good *for* you. Oranges contain generous levels of folate (folic acid), potassium, and thiamine, as well as some calcium and magnesium and, of course, vitamin C. They are also natural exfoliants. Mint is listed in the Chinese pharmacopoeia as an aromatic flavoring agent, a carminative (it relieves gas), and a soothing application to skin or mucous membranes. As a natural anesthetic, it can relieve pain or discomfort.

As you, the goddess, gently eat and exfoliate in this magical concoction, visualize *ese hombre que te tiene loca* that you have yet to meet. He can be movie-star handsome, tall and nerdy, short and teddy bear–like, funny in a sexy way. . . . It doesn't matter–he's your man and your fantasy, so be specific. And don't be shy! Just relax, enjoy, and revel in the magic. When you go out, even if you don't meet the *papi* of your dreams that night, at least you'll feel refreshed–and you'll smell even better than usual!

him, either. A self-respecting Latina also knows how to show her man *respeto*. So when dating a Latino, don't check out other brothers in his presence. Save your *coqueteria* for him, feed that part of him that wants to be *El Rey, el más especial*. When you show him *respeto*, you lift him up, and he's likely to return the favor. It's a "He is your king and you are his queen" kind of mentality: if he is El Rey, you are La Reina, and you expect to be treated as such.

2. Hunt, Don't Chase

There's a difference between hunting and chasing, *chica*, and I've never heard of a Latin man who likes to be chased. He'll revel in being hunted but freak out if you chase him. What's the difference? Well, you can hunt from the comfort of a bar stool or a chair at Starbucks. A glance, an inviting smile, a point of the finger and the international *ven acá, papi* gesture, and then, "Oh, I thought you were my brother's baseball teammate. *Perdón*, it's dark in here . . ." (even if it's noon on a sunny day). That way you can see him up close, check out the goods, *bien close*. That's an example of hunting. Chasing would be more like going up to him when he's barely finished checking you out, and asking, "Wanna dance? Wanna *cerveza*? What are you drinking, latte or cappuccino?" Your *sabrosura* has to be sweet and slow, the way you cook a chicken fricassee, because hunting is a sumptuous meal; chasing is fast food.

José is like many Latin men I've talked to about this. He tells me that he likes a woman who lets him know from the get-go that she likes him and wants to know him better. That's "I want to get to know you," not "I want to get with you." Assertiveness turns him on, but aggressiveness turns him off.

Subtlety is the key here. No Latino likes a woman to take the lead, whether in dancing or in dating. He likes to feel that he's made the first move, so give him the room to do it. If you jump before he's ready to catch, you might fall straight on your *nalgas*. For example, if you ask him to dance or ask for his phone number before he summons up the *cojones* to ask you, he'll feel emasculated. *Recuerda,* he's El

Hombre, and that means he needs to feel as if he "hunted" you, *mi hermana*–even if you and I know better.

If you don't believe me, try chasing him. Maybe he'll be okay with it, at least at first, even go along for the ride, give you his number, and anything else you dare ask him. But inside he'll probably feel uneasy, and maybe even a little scared of you. Is that the result you want? I didn't think so.

If you learn to hunt with *fineza* you can even ask him out first. Let's say you've been talking, dancing, and jiving and you're ready to go but he hasn't asked for your number. Sometimes he just doesn't know how to go there; men can be (and often are) fraught with insecurities that have nothing to do with us. That's when you have to use your Latina intuition. Give him your card or ask for his. Tell him you'd love to see him again and ask him if he'd like that too. If he says yes, give him your number, then walk away. (Give him your work number if possible. I always find it safer to give a complete stranger my work number. That way, if he turns me off or I change my mind, I can always say, sorry, I'm busy!)

But what if he says no? If he does, or stumbles just a bit, forget about it. Just walk away. He had his chance. Rejection will get easier with age and experience, I promise. And believe it or not, you shouldn't take it personally; he may actually be doing you a favor. (He might have a wife and six kids, or neuroses you don't even want to *hear* about . . .) Besides, *camarón que se duerme se lo lleva la corriente*– a shrimp that falls asleep will be taken away by the current. The current that brought that *camarón* will surely bring another.

3. PLAY, DON'T COMPETE

He's the man, a Latin man: let him be the *caballero.* Let him help you, and let him know you need him. This, of course, is not so true on the first date. But he should know from the get-go that you are not trying "to be a man," to compete with him.

We *latinas americanizadas* are a new breed. We have careers outside the home that are very important in our lives, and we see ourselves as more independent than our counterparts of a generation or two ago. Our friends, our careers, and our families fulfill us, and to some extent some of us have bought into the Anglo feminist notion that a woman doesn't really *need* a man. And, while technically this may be absolutely true, it's not the reality.

While you may have reached a point in your life where you don't need a man to pay your bills and buy you that fancy dinner, it's okay to admit that you need a man's energy *en tu vida*. Needing a man has nothing to do with being a *pendeja* or being incomplete without one. It is simply recognizing the equalizing energy that a man can play in your life. To show need doesn't mean that you cease to be independent, or that you lose your opinion, or that his opinion rules. You can admit that you need a man in your life and that at times you feel a little helpless or overwhelmed—yes, even you, independent honey. And to do this, coming from where you come from, shows tremendous courage and strength.

On the flip side, your self-reliant ways might rattle him as he's trying to figure what he means in your life. It's a pretty subtle thing that happens when you send messages telling a man "*no te necesito*": he'll get the hint.

Now, don't think for a minute that if you're a strong woman, you'll drive men away (more about this under Rule No. 8). There's a dumb old stereotype that says feminists emasculate the men in their lives, or cast them out altogether (if not both). Well, I'm a feminist, and I know tons of other feminists, and I can tell you right now that the vast majority of us love men and need them in our lives. They are our boyfriends and husbands, and also our brothers, uncles, fathers, sons, cousins—and friends. We'd be as lost without them as they would be without us—well, almost!

Latin men need to feel as if they can help. Everywhere a Latino goes in this country, he has to fight to be validated, let alone honored. He is constantly tested and demonized in mainstream society. He can't get jobs or cabs, and he's victim to police brutality, racial profiling, and border-crossing harassment; the last thing he wants is to be in guerrilla warfare *con su mamita*. And why would he want to feel like he's competing to see *quien tiene más cojones*? I know Latinas are born with ovaries and *cojones*–I see it everywhere, and I live the reality of it myself. But just because you have *cojones* doesn't mean you have to show them to him all the time. Again, I'm *not* saying you should ever take abuse or settle for less than you deserve. I'm simply saying don't *compete* with him. If you trust him, don't be afraid to show your softer side, to let him know that you have weaknesses as well as strengths; you'll bring out the *macho* in him. And there is a good thing in *machos* who've been raised to be strong providers–they have a yearning to feel needed, and your "needing" them (even for things you could and can do for yourself if you *have* to) answers this yearning in a subtle yet wonderful way. It also gives them a sense of responsibility that's been a little wayward in recent years.

Letting Him Take Care of You

This doesn't have to mean his making a great living so you can stay at home wearing your mink, getting pedicures, and eating bonbons (though that wouldn't be so bad, at least for a little while). It often means letting him–or asking him to–do things that you could do, or could hire somebody else to do. Forget about your chores; very few men on this planet are going to feel good about doing your laundry, washing your dishes, or shopping for your groceries (unless you're sick, and then he gets to be the hero).

Give him different chores. Ask him to take the air conditioner out of the window, hang a ceiling fan, program your VCR, hook up your stereo, or figure out "that funny noise" your car's engine is making, and nine guys out of ten will feel like they're about to go out and defend you from the fire-breathing dragon.

Even when they gripe ("What do you *mean*, 'I've never taken it in for a tune-up'? How could you *do* that to a car?!"), the unspoken thought that comes next is usually something like, "Lucky thing for her *I* came along. What would she do without me?" And it doesn't have to be household tasks like these–find out what he's good at (or at least better at than you are), and ask him to help you.

If it sounds like make-believe helplessness for you to let the man in your life do for you sometimes, think of it from the other side. Chances are, he knows how to cook for himself, arrange his own living space, buy himself a new shirt, or sew on a button. But when you do anything like that *for* him, you've just said, "I care about you. You matter to me," more powerfully than the words could ever express it. And your asking for his help is a way of welcoming him in, of letting him say the same thing.

One day a man I'd been dating for a while told me out of the blue, "You make me want to take care of you and do things for you." When I shared what he said with my best friend, she laughed, "Yeah, I see you pull that damsel-in-distress thing all the time!" She found it funny, but she knew there was a deeper purpose to the way I was with him. I was supporting a home, a son, and a mutt and thriving in my career—all the standard "I don't need you for nothing" stuff—and he *still* wanted to take care of me. Why? Because I never gave him that vibe that *says* "I don't need you for nothing." So don't be in control *todo el tiempo*. Don't make all the decisions alone. Let yourself count on him for some things.

And this is crucial.

Not long ago my friend Martin told me he's looking for a wife south of the border because he wants a woman who makes him feel valued—he wants to feel *que es un hombre*.

At first I was very suspicious. It sounded like this young, good-looking catch just wanted a "traditional" wife who wouldn't resist any overbearing I'm-the-man-and-I-make-the-rules-around-here machismo he wanted to pull. But as we talked about what he was looking for, I realized that he wanted a partnership, and that he felt that go-getting independent Latinas (like me) are too self-sufficient to want a real partner. In his mind, most modern (read: *americanizada*) women are too bossy, and don't really need him.

"Taking care of your lady" is a cultural practice our men have had instilled in them since the day they were born; while the attitudes about it can be misused (especially if a man thinks it gives him free rein to be the Boss), it can also be a very positive thing. So while you do set the rules of how he will treat you, make sure you leave him room to treat you with loving care.

4. Adiós, Cheapskates—Hola, Caballero!

Men who don't pay don't even get a chance to play in my board game. This rule is not about milking a guy or making him doubt your ability to pay for dinner, a movie, or a drink. It's a rule meant to summon his inner *caballero* to the surface.

I went on date once with a very good-looking, smart *papi*. He had everything going on—everything I thought was important. As we were going into a club, he went in ahead of me, paid for his entrance, and then turned to wait while I paid for mine. *What?* I thought. *How cheap!* I paid for myself, and once in the club, I danced the night away with everyone else but him. That was the last time I saw him. I feel that a man who is cheap with his money will be cheap with his heart. There are no two ways about it. I don't play that way, and you can't let your man play that game either.

If he doesn't pay for the first date, dump him! A man should pay for the first several dates, until you are comfortable sharing the costs of a date without offending your deeply ingrained notions of *caballerosidad*—and his.

Why not go Dutch? Simple: you're not Dutch, you're Latina. You didn't grow up with those values, and neither did he, no matter how much of a feminist his momma may have been.

Eduardo, a twenty-eight-year-old investment banker, said to me, "Women are like a bill. I always set aside money to take them out." While I thought it funny that Eduardo considers us a regular expense, I've got to offer congratulations to his mother and father; they raised him right. His dating philosophy is "If I can't pay, then I don't go out." By the way, he wasn't complaining when he mentioned that to me. He said he'd feel weird going out and having a woman pay. That was the way his chivalrous Latin father taught him and what his mother demanded.

Again, a man who is cheap with his cash is cheap with his emotions and definitely runs low on thoughtfulness. Give your man room to be a *caballero* and live up to the standards that give our lovely Latinos the "stereotype" of the Latin gentleman. It's those little things that I look for and expect: his walking on the curb side of the sidewalk to put himself in the way of anything that might be splashed or thrown at me (or, in the most recent interpretation, to clarify that he is not selling me—prostitutes walk on the curb side, the *viejo papi chulo* men tell me), his opening the car door for me before he goes around to his side, or letting me in the elevator first . . .

If the *chulo* you're hot for is too broke to pay for a movie, drinks, dinner, or something else, he shouldn't be taking you out! This rule doesn't mean "Only go out with guys who have money," though it's always a good idea to go out with men who have jobs and no *malas costumbres*. This rule is about the effort that he takes to court you. If he doesn't have or make a lot of money, he should say so, and suggest an activity that suits his finances: a picnic, a free concert, a walk in the park. That way he's not spending his rent to impress you, and when he *does* take you out for something fancier, you'll know how much it means.

There's another reason not to abandon the old-fashioned convention of the gentleman paying: gender economics. According to the 1999 census, Hispanic men got paid on average $405 a week, while Latina professionals made $348. So letting him pay is your way of equalizing the imbalance!

5. Be *la Mística*, Not *la Imposible*

He's not the enemy, and you don't want to confuse the man you want—at least not at the beginning! Don't fall into that high school drama of "playing hard to get."

No games where you have him thinking he's just one of many and has to compete with all the *hombres* out there. You're already a magical woman, opinionated, sexy, charming, full of interests and likes; you don't need to keep a Latin man guessing who you are or what you're doing. Keep it simple—*me gustas*. When you want to see him, let him know. Don't wait till he calls you; take the initiative. I don't mean that you should beep him five times a day, but I also don't mean that you should wait five days before you call him back!

We've all heard that we have to be mysterious to intrigue a man, and that part of the mystery is not accepting last-minute dates, because we shouldn't make ourselves too available, that men love the chase and the chaste. Well, that is just plain *caca*. There's mysterious and then there's just plain confusing, and nobody benefits from confusing. The old advice would be that if he calls you at the last minute to go to a movie, you should turn him down, no matter what (you have to keep him waiting); *I* say if you don't have plans already and you feel like going, go! That doesn't mean you're always at his beck and call; it means you're flexible when you can be, and you expect the same in return. It's not as if every time he's in your 'hood or in the mood, you drop everything to give him whatever he wants—that would be a *bobería total*. This is about fun, *mujeres*, but fun is not playing games with someone's feelings; so keep it real.

6. GIVE IT UP ON THE FIRST DATE

Perdón madre mía. I know what you taught me about girls who sleep with men on the first date, but hear me out. Now, this is a tricky one. Everyone says that this is a no-no, that men love women who play hard to get, that you will never see them again, and so on. But let me explain.

I think sex on the first date is fine if

1. It feels right.
2. You feel safe.
3. You don't care if you see him ever again.

I don't need to warn you that you're playing with fire—not least because there are diseases passed through sex that can hurt or kill you. (So please use protection whether you're on the first, second, or last date! And check out chapter 3, "The Healthy Latina.") Here is how I see it. This rule is really about your own sexual empowerment; about getting physical when you feel ready, willing, and horny; about setting your own internal when-to-have-sex timetable based on your internal clock and not by the fear *el que dirán* or that he won't "respect" you in the morning. The most important person that needs to respect you in the morning is you! Going for it on the first date does not mean that you are "easy," "*a cualquiera,*" or that you are not "picky." No, my beautiful *señorita,* it is about saying that you are comfortable and in control of your sexuality. Too many of us spend too much valuable time in the dating process trying to figure out exactly how long to wait before having sex—the first date, the eighth date, the third month, and so on because of what he or others may think and not because of how we really feel inside. If you could "respect" yourself in the morning, then what's the point of waiting for dessert—go for it, *mija!*

However, having said that, you should know, too, that there are two types of Latinos: those you sleep with and that's all you do; and those you want to sleep with *and* talk to after you've slept with them— men you want to keep around, *los meros, meros.* If you feel for a second that besides jumping his *chulería,* you'd like to talk to him, hold off and don't kick it on the first date. Sex, as I'm sure you know, is not the same as intimacy, nor does it build intimacy or hurry it along. You can "catch" a good Latino by giving it up on the first date, but to keep him you must make him wait. The point of the waiting is not just to build intrigue about the good sex you'll have with him eventually or to pretend that you are a "good girl"; rather, to create a sense of all the good things you'll share together *besides* sex.

When you sleep with a traditional Latin man on the first date, this is what he's thinking: "*Esta seguro que lo hace con todos.*" It doesn't matter if you're thinking the same thing about him, because our skewed gender politics sustain a big difference between a *puta* and a *puto.* No matter how generally enlightened he is, how Nuevo Latino he may be, he will feel a little funny about you for "giving it up" so easily.

Roberto, a Nuevo Latino catch, says Latino men will attest to this. "I'll sleep with her, sure, easy *punanni.* But in the back of my mind I'll always be wondering, 'Does she do this with all the guys?'"

Once you do have sex, whenever you decide to do it (and remember it *is* your decision), sex him up. Don't be shy about it—be a Latina lover like no other. If you've decided to go there with him, give it good and demand it good; let him know what you like (and don't like). But beware: if sex isn't good for the first two months and you see that he's not the kind of man you can train in your bedroom ways, dump him immediately. *Ahora!* Sex is important in a relationship, and if it's not at all good at the beginning, girl, chances are it will only get worse.

7. Mátalo, With Your Fashion Sense

Always look good and groomed. Don't confuse this with pounds of makeup, the latest Gucci sandals, and salon hair, because he won't notice. What he *will* notice is nice-smelling hair and body, manicured nails, smooth skin. All men are visual animals, and our own even more than men of other cultures, so don't fight it; don't show up at the movie theater in sweats. Whatever else is going on in your life (and believe me, I *know* it's a lot), make sure that before you walk out that door you are "together."

Don't do it for him—I'm not telling you to change your whole personality to get a man. If you happen to be into the grunge look, knock yourself out; but you should know that to many Latin men "grunge" is synonymous with *cochina*. Whatever you do that makes you feel sexy from the inside will be seen outside. Find a fragrance you like, a style that suits your personality, and makeup that fits your style. (My own sexy secret is to wear my thong, put on lots of lotion, and feel my skin silky smooth under my leather pants when I get ready for a date. It makes me feel *sooo* sexy.) Feel free to experiment with looks that are different from what you're used to, but the worst thing you can do is put on a style you think he likes (if it's a particular guy you're after) or "guys like." You'll never feel comfortable in it, and it's no different from lying about yourself to impress. As long as you're neat and clean (I just can't see our *papis* liking greasy hair or chipped nails) and put together in a way *you* feel good about, you'll be fine.

Harry, a third-generation *mejicano*, tells me that this rule couldn't be truer for him—he loves a woman who is well kept. "Appearance

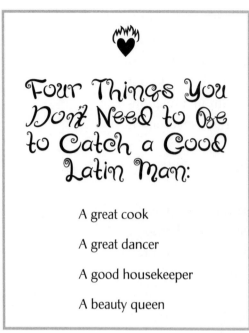

Four Things You Don't Need to Be to Catch a Good Latin Man:

A great cook

A great dancer

A good housekeeper

A beauty queen

makes a big difference to me. I don't feel attracted to girls who go outside just wearing anything or who don't take care of their hair." Personality is even more important, he says, but he wouldn't choose to get to know your personality unless he liked what saw first. Yes, *los hombres* are visual mammals.

If you think this rule's concern about appearance is superficial because it's only the *real you* that counts, think again: little things mean a lot. We all make judgments about people based on "little things" we see, and your outside is just as real as your inside. This rule is really about what Harry and many Latin men saw growing up: Mom dressed to kill before she stepped out the door. Styles have changed a lot since then, but a Latin man will still appreciate that his lady looks good for him. So even if you're really dressing for yourself, he'll still feel proud that you look great—for him.

8. Be Your Fabulous Strong and Opinionated Self; He'll Keep Coming Back for More

Don't pretend that you are a *mosquita muerta* because that's what *novela* heroines do. Don't play *la estúpida* because you hear that a good Latino doesn't like to be too challenged. And *por favor,* don't swallow your opinions because you heard somewhere that men don't like opinionated women. That's completely wrong; what men don't like are *bossy* women. (And who does? I know *I* don't!) A Latino likes his woman to tell it like it is. *No que lo maltrate,* but to be straight up. He likes her fire. A wimpy woman who doesn't share what she thinks, how she likes it, and what her rules are might as well wear a sign that says PENDEJA, because he'll walk all over her. Let him know from the get-go that he won't get away with that with you. Trust me: it works. But *why* do Latin men like women who are strong?

Think about this for a moment: Who was *la jefa en tu casa*? Even in a "macho," sexist, father-led household, it was Mom who was in charge. Think back to your home, think of your *tías,* your *primas.* Who really ran your house? It's like that old saying: we let them think that they are in charge, but *las jefas* are really *las mujeres. ¿Me entiendes?* Latinas run the house like generals, and that gives us tremendous power. What your dad wore, what he drove (maybe not the make, but definitely the color), where you sat, what brand of soap you bathed in, even your dad's underwear—all of these things were chosen by *mamá.* A Latina's strength can be quite sexy to a Latino, even erotic, I have been told. But it's also more honest: with a strong woman, a man knows he can't get away with shit, but he also knows where he stands.

This is what Jaime told me, and he could have been speaking for every other man I talked to about this: "The women I date all have minds of their own. They're not squeamish about letting me know what they like and don't like. Nothing's more boring than a woman who lets you make all the decisions and doesn't stand up for her beliefs. I *like* a woman who's independent and strong-minded."

For a long time I believed the myth that men are frightened by strong women. More books and magazines than I can count tried to tell me that this was the case, especially with *our* men. But I've come to see that there's a real difference

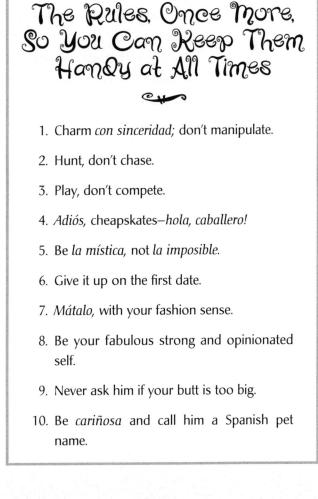

The Rules, Once More, So You Can Keep Them Handy at All Times

1. Charm *con sinceridad;* don't manipulate.

2. Hunt, don't chase.

3. Play, don't compete.

4. *Adiós,* cheapskates—*hola, caballero!*

5. Be *la mística,* not *la imposible.*

6. Give it up on the first date.

7. *Mátalo,* with your fashion sense.

8. Be your fabulous strong and opinionated self.

9. Never ask him if your butt is too big.

10. Be *cariñosa* and call him a Spanish pet name.

between opinionated and strong on the one hand and obstinate and bossy on the other. Don't try to hide your own strength; that's a trap. If you have to keep up with the *mentiritas* that you dropped here and there to hook him in, how can you ever relax enough to be yourself?

9. Never Ask Him If Your Butt Is Too Big

Few Latinos think a butt is ever big enough, but since we're bombarded with completely unrealistic notions of what's big, fat, thin, normal, and so on, we bring these weight issues to our dating situations. Chances are, he won't notice if your ass is bigger or smaller than Jennifer's, but he *will* notice it if you harass him with the silly question, "Am I fat?" Those extra pounds you think you should lose, that extra *longita* or *chicho,* are lost on him. In a 1998 *Latina* magazine sex study, 62 percent of the men we polled said that they like women with meat on their bodies. *Flacas* across the country were in an uproar over the results, but I think it's safe to say that *in general* our men don't go for the boyish and androgynous Gwyneth Paltrow look. However, if long and lean happens to be *your* body type, your guy will probably be perfectly happy with that. And no, I'm not contradicting myself.

You see, I find that what men really revel in is everything else you've got going for you. Sure, they like *curvas,* but more than *curvas* or straight roads, they like a *frescura* that shows confidence in your own skin. It's sexy for them that you love your *gordura* or your *flacura.* It all goes back to what Rosita, that elementary school vixen, taught me when I was a little girl: it's your attitude about yourself (including your body) that will reel him in. (So why even bring these issues up? See chapter 2, "*Que Bella Soy,*" and you'll understand.)

10. Be Cariñosa and Call Him a Spanish Pet Name

Cariño is such a Latino concept. To be affectionate from the very beginning—and we're talking about gentle affection here, not octopus style—is truly sweet. To give *cariño* and *dulzura* and, of course, to

Some Spanish Pet Names to Call Your Man

For some Latinas, pet names sometimes are associated with a skill of the man or the way he may look or sound. A friend had a boyfriend her family called *Cara de Hacha* (hatchet or small ax face), as if he had been struck in the face with it. Another friend had a husband who wore his hair like Elvis Presley; she called him *El Toche* and *Mi Toche*. Other pet names just don't make any sense at all. Whatever your *negrito* inspires, go with it. Of course, the diminutives are even more charming. These are just a few. See if your favorite made it to the list.

- *Nene, Nenito*
- *Negro, Negrito* (even if he is blond and has light skin)
- *Pa, Papito, Papi, Papasito* (or any derivation of *pa*)
- *Macho*
- *Mi Vida*
- *Mi Cielo*
- *Amorcito*
- *Chulo, Chulito, Chulango*
- *Mi Gordo* (even if he is *flaco*)
- *Mi Flaco* (even is he is *gordo*)
- *Chuleta* (even if he is a vegetarian)
- *Chino, Chinito* (even if he isn't Asian)
- *Papucho*
- *Mochito*
- *Mi Cuchi-Cuchi*
- *Mi Cholo, Cholito*
- *Mi Rey*
- *Guapo*
- *Prieto, Prietito* (even if he is light)
- *Guero, Guerito* (even if he is *prieto*)
- *Chupi*
- *Bebo, Bebé, Bebucho*
- *Tesoro*
- *Mi Tigere* or *Tigerecito*

expect it, is the big and final DO. One of the biggest "little" differences between Latino and Anglo culture is *cariñitos*. I often hear that part of Latina charm is that we are not *secas* or aloof. Affection is a trait most of our *familias* raise us with; like the Benny Moré song says, *besitos pa' quí, besitos pa' allá*. Women almost everywhere are socialized to be caretakers and nurturers, but none more than us, and that can be a good thing. So let it all come out, or relearn it if you've lost it. Give your man *cariñitos* and he'll go gaga over it. Our men yearn for that *chuleria*. Don't you? I know I do.

Cariño manifests itself in many ways, not just in public and private displays of physical affection. It also comes across in the pet names we give one another. Call a Latin man a pet name in Spanish, and watch him be *como agua para chocolate*. Roberto dates *mujeres* of all *razas*, but he says that names like *papito, nene, mi amor, mi cielo, mi rey,* and *mi macho* land differently in his ear than "babe" and "hon." A Spanish pet name is like a purr to your *papucho*, a soft pussycat purr that feels warm, gentle, and familiar, like a lullaby.

I think that it's the same for us—I know *I* like pet names. I don't demand them, but he'd better come up with a *chulería* to call me besides "Sandra"!

So hold his hands, caress his face, lips, and hair, scratch his back with your long nails, *tócalo, mimalo* (another thing I can't translate, but it'll warm his heart). And if something's out of place, don't tell him about it; just fix it: pick that stray lash off his eyelid, brush that lint off his collar, rub that spot of food off his cheek and then kiss it . . . and I can practically assure you entry to his heart.

A final thought on this very important subject: proceed in your dating and mating with reckless abandon, *pero con lo pies sobre la tierra,* as my mom always says (about *los hombres* and life in general—and she's always right).

A fierce Latina who made U.S. history . . .

 Before Selena, Jennifer Lopez, and Christina Aguilera, there was **Lydia Mendoza.** She was often referred to as "La Alondra de la Frontera." Lydia came from a musical family; as a young girl she performed with her parents and her sister Francisca in their family group called La Familia Mendoza. Born on May 21, 1916 in Houston, Texas, to Mexican parents, Lydia had a myriad of musical talents: she learned to play the fiddle, mandolin, and guitar by the age of seven. By 1934, Lydia, then in her late teens, started her solo career, which turned her into a Mexican-American musical legend. In one of her most popular songs, "La Pollita" ("The Hen"), Lydia is accompanied by her sister's mandolin playing. The song is a funny lament of the crazy, willful ways of a chicken who refuses to marry or to lay eggs and instead spends all of her time singing. This wonderful *pollita* could not be more similar to Lydia, who, having broken down the gender barrier of the Mexican-American music industry, has always rejected acting and thinking in a way people might expect.

CHAPTER SEVEN

LATINA SEXUAL MYSTIQUE:
The Hot Tamale, the Latin Lover, and Other Lethal Myths

For a long time, the only thing standing between an orgasm and me was God. It wasn't that I was ultrareligious; I'd never defined myself as a "church girl." The reason for my *Dios en la cama* complex is simple: I was raised Latina. While we may have a reputation for being hot in bed, the truth is that many, if not most of us, carry generations of religious and cultural baggage and taboos to our bedrooms.

All that *stuff*–passed from *abuela* to mother, and mother to daughter, and reinforced by the Church, *novelas*, and our communities–deposits a set of moral codes in the sexual pleasure zone of our brains. And these codes love to sneak up just when we're about to kick it, in the throes of kicking it, or recovering from the metaphoric touchdown.

So my lack of religious fervor did not save me from the indoctrinated lessons on Latina sexual behavior. In fact, these lessons became so much a part of my sexuality that anytime I delved into physical pleasure–alone with my hand or in the company of a lover–I'd feel shame and guilt, as if I were a *sucia*. Despite the "shame," I did it anyway, never sharing what I was feeling with anyone. Later I discovered that I wasn't the only one with a "God and the orgasm" complex. As the editor of *Latina* magazine and then the *Latina* website, soloella.com, I got hundreds of desperate letters and e-mails from Hispanic women who were longing for answers and a comforting *consejo,* Latinas weaned on the same traditional Latino values as I was. How would you describe the sexual mores you were raised on? In our homes, sex or, more important, sexual pleasure, is something typically left to the men. In the normal course of a developing Latina girl's life, sex and sexuality are not discussed openly. It follows that Latino sexual politics often leave grown *hermanas* vulnerable, frustrated, and horny. Vulnerable because we don't get the full story on sex; we're left to wonder or "*meter las patas*" (get pregnant or deflowered) or we're easy prey *para que nos cojan de pendejas* (be played by men). Frustrated because we can't take control of our bodies and fully explore ourselves as sexual beings, we can't really enjoy sex as a normal, wonderful, and healthy expression of our humanity. And finally horny because we're taught to give pleasure to men, but we're afraid to reach out and get some by ourselves or with a mate—without feeling guilt, fear of being judged, or shame for desiring something as natural as eating or breathing.

I lived a funny paradox that you'll probably recognize. As a Nueva Latina—growing up just a train ride away from New York City's seedy sex shops, coming of age in the sexually liberated 1970s and '80s—I thought those old attitudes were from *abuela* times and only happened now in Univision *novelas* or back in the homeland. Certainly not here in the swinging U.S. of A., not now in these hip times, and not to *me*! But oh yes, *hermana,* they did happen to me, and probably to you, too.

My sexual *complejos,* my cultural attitudes and taboos about sex and sexuality, are so deeply rooted in my Latina psyche that no number of years living north of the border, no amount of acculturation, apple pie and hot dogs, or even feminism classes could easily undo them. Let's look at where the seeds of these ideas are sown, how they're cultivated, and how—if we choose to—we can pull them out like weeds in our garden!

THE LATINA SEX CLASS

My first sex education class—and, I bet, yours—was in church. In fact, when I think back to my childhood church visits, I remember that sex was one of the most talked about topics after God, Christ, and the Holy Spirit. In one of the first Sunday school lessons I can remember, I learned about a precocious woman named Eve, her Garden of Eden, *papi* Adam, and those wretched apples that Adam knew better than to eat. But Eve, being the wanton woman that she was, was a lot more worldly than *pobrecito* Adam and seduced him to sin with her. In my Bible class, Eve became the ultimate *pecadora,* or sinful temptress. She was *la mala,* and her wantonness corrupted all humankind for eternity: sex weakened us, and made us all sinners! Future Sunday school lessons of woman-hood and female sexual behavior became a tad more sophisticated and perhaps complicated with the intro-duction of the Virgin Mary and her pregnancy by *El Espíritu Santo.* Unlike that bad Eve, *La Virgencita María* was *la buena*—this pure, self-less woman had chosen to become pregnant and bear God's son without even hav-ing had sex! Now *that,* I was told, is an example of a good woman. I didn't get it, but whenever I challenged my mom on these concepts,

Some Books on Latina Sexuality and Mental Health

The Sexuality of Latinas, by Norma Alarcon (Berkeley, Calif.: Third Woman Press, 1993).

Making Face, Making Soul, Haciendo Caras: Creative and Critical Perspectives by Feminists of Color, by Gloria Anzaldúa (San Francisco: Aunt Lute Books, 1990).

Lessons in Living, by Susan L. Taylor (New York: Anchor Books, 1995).

Amor, Intimidad y Sexo: Una Guía para la Pareja Latina, by Ana Nogales, (New York: Broadway Books, 1998).

Memory Mambo: A Novel, by Achy Obejas, (Pittsburgh: Cleiss Press, 1996).

Yesterday, I Cried, by Iyanla Vanzant (New York: Fireside, 2000).

she'd say that I was just a kid, or simply, "*Cállate,* you ask too many questions."

These Sunday school lessons gave me my first models of Latina sexual behavior: the seductress; the *puta,* the bad *mujer* who turned the world upside down and messed it up for humanity; and the *virgencita* Maria, the good and pure one who was *muy querida* in our families. Those models slowly turned into chains around my brain that had to be broken if I was ever going to have untainted pleasure, let alone the all-out full-body mind-bending climax magazines like *Cosmopolitan* kept promising me.

Needless to say, this *puta/santa* thing started looking very fishy to those of us who questioned it, especially the ones who were lucky enough to get an education and a career outside the home or who early on claimed our sexual power. For our *abuelas* and even many of our moms, there was little they could do to free themselves from those brain chains; to even try was to risk being relegated to the life of an outsider. The prospect of living a life outside *la familia* would have been even scarier for them than for us now, when so many families are already spread across cities, states, and the country. On top of that, their economic dependence on men made it hard to break out of the profile of how good women were supposed to behave.

We are fortunate to live in a place and time where Latinas are freer to explore sexually—maybe less free than our white and black counterparts, but certainly more free than Latinas of previous generations. We seem to have choices in our careers and lives, which by extension include our sexuality. But for many of us, those old codes came over with our ancestors, in their blood and in their suitcases. These values were sprinkled on our cornflakes as well as our rice and *habichuelas;* like the spicy food, mariachis, and boleros, they were as much a part of Latin life as our last names.

The residue of desexualization is still with us. And the struggle to reconcile the two—to be a sexually free Latina and to follow the traditions of our *madres*—is at the heart of our sexuality.

Diosas de las Américas

Xochiquetzal is the Mayan goddess of art, dance, love, and music. She lived on the top of a mountain above the Nine Heavens. It was said that those who were faithful to her would spend eternity in her paradise. Then came a flood, which destroyed all of Earth's creatures except for Xochiquetzal and one mortal man. Together they had many children to repopulate the Earth. Each child was born voiceless. Xochiquetzal called upon a dove to descend from the Tree of Heaven and give them each a unique voice and language. It was believed that all of the different races and languages came from these different children. Thus Xochiquetzal was honored as the Mother of the World.

CLOSE YOUR LEGS, *NIÑA*

"*Cierra las patas y abre la boca*" was a common *dicho* Mom told her three daughters—"Close your legs and open your mouth," meaning talk but don't give it up. That was about the only sex education we got. If you open your legs, you'll be a lost woman-child. Lessons about staying a virgin—the greatest dowry each of my mother's daughters had and all Latina daughters are told they have—usually began with those words. Any girl on the block who opened her legs kissed her reputation as a "good *muchacha*" and her future good-bye. Everyone in the 'hood, especially the *chismosas, le sacaban, el pellejo*—skinned her to death with gossip. She risked not only pregnancy but being ostracized from her family and community and becoming a target for the macho boys on the block. It won't surprise you that *I* didn't take that risk throughout my adolescence.

I didn't want to go to hell, live the life of a *pecadora*, or be the cause of family or barrio shame. I already felt like an outsider for challenging the gender privileges my brothers enjoyed, such as not having to wash dishes or clean house. They could stay out to play past sundown because *los hombres son de la calle y las mujeres de la casa*–the men are of the street, the women belong in the home. And my reputation was tied to my entire family's; in a small community, a reputation was a priceless commodity. So that code kept my *patitas bien cerradas* but it also kept everything else *bien cerradito*–no feeling up or down, no loose fingers down there (no tampons either because, as mom warned, they would deflower me), and certainly no oral or anal sex. I was a virgin in the brain and everywhere else.

LAS "SEÑORITAS" OF THE NEW MILLENNIUM

When Cleyvis, twenty-three, told her mother that she never wanted to marry, her mother lamented, "Then I guess you'll die a virgin!" And this is not a woman who'd just arrived from the homeland; she had raised her daughters in America, the land of the liberated woman!

Virginity in the twenty-first century may sound to many like an idea from the past, but I know that for a lot of us it's still very much in the present. Trying to hold on to your virginity nowadays can be very challenging, but it is possible, and the rewards are great–if you *want* to do it. But to remain a *virgen* because of others and not because of oneself is just a setup for a lot of suffering.

Jocelyn, a twenty-four-year-old virgin, told me that she firmly believed sex before marriage to be a sin, but that wasn't ultimately the reason why she had chosen to wait. "I'm waiting for the right person. A lot of young girls have sex without knowing what it means. I only have this body and I am not going to share it with just anyone because he buys me dinner or gets me a drink."

I see in Jocelyn the conviction of a sexually empowered young woman who wants to wait because of her own values. Sadly, though, that's not the case for many young Latinas today.

A 1998 *Journal of the Society of Pediatric Nurses* study examining the influence of cultural values on different aspects of Latina lives found that religion is the strongest influence on our sexual attitudes. The participants in this study were forty-nine Puerto Rican and Mexican American girls between the ages of ten and fifteen, and twenty-one of their mothers. The study found that these girls don't associate virginity with religious doctrine or practice but that their cultural values encourage them to lessen the risks of early and unprotected sexual activity. This suggests that Latinas may be moving away from sexual abstinence based on religion, but that our cultural values still urge many young girls to choose to abstain from sexual activity.

In my family, sex outside of marriage was considered a sin, a *cochinada*. Only married or divorced women were sanctioned to get it on, and of course even then with a lot of reserve. Good Latina girls didn't go there—until marriage. We saved ourselves for the husbands who, of course, didn't have to be virgins. For my brothers, and for most Hispanic males, virginity was of no concern—not for them, and at least not until it came time to choose a wife. They were free to have as many sexual conquests as possible.

My friend Cecilia tells me that her fourteen-year-old brother likes the "*putica*" on the block and that her mom is openly—and asking Cecilia to do so as well—encouraging him to pursue the girl. "He needs experience," her mom says. I asked Cecilia if her mom would have the same reaction if her brother were a girl and happened to like the "*putico*" on the block. "Of course not," laughed Cecilia. "She'd transfer her out of the school or move to another city!"

What a difference a vowel makes: a *puto* is what we expect from our men, a *puta* is not what we want of our women. Traditionally, a Latin male came to a partnership sexually experienced to teach his *mujer* about the pleasures of the flesh, and she came to him not even knowing what she didn't know. Even after vows, a traditional Latina understood that sexually she had to be *una dama*. She couldn't get too creative or introduce too many moves . . . it might give him the wrong impression about where she'd been before him. And that would risk her husband thinking she was the unbearable—a *puta*.

Usually the fun and "freaky" exploratory stuff would be left for . . . the mistress. (When I figured that out, I finally understood why some womenfolk in my family and many Latinas I know today actually insist on the pleasures of living life as "*la otra*"!)

Thankfully, not everyone believes these dangerous myths; even some men of the cloth have had the courage to oppose them. Listen to what Father Luis Barrios, an Episcopalian priest in the Bronx, New York, has to say: "Latinas are expected to be good *criadas,* good *putas en la cama,* and good *santas* when they walk out of the house. *Las mujeres* are expected and are responsible for conserving and consecrating the family and the marriage. It's a diabolical trinity, and a dangerous trinity that Latinas have to live up to."

Father Barrios asked me to think about the many images of *la virgen,* which I did for a second. "When have you seen a smiling and joyous depiction of any of our virgins?" Guadalupe, *Caridad del Cobre,* Santa Barbara . . . yeah, they all seem to be pretty much in agony.

He nodded his head. "Church teachings reduce women to giving pleasure; women are *not* supposed to want to receive pleasure. You dress a certain way to produce pleasure, you cook well and keep a good house for pleasure, you even *come* for your man's pleasure!" (His words, not mine, I swear.)

While this "religious" chauvinism is not unique to Latinas, it manifests itself with us in a unique way called *marianismo,* the cult of *La Virgen María.* The ideal woman becomes the pure and virginal and *sufrida* symbol of Jesus's mother, who was married but had Jesus by "*obra del Espíritu Santo*" and not the old-fashioned way—coital relations. It's probably safe to say that La Virgen didn't come (and neither did José, for that matter); she was too spiritual and pure for that kind of thing.

"The Church's teachings," Father Barrios says, "have been responsible for the ultimate objectification of womanhood—the ultimate assassination of her identity." And the weapon for that assassination is—you guessed it—guilt. Even the idea of a sexually liberated and guilt-free Latina is almost impossible to imagine—just ask Jennifer Lopez!

GUILT VERSUS PLEASURE—AND HAPPINESS!

In a 1999 interview with a British magazine, J. Lo was quoted as saying that one of her biggest life lessons that year was coming to grips with her Catholic school teachings about guilt; she said that guilt was a useless emotion. I don't know if she was thinking specifically about sex when she said that, but I wouldn't be surprised.

Yet even though those teachings mold (some might say "warp") our *minds* (and the minds of our mothers, fathers, brothers, grandparents, and so on), they don't control our *behavior*—very few Latinas behave like *santas* in their everyday lives! As Father Barrios says, "*Si la mujeres le hicieran caso* at all this bullshit ideology, *los hombres se estuvieran acostando con hombres*"—If women were paying attention to all this bullshit ideology, men would have to resort to sleeping with men. When I say they *are,* he counters, "But they would in bigger numbers, because most Latinas wouldn't want to have sex with them."

According to the good father, *marianismo* hits us hardest when it comes to pleasure and emotions. Our culture teaches us to express emotions when we are in pain, not when we are in pleasure: it's okay to cry, scream, *hacer escandalos* at funerals, but in bed we're supposed to be demure. And if you do show passion—which we do a lot—it had better be to affirm your man: "*Lo tienes grande, papi,*" "I love the way you do it, *papi,*" "You are the best, *papito,*" and so on.

Father Barrios sees this as one of the major reasons many Latinas today have issues with the "institutional church" and why we're leaving it in increasing numbers. "When it comes to dealing with the expression of sexuality, the church is an institution of social control." When he said that, I thought about the Church's stances on abortion, condoms, virginity, AIDS. . . . Listening to this priest, this man of God, validate what I had always suspected about traditional attitudes toward Latinas and sex, I felt liberated. I wish we had *all* had him for our Sunday school teacher!

THE CULTURE OF *SILENCIO*

"Latinos don't talk about sex." It seems you can't go a month without reading a newspaper or magazine story about yet another study that makes that argument. But I think those studies are missing the point: to say we don't talk about sex is to tell only half of the truth.

I grew up listening to sexual jokes and sexual double entendres—*los chistes colorados* were the jokes that made you turn the tropical red of an *amapola* (hibiscus). Children weren't really supposed to hear these jokes, but we did because we were always around adults. I also danced to *boleros, merengues,* and *salsas,* some with very sensual and sexually explicit lyrics—very poetic, unlike some of the raw stuff you hear today, but sexual nonetheless. Then there was the sexually suggestive clothing the women in my family loved and wore. The only way to describe this clothing is, well, barrio fabulous—the kind of clothing that accentuates *chichos* or *longitas,* massive butts and small waists.

Sexuality is all over Latino homes, in the way we dress, the music we listen and dance to, what we watch, and what we read. A friend told me that as puritanical as the Catholic Church seems to be, he thinks it is one of the most sensual institutions around. "The wine, the incense, the candles, the flowers, the altars, and the hymns make going to church a pleasure for all the senses." He said that as a young altar boy he would get turned on when he helped the priest feed the "body of Christ" to cute little Latina girls in his Union City, New Jersey, parish. Prime-time Univision and Telemundo shows are full of sex, and these *novelas* and programs are proof that in some ways we talk a little too much about sex. But as Father Barrios says, "We do it, *lo hacemos, pero no lo hablamos.* We don't talk about sex and sexuality through an educational perspective." In some ways you could say that, for all the focus on things sexy and sexual, we put more effort into talking *around* sex than talking *about* it with the seriousness it deserves.

And They Call It Qué?

My Puerto Rican mother called it *toto* or *tota*. It was a euphemism that she used whenever she wanted to ensure that I was washing real good "down there." The word's origin is still a mystery to me. And no, it wasn't because of Dorothy's dog Toto from *The Wizard of Oz*. What did your mom call your private parts?

Many Latinas I interviewed told me that their mothers would simply point and say, *"Bañese y limpiese ahí."* Their vaginas were nameless, reduced to simply being a location!

What is it about this six-letter word, v-a-g-i-n-a, that causes so much angst? Why do so many of us talk around our vaginas and not about them in a healthy and frank manner? As the talented playwright Eve Ensler reminds us in her critically acclaimed play *The Vagina Monologues*, the shame or *vergüenza* about our vaginas is not limited to Latinas; it is a worldwide problem.

My friend Maria's story about the *silencio* that permeates our Latina community is not just typical of her Mexican American family. It's a Pan-Latino phenomenon.

Maria's parents were both born and raised in Texas, though both grew up in farmworker families that migrated all over the Southwest picking cotton and other crops. Her mother spoke Spanish to her and her siblings and was a God-fearing, churchgoing woman who never, ever talked to her or her other children (as far as Maria knows) about sex, let alone used any words to describe her private parts. She just didn't.

While her parents didn't really speak English and didn't have much formal education themselves, they always pushed books, and Maria was lucky that they bought a medical encyclopedia. She says that it was very dog-eared by the time they'd all grown up, especially the section on the human reproductive system. The book and the streets served as sex-education teachers for herself and her six brothers and sisters. And although she's well into her forties now, married and divorced with a little girl, none of her siblings ever talk about sex to one another either, even to this day!

Maria remembers that when she was bathing, her *mamá* would say things like *"Limpiate allí,"* motioning to her private parts. That was it. *"'Allí.'* Does that even begin to tell you how much we didn't know about our vaginas or sexuality?" Maria asks me. But you know that Maria's story is really our collective story.

Another friend shared her mother's struggle with what to call her infant daughter's private parts. Claudia tells me that when she was growing up her mother referred to her vagina as "bunny" or *conejo,* and she had no idea why, until she asked her, a couple of years ago. Her mother said that was something the family's female pediatrician (who was *gringita*) had suggested; Claudia's mother had told the doctor that she didn't know how to refer to her daughter's genitals, and the doctor had suggested "bunny." I could only bite my tongue thinking, "Of all things, why a bunny? Did she mean that we multiply as if we're two-legged furries?"

Whether with *conejo*/bunny or *tota* or *allí,* our mothers did create a special language—cute and funny euphemisms—to refer to our vaginas when pointing and motioning was not enough.

Here are some Latina mother Spanish and, in some cases, Spanglish euphemisms. See if you recognize the nickname your mother gave your vagina:

la torta (as in cake)	*pips*
la tortita (a little piece of cake)	*la popa*
pan (as in bread)	*la popina*
pansito (a little piece of bread)	*la pepita* (seed)
chi-chis	*la semilla* (seed) or *semillita* (little seed)
el toto or *la tota* or any diminutive—*el totito,* *la totita*	*el tutu*
	tu cosita
el totin	*la cosa*
el toti	*la pípia*
la cookie	*la cucusa*
el popo	*ahí*
pipi or the diminutive, *pipicito*	*ahí abajo*

bollito (small loaf of bread; however, when
    referring to the whole loaf, it becomes
    a more "street," or *callejero* reference.
    See the box "Cuchie Names Around
    the Spanish Americas.")
	tus partes íntimas

	el bunny or *el conejito*
	el pipo
	la cucharita (the little spoon)

For Cecilia, a Miami-born Cubana raised Catholic, Father Barrios's words couldn't be more true. "When I was eight or nine, a boy in my neighborhood took it upon himself to tell me all about sex. I was disgusted and horrified. I told my mother the whole story. My mother's eyes kept getting bigger. When I was finished, I asked her, '¿Mami, qué es eso?' And she said, 'I'd rather you learn it in the streets.' My mother was too shy to tell me herself."

Cecilia's story is a perfect example of how we learn early on to be shy about the nuts-and-bolts physiological aspects of sexuality but seemingly open about all the externals. Another example of this paradox is our embarrassment about the most common and simple form of sex there is. Now, don't even bother thinking, "Oh, no, don't go there!" because I'm there already. That's right, *chica*—it's time to talk about masturbation.

TO MASTURBATE OR NOT TO MASTURBATE, THAT IS THE QUESTION

My son came home from school one day, fresh from his first health-and sex-education lesson (he was in fifth grade) and all eager to tell me about it. He told me that a girl in his class had asked Mr. Keen why her mom and dad's bed squeaked at night. "Because the springs are broken," said his teacher (according to BJ). *Ooh, good answer,* I thought to myself. Then it got a little deeper. Mr. Keen told them that masturbating was natural, and that many people do it.

BJ gave me a skeptical look. "Is that true?"

I answered him. "Well, yes, my dear baby-face. Many people masturbate, and it is natural; it's perfectly normal." Whew! But not quite— I wasn't home free yet.

"Mom, do *you* masturbate?"

El momento de la verdad! What do I say to my child? Do I continue the tradition of *silencio* about sex education, the same way Cecilia's mother and my own had done? This was my chance to break the chains of lies and *secretos*. Would I make the most of it or take the easy way out?

"Yes, sweetie. I masturbate sometimes." There—I said it! I just told my then ten-year-old son that I masturbate, and the walls didn't come crashing down around us. Actually, his response made me laugh.

With the grimace of someone who'd just swallowed cod liver oil, he said, "Yuck! That's gross, Mom!"

The next thing I knew, the conversation had shifted to Pokémon cards (much more important), but the lesson stayed with me. Perhaps if I'd had a conversation about masturbation with *my* mother when *I* was ten, it wouldn't have taken me till my late twenties to learn how to please myself!

Learning how to please yourself is actually the first step to a complete sexual experience and empowerment. It's a healthy sexual pleasure that, unfortunately, most of us are simply not comfortable with. Far too many of us think of it as the distant foreign country of *allá abajo*—down there.

It's not easy to ask about the masturbating habits of our *hermanas*. Rosa, a Massachusetts-based writer and mother of two, was shocked and angry when one of her friends—a famous Latina erotic writer—confessed to her that she had tried masturbating but couldn't climax because all the *cosas* in her *cabeza* were a block. This seeming hypocrisy spurred Rosa to research the subject on her own, and she set about interviewing hundreds of sexually active Latinas in the Boston area about their masturbating habits. She concluded that masturbation—and, by extension, sexual pleasure—among our peers, whether they were raised in the old country or here, professional or not, is still taboo. It's taboo as a topic of conversation, *con mucha verguenza*, and *ay Dios mio,* as an activity.

"We turn over the pleasure of our bodies to men. We're ignorant about our bodies and, in turn, we reject what we don't know. There's a complacency among Latinas about our bodies," she says. We know how to please men (there's the stereotype of the hot-blooded *chica*), but Rosa doubts that the majority of us know how to please ourselves.

Cuchie Names Around the Spanish Americas

When my mother overheard my sister and me talking about this list, she defined it as *"muy sucia."* "Why can't Sandra be a little more *sofisticada*? I don't know what kind of book she's writing," she mumbled under her breath but loud enough for us to hear.

"Precisely," I said to my sister (but not to her). *Respeto.* The idea is not to be dirty or disrespectful but rather to demystify the vagina and help begin breaking the silence around sexuality and our vaginas.

These nicknames are very "street" and, as some of my *amigas* warned, they are sometimes very embarrassing and said only among womenfolk in "hushed" tones. So, *mucho cuidado.*

This list may also save you from a potentially embarrassing moment if you find out that your childhood nickname, as it happened to a friend, really means "vagina" in some Latin American country.

In Venezuela, for example, the street name for the vagina is *la cuca* according to a friend who is a Cuban American. Her mom and *tías* called her "Cuquita" her whole life, and when her Venezuelan friends heard that, they quickly (between fits of hysterical laughter) informed her of the real meaning. By the way, no one in Argentina or Peru calls their girls Concha. Can you guess why?

Check out the list on the next page. See if your childhood nickname raises an eyebrow or produces laughter in some Latin American nations and Spain:

"We're dragging chains of *silencio,* years and years of sexual repression in our heads. I know a woman who has had five children, been married for over two decades, and not once does she remember ever climaxing, forget ever masturbating."

And even economically empowered Latina sisters don't escape the "indoctrination" lessons. I have a friend who considers herself well adjusted sexually, and she is economically and professionally at the

Mexico	*panocha, verijas, pepita, raja*
Honduras	*cusuca* (a hairy animal of the region), *pepita, tonton, cucusa*
El Salvador	*pupusa* (yes, it is the country's most popular dish too!)
Costa Rica	*rajada, tajada, panochote*
Nicaragua	*mico,* as in monkey; *chunche, pan*
Panama	*tonton, tontoncito, chucha, micha* (from a local bread called *palmicha*)
Venezuela	*cuca*
Venezuelan countryside	*chuchufleta*
Colombia	*panocha, cuca*
Peru	*concha* (a conch), *conchita, cucaracha*
Ecuador	*chucha, sapo* (yuck–that means toad)
Chile	*zorra* (fox)
Argentina	*concha, cachucha, chocho*
Dominican Republic	*crica, chocha, pollito* (chick)
Cuba	*bollo* (a loaf of bread), *papaya* (pawpaw fruit)
Puerto Rico	*chocha, crica, pájara*
Spain	*pájara, coño, parrocha, almeja*
Guatemala	*cuchunga, pupusa*
Bolivia	*concha, conejo, conejito*
Paraguay	*tatú, concha*
Uruguay	*uju, pichicha, concha*

top of her game. Well into her thirties, she has not ever masturbated. She tells me that there's no need for her to. "Why should I?" she asks. "I have a man in my life—he can get me off." When I point out that this has more to do with her own sexual pleasure and that it could heighten her pleasure with or without him if she knew how to get herself off—in his company or when he is traveling—she dismisses the idea, telling me that one thing (her ability to enjoy herself with him) has nothing to do with the other (her ability to masturbate). "Besides," she later confesses, "I don't know how to do it. I feel weird even trying." Why she feels uncomfortable is still a mystery to her. Is it to you?

Bueno, if you don't mind my asking, do *you* masturbate? (Yes, you–is someone reading over your shoulder?) Do you think it's healthy and normal? What are your thoughts about the subject?

Rosa thinks that it's as if we understand intellectually that it's okay to masturbate but, as they say, "*del dicho al hecho es un trecho*"– to know it is one thing, to do it–well, that is indeed a different *cuento.* Or as *Mamá* would say (although of course not about this subject), *No es lo mismo llamar al diablo que verlo llegar*–It's one thing to summon the devil, another to see him arrive! And speaking of arriving, let's talk honestly about orgasms.

Luz Maria, a twenty-six-year-old Los Angeles Chicana journalist, says this about her first orgasm with a guy, some ten years earlier: "I had dropped by my boyfriend's house just to say hi. Before you know it, we started fooling around. All of a sudden this . . . *thing* happened! I didn't know what it was–it was like an explosion. I was so bewildered, I threw on my clothes, jumped on my bike, and pedaled away as fast as I could. My boyfriend ran after me, calling my name; he called me at home and I wouldn't return his calls. . . . I didn't talk to him for more than a week! I just felt dirty, as if I had done something really bad. *Me sentí* like I was a *sucia.*"

Nowhere do the old ways clash more with "*nueva latina* ways" than when it comes to masturbation and orgasm. As honest as we can be in the intimacy of the bedroom, sometimes it seems like the cat swallows our tongue the moment we're outside it. Tell me something: have you ever faked an orgasm? If so, you may want to ask yourself why. Can you openly and honestly have a dialogue with your partner about the things you like in bed? Do you communicate comfortably about how you like to be touched and where? If the answer is no, then ask yourself why not, and what would have to happen for you to become comfortable.

Feeling empowered sexually means taking control of the situation when it is not working for you. I don't doubt for a second that we Latinas know how to please our men. However, because of the ingrained *santa/puta* dichotomy and all the "*caca*" mentioned earlier, I do have doubts about whether or not most of us feel really comfortable with the idea of seeking–or demanding–our own pleasure.

INCEST AND SEXUAL ABUSE

Not *all* our sexual dysfunction has its origins in the Church or in the values of traditional Latino culture; there's another negative influence that's probably the biggest taboo of all. Incest and other types of sexual abuse warp our ability to see sex as the healthy and beautiful thing it is. Being a victim of this kind of abuse can have a profoundly damaging effect on the way a woman views sex and is able to enjoy her body. It crushes her self-esteem, and undermines a woman's capacity to love herself. And, sadly, it's one of those topics still taboo in our society, let alone our own families. This is a sexual issue we don't even talk *around,* much less *about.* No society approaches this painful topic gladly, but we don't do it at all.

And it's not because it doesn't happen in our homes. Incest and sexual abuse occur in Latino families every day, but we fail to talk about it, deal with it, and protect our children from it.

The prevalence of child sexual abuse found in one study involving Latinas aged eighteen to fifty was frankly shocking: one in three reported incidents of sexual abuse. This figure was true regardless of acculturation or citizenship status. More than 80 percent of the initial incidents occurred by the age of seven. One of the most alarming aspects of this study was that they found that in four of the cases, the women were forced to marry their perpetrators. Other studies have found that Latinas tend to have higher rates of depression after childhood sexual abuse.

Latinas and Child Sexual Abuse

Very little research has been done on the topic of Latinas and child sexual abuse. In one of the few studies available, Gloria J. Romero and Gail E. Wyatt interviewed three hundred eighteen- to fifty-year-old Latinas of Mexican descent in Los Angeles county. Of the women who responded, 16 percent alleged sexual abuse at younger than age seven; 38 percent reported abuse between the ages of seven and eleven; and 46 percent reported that they were between twelve and seventeen years of age or older at the time of the abuse incident(s). The mean age of the victim at the time of abuse was eleven years. They also found that an alarming 59 percent of the women reported abuse taking place at the home of the victim, perpetrator, someone known to the victim or perpetrator, or the victim and perpetrator's home.

Victims reported the abuse lasting from one day to several years. For 63 percent of the victims, the abuse consisted of one incident. One third of the women reported being abused more than once. Thirty-six percent reported incidents that lasted from more than one day to several years. Almost half (48 percent) of the victims reported abuse from a perpetrator within their own family. Whereas 51 percent of the alleged perpetrators were twenty years or younger, 28 percent were between twenty-one and thirty-nine years, and 21 percent were forty or older. Sadly, more than half of these women (60 percent) did not report the abuse to anyone. When Romero and Wyatt further examined level of acculturation and disclosure, they found that the less acculturated the woman was, the more likely she did not report the incident to anyone (68 percent).

According to the U.S. Justice Department:

- Males are more likely to be victimized by a stranger; females are more likely to be violently victimized by a friend, an acquaintance, or an intimate.

- In 1999, almost seven in ten rape or sexual-assault victims stated the offender was an intimate, a relative, a friend, or an aquaintance.

- Women aged sixteen to twenty-four experienced the largest per capita rate of intimate violence.

Lucia, a twenty-seven-year-old second-generation Mexican American raised in East Los Angeles, is still figuring out what effect childhood incest had on her sexually and emotionally. "I was molested by a male cousin and it broke up my family. They didn't consider it molestation because he was seventeen and I was five, so they decided to ignore it. I considered my cousin like a brother, so it was really hard to stop talking to him. That's the victim mentality—try to befriend your attacker, make nice with him; it's a defense mechanism: 'You didn't hurt me that much . . .' But it *did* hurt. I don't think it matters how old the molester is."

Like Lucia and countless other Latinas, I was molested as a child by a relative. I was six when it first happened. My mother's then lover would go into my room at night and stick his tongue in my tiny mouth and play with me. This went on until we moved to the United States four years later. I always pretended I was asleep so he would leave me alone, but he never did, so I pretended to myself that it was a dream. Way into adulthood the dream turned into a secret and internal *pessadilla*—internal baggage—that I would eventually have to deal with in order to heal. My having been a victim of sexual abuse manifested itself in ways that wounded my soul. I chose mates who were verbally abusive, and worse. I stayed in bad relationships long after I knew they were bad. I disrespected my body and soul with too much booze and with sex with the wrong people. I rushed intimacy too many times, and turned away love because I was afraid that it was real but I didn't deserve it. I lived in a hurtful cycle of self-abuse, and sometimes I wondered why—I was a smart, attractive, and successful woman who kept finding herself in unhappy or even dangerous circumstances. In hindsight, I see that I lived in a self-imposed prison, where the bars of my cell were made out of fear and shame.

Healing from sexual abuse and incest, where trust is violated and destroyed, takes a lifetime, but it *is* doable, a day at a time. I discovered that I'm not alone; meeting Latinas who have lived and survived incest, sexual abuse, and rape was and is empowering. Letters I have read over the years from Latina victims of incest and sexual abuse

Mental-Health, Sexual-Abuse, and Assault-Related Hot Lines and Resources:

◦⊹◦

- Rape, Abuse and Incest National Network (RAINN), 1–800–656–HOPE or www.rainn.org.

- Voices in Action (Victms of Incest Can Emerge Survivors), 1–800–7–VOICES–8 or 847–753–9273

- National Clearinghouse on Child Abuse and Neglect, 1–800–394–3366

- National Latina Health Organization (NLHO), 1–800–971–5358

Books, Videos and other resources for survivors:

The Courage to Heal: A Guide for Women Survivors of Sexual Abuse, by Ellen Bass and Laura Davis (New York: HarperPerennial, 1994).

The Maria Paradox: How Latinas Can Merge Old World Traditons with New World Self-Esteem, by Rosa Gil and Carmen Inoa Vazquez (New York: Berkley Publishing Group, 1996).

Sexual Healing Journey: A Guide for Survivors of Sexual Abuse, by Wendy Maltz (New York: HarperCollins, 1992).

Finding Our Way: The Teen Girls' Survival Guide, by Linda Villarosa and Allison Abner (New York: HarperCollins, 1995).

The Confrontation: Latinas Fight Back Against Rape. Videotape. By Women Make Movies; www.wmm.com.

Dolores. A 1988 movie about family violence; www/cinemaguild.com.

National Alliance of Sexual Assault Coalitions; www.connsacs.org.

Network for Battered Lesbians, (617) 424–8611

who are healing from their experiences gave me comfort and courage (even as they fanned the flames of my anger about the issue). In being open and talking to my intimate friends about my experience, I have also learned that many of my closest friends and colleagues are incest and rape survivors. These honest conversations about the pain and personal victories have helped me grow and heal.

If you have been a victim, there are three things you must know: you did not deserve it; you did not provoke it; and you are not alone. I share your deep pain, your profound sense of shame and inadequacy; so do more women than you could possibly count. And even though you know intellectually that you did not bring it on yourself, you will learn it in your heart (if you haven't been lucky enough to do so already). Many of us come to believe during or after the experiences that we somehow caused it, in the same way children worry that they are at fault for friction between their parents; this is simply not true. Sometimes we used the coping mechanism of forgetting, "fooling" our mind into thinking "It didn't really happen . . ." The danger of this "trick" is that your soul *never* forgets—information you lose *consciously* has a nasty way of coming back *unconsciously* and acting itself out in self-destructive choices and behaviors.

But just reading these words won't heal you. The recipe for healing starts with the self. A woman who has lived through incest and sexual abuse must face it and look for ways to heal from it so she can have a healthy sexual and loving relationship with herself and with her mate.

For several years I invested time and money in psychotherapy—I dared to see a "shrink" *and* tell my family about it, knowing they'd probably think it meant I was a certified *loca*. With the help of my therapist, I explored my fragile self-esteem; I explored my sexually promiscuous behaviors, and I worked to discover patterns and then break them. Then I went deeper: I explored my shame and my guilt, not the kind that comes from the Church, but the kind that comes from a violation of trust. I had been living a shame that made me feel like dirt, and as if I must have *done* something bad to *feel* so bad. I cried. I screamed. I dug and continue to dig deep inside. I give myself

How to Keep a Journal

Writing about any type of violence that you have experienced in a journal or a diary is one of the best ways to begin healing. It's the first step before talking about it. Many women find it less stressful to write than to talk. Putting pen to paper provides a space where you can safely purge what causes you pain. It is also a place where *you* call the shots; you control how much you want to reveal, when, and how quickly.

It is never a "perfect" time to start a diary, but Dr. Lozano-Vranich encourages journals as part of therapy. She recommends that there be no major upheavals in your life—moving, a new job, a death in the family—at the time you start the process. And be sure that you have a strong support network of trusted friends and family around you. Also, you may find that as determined as you are to begin the journal, starting is the most difficult part. It is daunting and scary, and it will open old wounds. If you have decided to keep a journal, congratulations. Please keep in mind the following:

- Write a page a day. Don't worry about punctuation, grammar, or eloquence. Just write. If you get stuck, write that you are stuck and what you are feeling at the moment. Block out a time when you can write without interruptions. You can work up slowly, first to two pages a day, then until you write as much as you can.

- Do start writing about what you are feeling at the moment and not necessarily from the beginning of your life, such as, "I was born in Madison, Wisconsin, on January 1." Write about how you're feeling now, or how the abuse made you feel.

- Keep the journal in a safe place. The sexual abuse you suffered destroyed your sense of trust, so it is really important that you feel comfortable that no one will have access to it. Safekeeping

emotional root canals, asking the tough questions, listening for answers, and finding new ways to heal.

The work I've done on these issues—in therapy and out of it—has made my life richer and more rewarding than I could ever have imagis especially important if you share your home with family, roommates, children, a partner, or any combination of the above. Dr. Lozano-Vranich recommends that you even go overboard with the safety of it. Of course, don't keep it in such a safe spot that when you need it you don't remember where you put it.

• Don't read what you write immediately. You need time to let it sit, and you don't want to go back and edit what you have written.

• Expect to have dreams or to remember things that were long forgotten. (One of the most common symptoms of incest survivors is to be "forgetful." That is one way that your body/mind/soul protects itself from hurting.)

• Be aware that you may experience symptoms such as crying in the middle of the day, at work or in the supermarket, for no apparent reason; the inability to sleep; and the more serious consequence, flashbacks.

• Tell your best friends and trusted people in your life that you are doing this and call them when you need encouragement. Dr. Lozano-Vranich says that you may want to tell people what *you* need to hear, as opposed to expecting them to tell you what they think you want to hear. We often expect that our loved ones know exactly what to say, but more often than not they don't. For instance, I may want to hear that I'm special, kind, and beautiful. That I am loved. That I am a good person. That it did happen, but it's over and it won't happen again. Choose words that are special, beautiful, and comforting to you.

• Finish each journal entry with a personal and uplifting mantra. An example of one of my mantras is: "That chapter of my life is over; I didn't have choices then because I was young. Now I have choices; I am special. I am kind and I am loved." Use language that is positive and comforting to you.

ined. In healing I continually relearn how to love myself as the beautiful and precious soul that I am. But I'm not unique; I don't have any special gifts or superpowers that make it possible for me to heal. What I'm saying is, if I can do it, you can do it.

As powerful a tool as therapy can be for working through the after-effects of sexual abuse, it's not the only one out there. And as women of color and survivors of historic oppression, we must ensure that our healing is culturally relevant. I recently consulted Pati, a trusted friend and wise *curandera,* who I believe could heal a broken heart given the chance. I wanted her to cure the hurt that had been inflicted on my soul, that had robbed my innocence, faith, and trust and limited my sexual being.

In her tradition, *curanderismo,* she explained, they work with the child spirit, that child whose spirit was broken. What happens when a girl (or anyone) suffers sexual abuse, incest, or verbal or physical abuse is a big *susto,* or a sort of post-traumatic stress disorder like the ones suffered in war. That *susto* gets lodged inside our little hearts and stays with us, manifesting itself in physical and mental illnesses, in self-abuse, and in many, many other ways. The *susto* ultimately limits the capacity for our spirits to soar—sexually and otherwise.

Pati's healing session for me involved lots of prayers and affirmations to Mother Earth, the moon, the ocean, the air, and all the energies of the gods of the east, the west, the south, and the north. It also involved *baños* of flowers, rose petals, daisies, and the healing plants *romero,* or rosemary, and basil. But this was more than a recipe cure: it demanded my own faith to heal, the faith that Pati could help me uncover, and my willingness to go into a deep hypnosis to get in touch with a little girl I'd forgotten long ago. To talk to Tita (my childhood nickname) and tell her that she is loved and forgiven, that she will forever be protected. This session was the first time I remembered myself as a lovely, sweet, curious, happy, innocent spirit child, and it was the first time I told her that nothing and no one would hurt her ever again. As a grown woman, I had the will to draw a line in the sand. Pati warned me that the healing journey wouldn't end when the session did, and she was right. It continues forever.

The healing process has been a profoundly painful and sometimes lonely one for me, but it has always handsomely repaid whatever effort I put into it. So seek the help you need, pray for it, and have faith that those who will help you heal will show up. You are not alone, though sometimes you'll feel like you are. Learn to trust again—trust an *amiga* or *amigo* or family elder or member with your story. Go to a therapist, a priest, a minister, or a *santera a curandera*. Read books on the subject; keep a journal. Each of us must walk our own journey. Every one of these healing roads is the right one.

OUR DIRTY LITTLE SECRET, LATINO HOMOPHOBIA

As if dealing with the Church and healing from the violent sexual experiences we may have lived through as children were not enough, those of us who are bisexual or lesbians often have to deal with the entrenched homophobia within our own families that limits our ability to openly and shamelessly express our love for other women. It's too often the case that a gay Latina sister feels she has to stay deep in the closet or lead a secret, painful life behind the backs of her loved ones because of fear of rejection, family shame, or both. Luis, a straight macho from the 'hood and a staunch gay and lesbian activist, tells me he is passionate about Latino gay rights because of the pain he saw his sister live through. "When she realized that it would be very difficult to live life as an open *lesbiana* and that our parents would reject her, she went wild and became a certified *puta*. She understood that the family would have a better time dealing with promiscuity with men and her drug use than her gay life." She recently died of AIDS, and Luis has joined the struggle for gay rights in hopes that his sister's story will not have to be repeated.

Many lesbians I spoke to say they lived with personal shame and feelings of inadequacy and fear prior to accepting themselves and coming out of the closet to their friends and families. Fortunately, in the United States, more and more support groups for lesbian Latinas are springing up, allowing an extended *familia* to take the place of *la sangre* when it does not accept their lifestyles.

Gay and Lesbian Resources

The Bi-Women Newsletter

The Boston Bisexual Women's Network
PO Box 639
Cambridge, MA 02140

National Latina/o Lesbian, Gay, Bisexual and Transgender Organization (LLEGO)
www.llego.org/casa.htm

"I didn't want to accept that I was gay until I found myself divorced with three children," says Wanda, a third-generation California Chicana. "And it was no piece of cake coming out to my children and family. My mother still thinks that I can find a good husband." Despite the *escándalo* that her coming out caused, Wanda says that, in retrospect, she would have done it sooner, knowing the tranquility and happiness she now feels, living out and proud. "I have absolutely nothing to be ashamed of."

Despite the countless Latinas accepting and embracing their sexual preference openly, much work needs to be done for our culture as a whole to accept and embrace all its members, regardless of their sexuality.

As little as we hear serious talk about "straight sex," we hear even less on the topic of homosexuality. "*La tía que nunca se casó* was simply unlucky in matters of men," we are told about many of our lesbian family members from generations ago. And just as with racism, homophobia is a topic that we don't openly deal with as a community or in our families. For the young lesbian coming of age in a traditional Latino home, the same feelings of shame, rejection, hurt, and confusion that so many of us victims of molestation suffer are part of her developing sense of sexuality. Afraid to deal with it openly, without a strong support network of understanding friends and relatives, too many lesbian Latinas resort to leading a *doble vida* of sorts or, as in the case of Radoyka, become completely estranged from their culture and family.

"Being gay in Latino culture is like not being part of Latino culture," Radoyka, a twenty-five-year-old Portland, Oregon, lesbian tells me. "It's the biggest oxymoron I know. You are Latina in one aspect of your life, but gay on your own time. You just keep doing it on the sly. I've reached a point where I have chosen being a lesbian over my family and over my culture. I had to decide which one affords me more sanity and more happiness." Radoyka said that in admitting the truth about her sexuality to herself, she felt as if she had chosen to add another strike to her life.

Radoyka and others in her situation shouldn't have to feel that way, and neither should any Latina. No one chooses to be gay, just as no one *chooses* to be straight; sexual preference has as little to do with choice as does eye color. And so much education needs to happen on this topic. Thankfully, the gay and lesbian movement in the United States has empowered a generation of Latina lesbians to openly and proudly embrace their gayness. Chicana writers like Gloria Anzaldúa and Cherrie Moraga, and Achi Obejas have served as role models. The question of coming out to your family is a very personal one. For Wanda, it was the lies that kept mounting that prompted her to confront the issue head-on.

The gay pride movement, though pretty much white and male, has at least made some inroads in addressing the needs of our lesbian sisters. And if we force the issue to be part of the political debate, the conversation will trickle down to the family level, so that more and more of our gay sisters can live happy and openly lesbian lives.

The way I see it, until our *hermanas lesbianas* are as warmly and unself-consciously embraced as are *hermanas, hijas, primas, tías,* and *madres,* we won't have fully earned the right to call ourselves a "community."

EL CONDOM, EL SOMBRERO, EL GORRITO

Latinos just don't like to wear condoms. I hear this a lot, and my own experience goes along with it. Even Willie Colón dedicated a song to the condom and the Latin man who refuses to wear one. Just try asking a man to use one without feeling like a *puta*–and without him responding as if he thinks you're a *puta.*

Coming Out to Your *Familia*

So you have decided to come out of *el closet. Felicidades, mujer, y buena suerte.* As you know, no family is the same. Therefore, every family's reaction will be unique. In the best-case scenario, you will eventually be embraced and accepted. At worst, you will be kicked out of your house or even disowned.

A friend's mother swore that she would commit suicide if her daughter "didn't change her mind and be straight again." It took this mom two years to accept her daughter's lifestyle, but she did come around. Another *amiga* told me that when she was "outed" by a cousin, her mother stopped talking to her. It's been three painful years since she came out. Her traditional Mexican mother refuses to speak to her or even take her calls, despite tearful pleas from the other siblings. The bottom line is that your *sangre*'s reaction may include shock, denial, guilt, or disgust. And much like when dealing with death–*la hija* (the assumed straight *hija*) *que yo conocía is gone*–they will need time to process the information.

All the *lesbianas* I spoke with who successfully came out agreed you will need to arm yourself with four things: clarity and comfort in your own sexuality, patience, financial independence, and a strong network of friends.

Here are some things to consider:

¿Mija estas segura que eres lesbiana?

Are you sure that you are lesbian or bisexual? Don't bring up the subject unless you can answer the one question you will be asked: Are your sure about this, *mijita?* Any doubt on your part will create confusion on their part.

What does it mean to be a *lesbiana?*

You better be prepared to answer that one. The truth is, there are many stupid myths about homosexuality. Arm yourself with the "truth versus fiction" facts. If you are the only "out" gay member of your family, expect to take on the role of *"maestra."* In a weird way, Leticia tells me, you may become their "parent" for a bit. You'll likely end up answering the same questions repeatedly until they get it; be prepared with the facts and have brochures on gay life handy. In addition, you may want to have a list of gay and lesbian hot-line numbers for them to call, should they so choose.

Are you gay and proud?

If you are still struggling with your sexual orientation, are guilt-ridden, or even are suffering with bouts of depression, it's better to wait until you are more comfortable with your own feelings. I cannot stress how important it is for *you* to feel profoundly clear and proud and not ashamed or guilty about your sexuality.

Why come out now?

Pressure from peers? Sick of living *mentiras o una doble vida?* Love for them? A growing rift between them and you? I don't believe that everyone needs to know your sexual orientation—that's right, not even your beloved *familia.* So if you decide to come out, be clear about your reasons. And most of all, no matter what insults are hurled or hurt has been caused, don't demonstrate anger or frustration if they don't accept or embrace you immediately.

Have you come out to other people?

Do you have a strong network of friends or anyone in your life who accepts, embraces, and supports your lifestyle? If not, wait until you do to come out to your family. Regardless of your family's reaction, you will need to speak with a trustworthy or intimate friend about this, since the process is not "one, two, three, I told 'em *y ya!"* Validation and a shoulder to cry on are crucial for you at this time.

Is there a perfect time to come out?

No. However, pay attention to what is happening in their lives now. Though there is never such a thing as the "ideal" moment to have a sit-down, choose a time when there are no "major" upheavals in your home. Things like recent deaths, health problems, or even economic issues can aggravate an already delicate situation.

Do you have the patience of a santa?

Tu familia will need time to process the information. They may not want to talk to you about the issue for months or ever again. This may be a sore point forever and the reason for constant *batallas.* If you are lucky, they may want to engage you immediately. Experts say that this "processing" period can take anywhere from six months to two years.

Can coming out make you homeless?

If you need your family's financial support, whether you still live with them or they pay for school or help you out occasionally, wait until you are financially independent to come out. *¿Por qué?* You never know what their reaction will be. When I was a youngster, my teenage Latina neighbor was kicked out of her home when she came out. My mother took her in for several years. So if you have no place to stay or if you depend on them economically, *esperate un poco.*

Are your parents or family homophobic?

Are your parents flexible or open about the issue? You know them best, so gauge the situation. I know that my dad would rather see me a *puta* than a *lesbiana,* so openness and flexibility on the issue is impossible in his life. However, I do know how Mom stands on this topic. My ex-husband once suggested that I was hanging out with too many *lesbianas* and called my mother to "tell" on me. But Mom was clear with him: it's Sandra's *chocha,* and she can give it to anybody she wants. (My sister was the one who shared this years later.) Find out where your loved ones stand on the issue.

Es un pecado, mija

"If God wanted us to be with women, he would have made *Eva y Eva,* not Adam and Eve" is one stupid thing I hear over and over again from homophobes of all backgrounds. Churches—almost all of them, that is—are some of the most homophobic institutions around. And to your God-fearing parents, what their church has preached to them is what their first reaction will be. Be prepared to remind them what my mom always said to me: *Todos somos hijos de Dios.*

Amanda, a twenty-seven-year-old Puerto Rican, told me the following story.

I am not a promiscuous woman. I have sex only with men I love, and there haven't been that many of them. The last person I was

Do you have a lesbian or gay relative who is out?

Are they trustworthy? If so, talk to them first. Get *consejos* from them. How did they come out? What was your family's reaction to them?

¿Que dirá la familia? Tu padre? Tu abuela?

This is something all mothers ask themselves when their daughters do anything that is "not traditional." What will the family say? Many may think that it is somehow a shameful thing to be a lesbian. One woman told me that her mom asked her immediately who knew and to please not tell anyone else. "Let this be our secret," she said. What she needed, however, was time to process the information and find a way to *decirselo a tu padre*. While you should make it very clear that there is no shame in being gay, you need to be open and flexible about who they want to share this knowledge with and when.

¿Fuí mala madre?

Why are you doing this to me? Why do you want to hurt me this way? Your mother or father will probably wonder whether their own parenting contributed to your homosexuality, or whether you are doing this to "hurt" them, as crazy as this may sound. Therefore, you will need to explain that this has nothing to do with them or their "failure." Explain the different theories about *lesbianismo* and clear up myths about the issue, again and again.

Do you have the compassion of Mother Teresa?

Above all, be gentle and understanding and display compassion to them. Just as you have struggled with the issue and its attendant depression, anger, confusion, frustration, and shame, so may they. Single mothers may feel this more profoundly since they are "single-handedly responsible" for having raised you. Moreover, they don't have the support of a husband to "deal" with the issue. Finally, as much as *you* need them to support you, the truth is, *they* need you to be compassionate about what all of this means to them.

---

with was one of those movie romances. We instantly fell in love with each other and got along so well. He was so loving to my daughter and treated her as his own. He had to move to the Midwest while our relationship was still very new.

Anyway, he never liked wearing condoms. I understood that, because the men I had dated in the past didn't either. They would use condoms at the beginning of the relationship, but only if they were with girls that were sucias—*if you were their girlfriend, there was no need to use a condom. Besides, he said, he didn't sleep around and neither did I.*

When he asked me to move out there with him, it was difficult for me to up and leave my family, but I thought he was it. I moved, and we were having a great relationship—until I started to experience pain and discomfort during sex, and I broke out in my vaginal area.

I didn't know what was going on with me until I went to the doctor and found out I had herpes. I didn't have herpes before I started dating him. When I brought it up, I realized that he already knew *he had herpes. Our relationship ended.*

Fijate

U.S. Hispanics bought a total of 3,255,000 condoms in 2000.

The total adult condom purchases were 24,339,000. Men bought 16,048,000 condoms. Women bought 8,291,000 condoms.

Dr. Lozano-Vranich tells me that she has seen more and more Latina clients become comfortable with the issue of carrying and asking their partner to use condoms without *verguenza*. But at the same time, she sees that condom use often ends three or four months into the relationship. "When you become his lady, his girl, his *novia*, the condom goes out the window."

The condom issue also brings up the issue of shame. If "good girls" don't initiate sex, or even plan for it, why would we buy condoms at the local deli or bodega or pharmacy and risk having someone who knows us see us and say, "*Que dirán . . .* is that woman a *puta*?" If I carry them in my purse, what will he think of me, and how will he judge me? Are you comfortable buying condoms at your local store? Do you think that it is *your* responsibility to buy them and carry them, or is it his?

It's a problem, Dr. Lozano-Vranich says, for Latinas of all classes, backgrounds, and religions, and it starts with the fear of "*el que dirá*"— what will my man think? In other words, a Latina fears being judged loose, or *una cualquiera*—a slut. Some Latinas even confessed that they feared that their men would think that they were cheating on them.

But if you begin to process and take responsibility for your sexuality, the condom can become part of foreplay–*sin susto* or judgments. We are living in dangerous times, and a single slip today can cause a terminal disease or an STD (see chapter 3, "The Healthy Latina"). So if you need an incentive, something to give you strength to demand condom use, just remember the stakes: it's your life!

TU CLITORIS, YOUR CENTER

While the most important sexual organ is the brain, there are real physiological issues that can prevent us from enjoying sex completely. In their revolutionary sexual guide *For Women Only,* psychotherapist Dr. Jennifer Berman and urologist Laura Berman explore sexuality both scientifically and mentally. The Berman sisters have a practice in UCLA and see women of all ages, nationalities, and religions who live with sexual dysfunction. They remind us that for years pharmaceutical companies have spent millions to research male sexual dysfunction (hence Viagra), while only recently beginning to recognize female sexual dysfunction as a medical problem.

One of the most startling revelations in the Bermans' book is how little is known about how the clitoris and vagina work; hence we can't figure out how to "fix" them when things go wrong. "It was not until 1998 that an Australian urologist, Helen O'Connell, discovered that the clitoris is twice as large and more complex than generally described in medical texts," the Bermans write. This brings me to a very important question: Does your gynecologist check your clitoris during an examination? I don't ever remember mine doing it. Until I read *For Women Only,* I didn't even know that doctors were supposed to actually examine the clitoris. So if your libido is down or you can't have an orgasm, don't assume that it's all in your head and there is no help available–get yourself checked out physically first to make sure it isn't your body getting in the way of the pleasure you deserve.

CLAIMING YOUR SEXUAL POWER

Sexual liberation begins and ends—like every journey—with you. If I had been part of the founding fathers of this country (or any country, for that matter), I would have included orgasms as a guaranteed female right, immediately after free speech. I believe that it's your *right* to climax, not a privilege. Imagine all the men who would be hauled to court for denying us our right! And if you think that's a funny picture, imagine *us* being arrested for denying *ourselves* the pleasure that is our constitutional right!

Until we get that amendment passed, sisters will just have to do it for themselves. Can *you* be sexual with yourself, or do you need a man or a partner to feel sexual? Are you curious about your vagina? You should be. To be in control of your body is to affirm that you can be sexual with yourself—that you know your hot buttons, and that you can get off on your own without feeling one iota *sucia*.

I remember the first time I saw my vulva and clitoris in a mirror—it was like seeing a foreign country I'd never heard of, let alone visited. But the more I looked at it, the more comfortable I became with the way it looked and the way it felt when I touched it; and the more willing I was to accept the pleasure it gave me to touch it or have someone touch it.

Here's a sexual recipe you can try at home. It's right out of the pages of the feminist-health manifesto *Our Bodies, Ourselves*, which is now also available in Spanish,

---

Books on Women's Health and Sexuality

Our Bodies, Ourselves, by the Boston Women's Health Book Collective (New York: Simon & Schuster, 1976). Now available in Spanish, edited for Latinas.

Nuestros Cuerpos, Nuestras Vidas: La Guía Definitiva Para La Sallo de la Mujer Latina (New York: Siete Cuentos Editorial, 2000).

For Women Only: A Revolutionary Guide to Overcoming Sexual Dysfunction and Reclaiming Your Sex Life, by Jennifer Berman, M.D., and Laura Berman, Ph.D. (New York: Henry Holt and Company, 2001).

---

including lists of Latina resources throughout the United States and Latin America.

Take a mirror big enough to reflect your entire God-given vaginal glory and see it for what it is. Look at it first as a scientific and purely physiological experiment; locate your clitoris, your vaginal opening, and your labia. Discover them not with the eyes of fear—the disgust of a little girl who shouldn't be touching herself down there—but with the eyes of wonder. Can you appreciate their beauty without turning red? Try this for as long as you can discover something new, a mole, a line, a scar. . . . When you are ready to move on beyond the scientific, touch it; explore where and how you like to be touched. The clitoris and labia are among the most sensitive areas of our bodies—and probably the least understood. But for sexual and mental liberation, it's up to *you,* and not necessarily your lover or partner, to discover the wonders of it. (If you have already discovered the joys of masturbation, I encourage go to the next level, the use of a vibrator—for yourself *and* your partner.)

We are at the dawn of a new age when it comes to sexuality and sexual pleasure for *all* women. For Latinas, the journey starts with *Papa Dios* and "tradition." With all the *respeto* that God and *tradición* deserve, exorcise them out of your bed and head now if they are interfering with your ability to enjoy yourself sexually! Though many people may have denied you the truth, sex, healthy sex, is central to your life. Sex, of course, is not the same as intimacy, but it's a crucial element of it, tightly linked to who you are and your quality of life. Accept this truth as your truth, without reservations or *peros,* then move forward—get any help you need, communicate, discover, honor, and enjoy your body. Healthy sexual pleasure is a *receta* for joy.

A fierce Latina who made U.S. history . . .

Before there was Cesar Chavez, there was **Dolores Huerta.** Huerta and Chavez cofounded one of the most important labor unions in the United States, the Farm Workers' Association, which later became the United Farm Workers' of America. Born on April 10, 1930, in northern New Mexico, Dolores was exposed from a very young age to the plight of the farmers. She attended the University of Pacific Delta Community College (now known as University of the Pacifica, Stockton) and received a teaching degree. It pained her to teach the children of farmworkers the ABC's when they simply wanted food. She felt she could do more for them by organizing their parents. This fearless single mom of eleven children was nicknamed the Dragon Lady by the grape growers because of her fierce negotiation tactics on their behalf. She was instrumental in the passage of legislation allowing voters the right to vote in Spanish, and the right of the individuals to take their driver's license exam in their native language (in California). Dolores often spoke out against toxic pesticides that threatened the health of farmworkers, consumers, and the environment. In 1993, Dolores was inducted into the National Women's Hall of Fame. She has received numerous awards, all celebrating her social consciousness and her passion for the rights of underrepresented people. In the 2000 presidential election, while recuperating from a difficult operation, she voted in abstentia from her hospital bed and encouraged all Latinos to vote.

CHAPTER EIGHT

LOVE AND RELATIONSHIPS:
La Novia, la Esposa, and the Case of the *Casi-Esposa*

Wife. *La esposa.* It's what we were raised to be. It doesn't matter if you grew up in the suburbs or the projects, topped off your education with a Ph.D. or a GED, ate off paper plates or gold plate. It doesn't even matter if you've been "boy crazy" since kindergarten or knew you were *lesbiana* from the first moment you saw Iris Chacón shake her bonbon: little Latina girls, you and me, are groomed from birth to become *las esposas.*

As a people we are so obsessed with marriage that it defies all logic. You could be the highest-ranking Latina judge in the nation or the first Hispanic female to explore the planet Mars; heck, you could be the first Latina president of this country, but as far as your family's concerned, if you're not married by the age of thirty, *olvidate!* If your family is like most, none of your professional achievements rank as high with them as the personal "achievement" of marriage. Once you hit thirty, if you don't hear "*¿mija, cuando te vas a casar?*" at least once per visit or phone call, you know somebody must be sick or hurt. And when *vecinos chismosos* ask you, "*¿Qué pasa?*" they don't care what's going on in your life—their quizzical faces translate "*¿Qué pasa?*" into "Nice-looking *mujer* like you, out of college how long now, and still not married?!"

There is no stopping us now

Hispanic income has been rising over the past five years. The purchasing power of U.S. Hispanics has risen at a compound annual growth rate of 7.5 percent. In comparison, the purchasing power of the rest of the U.S. population has risen at a compound annual growth rate of 4.9 percent.

They can barely hold back their tongues from passing commentary till you walk by: "*Esa pobre muchacha se va a quedar jamona . . .*" Yes, the tragedy of the aging Latina spinster, tsk-tsk. But, as you already know, even marrying doesn't put an end to all this scrutiny and "concern." Once a *mujer* "graduates" to *esposa,* there's a new question and pressure: "*mija,* when are the little ones coming?" This is because getting married is only the first part of the traditional Latina destiny; becoming a *mamá* fulfills it. For as long as I can remember, I've rejected the notion that I had to live out this role to be a "complete woman." But this rejection wasn't disrespecting or disdaining my culture, marriage, *esposa,* or motherhood. Actually, it was just the opposite: I am hopeless romantic who believes in the institution of marriage and takes pride and pleasure in being a doting mom, and I'm a nurturing *novia,* thank you very much!

It's just that I've always thought that there are so many other things that could complete me. At the same time, I did worry about what I saw happening to so many women in traditional Hispanic marriages: strong, smart, amazing *mujeres* slowly losing their sense of identity and becoming the dreaded *sirvienta.* I was often told that with my kind of *liberada* and independent attitude, I would never find a husband, especially a Latino one!

As women who live in a delicate cultural middle, we are constantly deciding which traditions we are going to keep and which ones no longer fit our lifestyles. Sometimes it feels as if there's an ongoing conflict between the Latina we are outside, in the world—the student, the professional, the go-getter, *la luchadora*—and the woman we are expected (and often want) to be in the privacy of our homes, families, and relationships.

Given the oppressive wifely roles that so many of us have seen and still see, it's no wonder more and more U.S.-born and -raised Latina sisters are saying no to the traditional Hispanic marriage: "Hell, no!" "Not us!" "We are not going *there*!" Then we fall in love. And just like the character in Angeles Mastretta's novel *Lovesick,* we fall in love the only way intelligent women know how to fall in love: like complete *idiotas. El amor nos convierte en pendejas.*

We become the *novia,* the live-in, *la chilla,* the partner, the *casi-esposa, la mujer,* the wife, and, ultimately, the mother; and then something else happens. An automatic *sirvienta* button most of us didn't know we had (or thought was long gone) is pushed. My friend Sandra Angelita says that we also get an acute case of *mamitis agudi-tis,* or acute mothering when we are in deep like or love. It's like we become the lover's *madrecita.* "It's sick," she laughs and shrugs, "but it's true." Maybe not always, but all too often!

Marriage or a committed relationship takes us to territory that will bring out our mothers or *abuelas* in ways we didn't expect. And when we find ourselves in that territory, boy, do we struggle against her—that traditional wife who carries her home on her back. We fight like hell against the automatic servant and nurturer in us. Some *hermanas* call this the dreaded "Mexican-maid complex."

The challenge of the contemporary Latina wife for us *nuevas lati-nas* begins in the sacred space of love. And we struggle with such questions as: How do you balance this desire to express your love the way you were taught to express it (nurturing, taking care of your man and your kids and your house) without losing yourself in the process? Can you forge a healthy relationship without surrendering yourself in him, in the relationship, and in the expected responsibilities of it all? Can you put your needs first, before him, before the children, without feeling like a complete *mala esposa* and *mala madre*? Can you be a Latina wife and not a *sirvienta*? And, finally, are there any straight, fine Latinos with a job and no illegal bad habits who want women like us—women bent on flipping this part of our culture?

WHO IS THIS NEW BEAST CALLED
LA NUEVA ESPOSA AND IS SHE FOR REAL?

I call them "the new Latina wives," and these fierce babes exist all around us. Thousands of twenty-first-century Latina wives and partners are breaking new ground on love, reinventing marriage, girlfriend-hood, *esposa*-hood and *madre*-hood even as you read this. We have found that we can *selectively* embrace the traditions and trappings of a traditional Latina—be a loving caretaker, partner, and doting mother—without accepting old-school customs about endless thankless giving and noble silent suffering. In the words of our younger sisters, Nuh-uh!

Las nuevas esposas never assume that suffering—*la cruz del marido y de la casa y los hijos*—is an admirable quality. We know that's the way it was, but we don't believe that's the way it is or has to be. We know we can bring home the bacon, fry it up in a *caldero,* keep an awesome *casa,* treat a man well, and all that. But we've learned to reconcile that part of giving and loving is getting the same in return. As a fierce Tejana grandma told me in a middle of a presentation not too long ago, "*mija,* I am proud to have the *sirvienta* button, *pero* I only unleash it when I want to!"

I won't kid you: living the life of the new wife isn't easy. A new Latino relationship takes work, *cojones,* conviction, and, of course, a willing *papi* (or *mami,* if that is your case). All the fierce twenty-first-century Hispanic men and women who embrace a balanced Nuevo Latino relationship continually have to *unlearn* what we were taught about relationships and marriages. We have to keep ourselves in constant check. And we have to toss out the dominant (read "male-privileged") script that was handed down to us by mom and dad and tradition.

New Latina wives in modern relationships have to learn to embrace the secret of self-esteem before any other kind of love, the power of delegating and negotiating responsibility, and the concept of learning with our mates this very new dynamic.

> *Culture forms our belief . . . dominant paradigms are transmitted to us through culture. Culture is made by those in power—men.*
>
> —Gloria Anzaldúa,

FIRST COMES LOVE, THEN COMES *NOVIA* . . .

A Latina about to take the plunge into a serious relationship may want to ask herself, "What kind of a *novia* am I?" Be on your guard against becoming that dreaded creature, the *casi-esposa*. We Latinas too often go from dating to *novia* to *casi-esposa* in no time, faster than homemade *pan dulce* goes stale.

Therapist Dr. Lozano-Vranich breaks it down for us. She sees women who struggle with this issue, and she is challenged by it herself. "On the first couple of dates we don't really worry too much about what he is eating. But by the third date, we notice that he didn't touch his *ensalada* or his *arroz,* and we ask, *Papito, no comiste, tienes que comer, qué te pasa,* are you sick?" Sound familiar?

"We become the quasi-wife, and then we're taken for granted because we take on the responsibility of the relationship really fast," she adds. Often, she says, we tend to *assume* the responsibility of the relationship, as opposed to the other person delegating it to us or demanding anything!

The *novia* you are tells you what kind of *esposa* you will be (unless you take conscious steps to change). As a *novia* you are writing the wife role that you want to play in your marriage. You are setting the stage; you are in dress rehearsal. So, *mija,* pay close attention to how you behave, how your honey behaves, the expectations you place on your partner *and* yourself, and the responsibilities you assume. Do that, and you can begin to flip the cultural script right from the beginning.

THREE GOLDEN RELATIONSHIP RULES FOR THE NUEVA LATINA

1. HAVE A RELATIONSHIP WITH YOURSELF AND GAIN A STATE-OF-THE-ART *CABRÓN* DETECTOR

I'm sure you've heard this one before, but every one of us needs to hear it *otra vez:* to have a spiritually, physically, and emotionally healthy relationship with someone else, you have to first have a sacred and fulfilling relationship with yourself.

Women have to be careful about when and why we enter relationships. Many of us enter relationships not knowing or loving ourselves completely, with expectations that the person we fall in love with will make us feel whole, happy, special, beautiful, or simply loved. We expect this mate to complete us. The fact is, it's grossly unfair *and* unrealistic to expect the person we fall in love with to make us feel things we don't already feel for ourselves. No one can make you feel special, beautiful, smart, or complete but you.

It is often said that love has no logic, but it seems perfectly logical to me that a relationship built with one member feeling incomplete will be full of misery, frustration, and drama; it will crumble. Trying to establish a long-lasting relationship on a shaky foundation is like building a castle on quicksand.

Some of us enter or stay in bad relationships because we fear being alone. This fear of being alone makes us settle for less than we deserve. We allow all kinds of *humillaciones*, physical and mental beatings from the people who say they love us. Maybe the lack of self-love and the fear of being alone can explain the disturbing increase in the number of Hispanic women dying at the hands of lovers or husbands. One in three Latinas is beat up by a lover or husband. It happens in lesbian relationships, too. According to research psychologist Richard Niolon, domestic violence in gay and lesbian couples is a serious problem. Until recently, he said, the problem had been completely discounted and thus unnoticed.

"The incidence of domestic violence in gay and lesbian couples is probably at least as high as in heterosexual couples, if not higher." And according to a Rutgers University study, Dr. Niolon's research is right on. The study found that "violence in gay and lesbian relationships occurs at the same rate as in heterosexual relationships."

Violence has no sexual preference. If you find yourself tempted to get into or stay in an unhealthy relationshiop, remember the wisdom of this *abuela*-ism: *"Es mejor estar sola, que mala acompañada."*

It's easier for a woman to surrender herself to another person in a relationship if she does not love herself, if she's not grounded, if she feels that she does not deserve better, or if she has no life outside of her romantic relationship. If a woman has suffered abuse as a child—sexual or otherwise—the issue of love gets even more complicated. (See chapter 7, "Latina Sexual Mystique," for more on this issue.) Although it seems like an oxymoron, being in a relationship has more to do with your feelings about and relationship to yourself than anything else. If you find yourself gravitating toward the same problematic type again and again, it's time to take stock of your self-esteem. It's not always them, baby; it can be you. Before you focus all your energy on finding Señor Right, spend quality time finding out who you are and what you enjoy. My thirty-two-year-old second-generation Latina sister-in-law recently took a day for herself for the first time in her life. She went window-shopping and clothes shopping—alone. Once the initial feeling of "I wish I had someone with me—a friend, Mom, a niece, my husband . . ." wore off, she told me, she relaxed. One of the marvels she discovered

Domestic Violence

Domestic violence perpetrators fall into three categories:

Psychotic: "Psychosis" is a kind of umbrella label for a number of severe mental disorders, but in general this type of person lacks empathy and impulse control, often seeming disconnected from reality. If you think your partner is manifesting behavior indicative of mental illness, work with family members to get him or her in for an evaluation.

Chronically angry: What defines this type of person is not what he or she looks like or what he or she does in his or her downtime, but his or her ability to go from zero to sixty on the anger meter within seconds: one minute laughing and playful, the next in a blind rage. Alcohol and drugs frequently play a role in mood swings, and unfortunately, over time you may become target *número uno*.

El que no rompe un plato: This individual can be the most insidious of the bunch. In public he or she appears normal and possibly even engaging. Home, however, is a different matter entirely. His or her violence, anger, and psychological abuse center almost exclusively on his or her partner and children. It is also common for the frequency and degree of the violence to escalate over the years.

was that she could take her time in the sale rack without the pressure of others; she could move at her own pace. At the end of her excursion, she called to thank me for encouraging the "*sola*-expedition" and said, "I need to do this again and again." I promised her, and I promise you, that the more things you do by yourself, the more you'll get to know yourself—and as a fringe benefit, the more interesting and ultimately satisfied a partner you'll be.

BESAME MUCHO: Where are you on the "I Love Me" scale? Ask yourself the following questions:

- Am I the woman I want to be?
- Am I waiting for that special someone to awaken the woman I want to be?
- How many ways do I love myself?
- *Do* I love myself, with all of the *cositas lindas y feas* that make me who I am?
- Do I find myself beautiful, smart, special?
- Do I feel incomplete without a relationship?
- How desperate am I to be in a relationship?
- Am I comfortable doing things by myself, or do I always need him or others to go with me everywhere?

Diosas de las Américas

Spider Woman, or **Sussistanako,** appears in the myths of the southwestern Native Americans as a resourceful helper who spins magical charms and each person's fate. No matter what problems or obstacles you face, Sussistanako, creates the right network of energy to put you on the road toward accomplishment. The Native Americans believed in the legend of Spider Woman; what happens at one part of the web influences all parts of the web.

Make a list of all the reasons you *want* to be in a relationship. Now make *another* list, this time of things you *expect* from a relationship. Have these questions and lists given you a picture of your "ideal" mate? How do you want to feel with this ideal mate? Finally, write down all the things you would want in this "perfect" relationship. It seems like hard work, but try it and you will be looking at a relationship mirror that is you, yourself in terms of relationship.

A relationship therapist explained to me that most of us have an image of a perfect mate that we devised in our teenage years. He is a combination of the things we loved or wanted in our fathers, our favorite *tío,* and the salsa or rock star we so loved. But while this mate may have satisfied us in our minds when we were fifteen, he does not function when we are twenty-five or thirty-five. Besides, he does not exist.

As you reflect on these questions, listen to the whispers of your intuition, to the voice that may have been drowned by self-doubt, low self-esteem, or past heartaches and experiences. You are bound to hear the answers to these questions. I promise you that they are inside, in your heart. Even if your answers seem absurd in black and white, they will tell you a lot about yourself, and possibly what's been frustrating you in your life.

But let's get down to the nuts and bolts of Golden Rule No. 1: How *do* you have a relationship with yourself? For starters, you have to take care of business, and you *are* your business. Getting to know and love yourself is a delicate and lifelong journey. It doesn't happen in one night, by answering quizzes, making lists, or reading a self-help book, though these things are all part of the journey. It takes conversations, *contigo misma,* many years of introspection and reflection. It takes doing things by yourself, *sola,* and making mistakes, and never losing the lessons. And because you never stay the same, the process of knowing yourself never ends.

I was married and had a baby before I turned twenty-three, within two years of graduating from college. Unfortunately, I was a baby myself: I certainly didn't know and love myself completely enough to

Your Ideal Mate

I believe in the concept of soul mates—that there is a person out there who is a perfect fit for you. And I believe in the power of visualization, affirmation, and prayer. Here's a quick recipe for love:

- Don't wait for him to complete you. Become the woman you dream of being.

- Make a list of *all* the characteristics you want this soul mate to have, and don't be shy—it's your list! There's just one condition: you can't put things on the list that you are not. For example, you're not ready to write that you want a man with a sense of humor if you can't laugh yourself.

- Don't invest time or energy in someone who doesn't fit the most important profile you made for yourself.

- Be open to meeting all kinds of people. Don't get stuck on the perfect abs or height or job. This short guy who doesn't have rhythm *may* have the "qualities" you desire. Let time and him tell.

- Be patient and have faith that he or she is out there getting ready for you. If you have so many heartaches or have been with so many *cabrones,* it is easy to lose faith. Keep focused and don't embrace negativity. Don't lose faith in the magic of love.

- Be practical; after all, adult relationships are about compromise. He may not be the millionaire you wished for, but he may be a really hardworking cabdriver who has everything else you want.

- Don't settle for less than you deserve, *nena,* and you deserve *lo mejor*!

build a solid, healthy union. I found a man I hoped would complete me and make me feel things about myself that I didn't feel on my own: beautiful, lovable, and special.

Of course it didn't work, but I don't regret my choices. That failed marriage was a life lesson that I turned into a victory. Twelve years of life as a single mother and a journey of getting to know and adore me–warts and all–has given me the power and clarity to view relationships with a different set of eyes. How many hearts have I broken in my journey of getting to know me? I hope not too many. How many times has my own heart been shattered? *Muchisimas veces* . . . but I refuse to settle! It isn't that I won't compromise, but I won't stay with the wrong partner just because I want to be married or hooked up with whomever.

Because today I know and love myself, I have the strength and conviction to make and keep boundaries in a relationship; I establish ground rules for those who wish to enter my life. Can you draw lines in the sand and not feel bad about it? This self-knowledge gives me the ammunition to be a master negotiator, too. We know how *difícil* it is to negotiate under the weight of love–*el amor es ciego,* as the *dicho* goes. But it's even harder to negotiate what you want when you're not clear about your needs. *Mi hermana,* you set the example of how people will treat you. When a woman is clear about who she is and how she expects to be treated, there is no stopping her in matters of love.

Knowing myself has given me the courage to make no excuses about the kind of partner or relationship I want in my life. It has given me the power and conviction to walk away forever when things are not right. And most important, it has given me a state-of-the-art *cabrón* detector.

2. DESTROY THE POWER CENTERS OF YOUR HOME AND REBUILD THEM TOGETHER

There's an old *chiste* I really love. A groom tells his bride the rules for their new marriage: "On Mondays I go to work, and after work I head for the gym, dinner around eight P.M. Tuesday's bowling night, and I come home about nine P.M. to a home-cooked meal. Wednesdays I work late, so I'll be home around ten P.M.—don't wait to have dinner with me. Thursday is boys' night out, so don't expect me to get home till after midnight. Fridays, I visit my mom, so I'll have dinner over there. Weekends I relax and get ready for another work week. You okay with that?" he asks. "Sure, *papi*," the bride calmly responds. "I have only one rule. In my house I screw every night at eight P.M.—with or without you!"

Take a long and hard look at the power centers of your home and relationship, destroy them, and create new ones with your partner.

There are always power dynamics in every relationship, however subtle they may be, and there are four areas where most power is concentrated: sex, money, household chores, and child rearing. Here are a few questions to ask yourself about those power relations:

- Who is deciding what?
- Who is doing what?
- Do you feel silenced in your current relationship?
- What power do you have over major decisions in your partnership?
- Who decides when to have sex, and who initiates sex?
- Who brings home the money? Who manages it?
- Who is in charge of the cooking, the cleaning, the decorating, the shopping, and so on?
- If there are children involved, who is responsible for caring for the kids and disciplining them?

One of the best ways to find out where you are is to take a cold look at your relationship in each of these areas. Pretend that you're looking at a movie where you are the central character, and you're analyzing this character's interactions within each of the four areas. After you determine who is doing what, and who has the power to decide what, knock those power centers down and rebuild from scratch—together. Remember the *dicho* that says no one can take power unless you give it away.

The problem with marriage is that it ends every night after making love, and it must be rebuilt every morning before breakfast.

—GABRIEL GARCÍA MÁRQUEZ, *Love in the Time of Cholera*

Marta Lucia, twenty-nine, who had recently moved in with her boyfriend of two years told me that she constantly found herself "checking in" to make sure that she wasn't losing herself in the process of living with her love.

"It's hard, it's a pain—to constantly ask myself if I am doing too much, if I am taking on too much of the responsibilities—but in the end, it's all about balancing my heart, my mind, my soul, my mental health, and my love for me and him."

Whenever she referred to power plays among men and women, my mom would always say that men were like monkeys and women like trees; a monkey knows the tree it will climb. "*Si te dejas montar, te jodes.*" If you let him climb all over you, you're screwed. In other words, if a tree is too difficult, treacherous, challenging, or plain hard, the monkey will respect it and tread carefully. Show some spine, negotiate your turf. You have the power and the responsibility to you, your man, and relationship to determine what your relationship will be within each power center. Negotiate and compromise with your partner. These power centers have no genders. If your man wants to stay home and take care of the kids, for instance, and you work and you can afford it and it's what you want too, let him do it! If you're the disciplinarian and he's the "doting *mamá*" parent and it works for you both, that's fine. There's no right or wrong here, only what makes sense for you and your honey in the sanctity of your private space.

El mono sabe el palo que trepa.
—Popular *dicho*

LET HIM DECORATE THE HOUSE EVEN IF HE'S COLOR-BLIND; LET HIM WASH DISHES EVEN IF HE DOESN'T KNOW HOW. My friend Rossana says that a lot of Nueva Latinas are full of *caca* when it comes to living a new *matrimonio* concept. She says that we want partners but we don't really want to give up the power we have in the home. Intellectually, I know that I'd gladly give up my cooking and cleaning duties to Mr. Right. But when it comes to, say, buying the kids' clothes or redecorating *la casa,* I admit I have second thoughts. I am like many other *mujeres* who say, "No, *papi,* I'll do it."

And we come up with all kinds of nifty excuses: *los hombres no saben de esas cosas,* or they don't know how to color-coordinate, or "He just doesn't know how to do it (wash the dishes, clean the house . . .) the way I like it!" So many of us end up doing it ourselves. We pride ourselves in knowing how to do certain things, including rearing kids and keeping house. Sound familiar?

Many of us set the patterns we ourselves grow to hate: we don't delegate from the beginning, we don't know *how* to delegate, and we're uncomfortable with the idea of what our mates can do. Sometimes our mates resist change even when we're ready for it. Sometimes we are afraid use the power we have, or don't realize that we have it. Other times, we're afraid to let it go. The power of running the house is especially hard to let go. *But we can't have it both ways.* We have to learn to release our control, even if the kids end up with ugly shoes or he missed sweeping under the bed. *¡Que aprenda!*

THE CURSE OF *LA SUPER-ESPOSA.* Anneci, a thirty-four-year-old Latina professional, told me that when she first married, she decided she would be a traditional wife. "*Bueno,* my husband would come home and wait for me to do everything. He relaxed from a hard day's work while I cooked, set the table, did the dishes, and, later on, gave him some. I really *wanted* him to come home from work and relax." Now, I should point out that this woman is no one's definition of a doormat or *pendeja.* A therapist herself, she manages a mental-health clinic for abused children during the day, is a community leader, has a private mental-health practice, and is a sex and relationship counselor for a national website. To top it off, she is the mother of a pre-teen girl. However, she wanted to express her love for her man just as her mother did for her father, without getting much help on the domestic front in return, save for his "*Gracias,* babe, the lasagna was kicking!" She tells me that her husband, who had been raised by strong Hispanic women who encouraged him to do for himself, was surprised by her insistence on doing things as they were done in the "old school." But as you might expect, he was okay with the arrangement. He told his wife, "Knock yourself out, Mami."

"Then it all became so overwhelming," she said. "I was running myself into the ground." The couple had to start from the beginning and revise the responsibilities—the power centers—because the stress of her trying to be his everything and do it all was tearing her and the marriage apart. Her husband learned how to cook and today boasts about his culinary skills. They have found a balance in their lives, and this *nuevo latino* relationship is stronger than ever.

SEX IS NOT A WEAPON. *PERO . . .* Simply asking for what you want often works, though not always. *Repeated* asking becomes nagging, and nagging almost *never* works: you get tuned out, or if you get your way, it might be at a very high price (such as his respect for you). Sometimes you have to take seemingly drastic measures to break patterns that exact a toll on you and your relationship.

Early in my first marriage I learned this one from my neighbor, a streetwise Latina who seduced a priest and then married him. She'd wrestled this good guy from God, so imagine how much she knew about the male mind. One day I complained to her that I was sick and tired of doing most of the work *en la casa,* taking care of the baby, cooking, and cleaning after coming home from a hard day's work as a reporter. My then husband wouldn't do his share. She asked me if I had sex with him every night.

"Yes," I told her. "Why?"

"That's your mistake," she said. *"No se lo des!"*

"What?!"

"Be stingy with your *cuchie,*" she said. I told her I thought that was crazy and archaic, but she said, "*Niña,* go on a sex strike for a week. Sweetly tell him you *want* to get it on, but you can't because you're too tired from doing all the stuff at work *and* in the house. You *need* his help, or you can't be the pussycat that he wants you to be."

I thought it was crazy to deprive myself of something I liked, and wrong to use sex as a negotiating tool. But she argued that I had given up the power in several areas of my relationship: I was helping bring home the bacon, I was responsible for the child and home, *and* I was being the dutiful wife past midnight. This woman reminded me that I had to reclaim *one* of those power centers. So I tried this older *vecina* wisdom and declared a sex strike.

Mujeres, it worked. No *cuchie* for a week, and my husband was washing down the bathroom and kitchen squeaky clean the next weekend. But it doesn't have to be a sex strike. You can go on a cooking strike, a laundry strike . . . there are all kinds of strikes and slowdowns to get your partner to the negotiating table! Labor leaders do it; you can too!

3. BECOME HIS *MAESTRA*

Our men are not stupid or ignorant, and they weren't born on Mars. They're not born *machistas,* either. But they *were* socialized into being and expecting certain things from us and society. This doesn't excuse *machos* who revel in male privilege, but we need to understand their behavior if we hope to change it. *La cultura* empowers them, the Church sanctions their supreme role, and the *madres machistas* who raise them perpetuate it all. Our men, too, have been "victims" of *la tradición.*

I was witness to a *machista* mother who raised two little Hispanic *príncipes.* My brothers didn't especially want to avoid the housecleaning rotation, but they were raised by a mom who didn't think it was a man's place to be running around with broom and mop in hand. *Esas no son cosas de hombres . . .* I'd go on furious (and now infamous) tantrums protesting that Mike and Alex should be put on the dishwashing rotation just like the girls. "No," said Mom, *"ellos son machos,"* and with that I was supposed to understand why they had been excused.

Fast-forward to today: my brothers are Nuevo Latino husbands. Mike is a certified Mr. Mom. And their Nueva Latina wives—my sisters-in-law—tell me that, despite excessive pampering from *Mami,* my brothers are troupers. They respect and honor my sisters-in-law as wives and not *sirvientas.* They understand the true meaning of a partnership. They have made major adjustments to fit this prototype of a

Many of our men are oppressed by a cultura that dictates the way they should be as opposed to what they could be.

—MARTA LUCIA, HIGH SCHOOL TEACHER AND WRITER

relationship that was being demanded by Latinas raised in a new era and country.

So just as I unlearned my traditional role, my brothers unlearned theirs. The *machista* paradigm *can* be undone! We women must often be the teachers, but both men and women have to be willing to take on the challenge, and to meet it together, a day at a time. By establishing *your* rules, you are teaching your man to be the best *esposo* that he can be.

A MACHO MOMENT. Of course, there are always moments when it doesn't work the way we think it should. We were at a family dinner last year at my brother Mike's place. After everybody ate, the women hurried to the kitchen to clean up, and the men in the clan (including my fourteen-year-old son) retired to the living room to watch TV. As I stuffed leftovers into a garbage can, I looked at the scene and asked my *cuñadas,* "What's wrong with this picture?"

They told me that when my mother was not there, my brothers were all in here doing their share. I turned to *Mami,* and she said, very matter-of-factly, "Well, *qué quieres?* For them to be here in the kitchen?" The scene made me think again about this new woman and the perpetual Latina challenge that we face in the home. The more I thought about what my *cuñadas* said—"When your mother's not around, they're different"—the more sense the whole scene made.

There are some situations where we might *temporarily* choose to take on traditional roles. Maybe it's to let our men save face in front of relatives and friends; we don't need to "humiliate" them in public to make a point. If your man understands that in *your* intimacy he should be in the kitchen too, doing his share, then it's okay to let him slide in "public." We are not going to change their mothers: they still will say under their breath that we, *las mujeres de hoy*—meaning *las nuevas esposas*—no sabemos cuidar a sus hijos. Or worse: some will even say that we're turning their sons into *maricones* by demanding that they do traditionally "female" tasks. Most of these mothers were born in a different era, so we can keep their prejudices in perspective, but we don't always have to bow down to them. I have a friend who will do the dishes when she visits her mother-in-law, but she makes sure that her partner—this woman's only son—keeps her company *en la cocina* and doesn't retire to watch TV with the boys.

There's another good reason why we might not want to demand that all the *varones* march into the kitchen with us. My honey pointed this out to me when I mentioned how upsetting the living-room scene made me. He said, "Maybe your ma has secrets she wants to share with you and the rest of the womenfolk in the absence of the men."

Now, there's a thought! There *is* magic in the *madre-hija-hermana-cuñada-tía-abuela chisme* banter that takes place our kitchens. It's the place where family *recetas* and *cuentos* are passed on for future generations. I thought for a moment about all the kitchen *cuentos* and family *chistes* I got to hear from my mom, my *tías*, my sisters, and all the womenfolk growing up. So when I'm at family gatherings now, I pause before asking my man to come in and help out with the *platos*.

EMBRACING, WITHIN LIMITS, THE *SIRVIENTA* WITHIN. I have come to accept that I am a nurturer and that it's okay to revel in what that really means. Being a nurturer doesn't make me any less a *feminista* or Nueva Latina. It gives me strength, because I'm able to provide strength. However, I do need balance: nurturing has to come back to me. In new relationships the motto is "*Cuidame, mi vida, que yo te cuidaré.*"

Becoming this *nueva esposa* will depend on you, as well as on the mate you hook up with, and on the compromises both of you are willing to make. It takes constant temperature checks on yourself to ensure that you are nourishing and replenishing yourself as you go about creating this new relationship. We are all bound to break new and difficult ground as we build strong and fulfilling *nuevo latino* relationships that allow us to honor ourselves, our *familias,* and our *tradiciones,* while creating our private and special space in the mix.

A fierce Latina who made U.S. history

Before Serena and Venus Williams, and before Chrissy Everett, the game of tennis saw Latina tennis champion **Rosemary Casals.** And long after this powerhouse left the nets, the game and, in particular, the way women were treated would never be the same. Thanks largely in part to Casals's efforts, today's female tennis stars are still benefiting from her achievements. Rosemary was born in 1948 in San Francisco, California, to parents who had emigrated from El Salvador. Because her parents were very poor and unable to care for her and her younger sister, a great-aunt and -uncle raised both siblings. The *tío* would inspire and teach Rosemary the sport that made her a part of American history. Rosemary, who perfected her game in San Francisco's public parks, won more than ninety tournaments in her professional career and was a force to be reckoned with when it came to changing the perception of women's tennis. She often competed against opponents who were older and had more experience than she did, in an effort to improve her game. In 1965 by the age seventeen, she ranked eleventh in the country—and that included both men and women. In 1966, she and Billie Jean King, who was her doubles partner, won the U.S. hard-court and indoor tournaments. In 1967, Rosemary and Billie Jean took the doubles crown at Wimbledon and at the United States and South African championships. To this day, they are the only doubles team to have won U.S. titles on grass, clay, indoor, and hard surfaces. During the time she was winning doubles titles, Rosemary ranked third among U.S. women. Among her most notable achievements was her fight to change unfair traditions in professional tennis. She worked for an arrangement that would allow both professional and amateur players to compete in the same tournaments. She also fought pay inequity in the game. Because male players were awarded more money than female players were, Rosemary along with other players threatened to boycott traditional tournaments. However, the USLTA refused to listen, so she organized, along with other players, the Virginia Slims invitational. The media attention generated by this invitational soon brought about other tournaments specifically for women, increasing the amount of money they were awarded. Rosemary retired from the game in 1978 after undergoing knee surgery. Since 1982, she has been president of Sportswomen, Inc., a California-based company she formed to promote women's classic tours for new chances to improve the game of tennis.

CHAPTER NINE

MARRYING OUTSIDE *LA RAZA:*
Eight Things to Know Before You Marry a *Blanquito*

(Take this test before you marry him!)

So you've finally met the *papi* of your life—he's tall, fine, smart, funny, charming, and in touch with his feminine side and chivalrous roots. San Antonio, the Latin Cupid, patron saint of single *chicas,* whom you may have dunked upside down in a glass of water so that he could find you a man, has answered your prayers. Well, kind of— the man of your dreams happens to be John, not Juan. He is, as your *abuelita* might say, a *blanquito.*

While somewhere inside your head you may hear the old racist *dicho* that says, it's okay, "*voy a mejorar la raza,*" another louder and more imposing voice might be telling you to back away from your newfound *amigo.* Are you right to worry? Will you be messing up *la raza*? Should you light some more candles and dunk San Antonio back in the cup so that he will take him back and exchange this Smith for a Rivera?

Calmaté–don't return this guy just yet.

First, you should know that you are in a good company. San Antonio has been going a bit *loco* and pairing many *hermanas* and *hermanos* across this nation with non-Latinos. According to the 2000 United States Census, almost one-third of U.S.-born Hispanics ages twenty-five to thirty-four were married to non-Hispanic whites. In addition, numbers show it is the Hispanic female—not the Latino—who is leading the trend to marry outside *la raza*. Most often, we end up marrying white guys. (Check out the "Who Is Marrying Who" box.) This trend shows no sign of slowing, either. National government demographic studies show that by the third generation in this country, nearly half of Hispanics marry outside their group.

Although dating within *la raza* is no guarantee of happiness, dating outside *la raza* does add complications to the "regular" challenges of a relationship. That doesn't mean you can't be happy, but you should both be aware of the extra challenges that *will* come up!

Yours will not be a traditional union. It will be a relationship that even in the smallest ways brings together two cultures, two experiences, and two very different worlds. The faster you recognize the potential *complicaciones*, the better it will be for you and your newfound man.

MAKING IT WORK

The key to making your special combo work is, as with any other relationship, communication—whether it's in Spanish, English, or (as with many of us) Spanglish!

There is a reason why the 1997 movie about the ultra-Anglo Matthew Perry and *muy* Latina Salma Hayek was called *Fools Rush In*. In the movie, their characters rushed into marriage three

Who Is Marrying Who

In 2000, 932,000 Latinas were married to non-Hispanic males. Of those guys, 824,000 were white, 72,000 were African American, and 35,000 were other.

That same year, 811,000 Latinos were married to non-Hispanic females. Of those women, 723,000 were white, 41,000 were African American, and 47,000 were other.

However, the bulk of our unions were to other Latinos, with 4,739,000 marriages where both spouses were Latinos.

The Networks

According to Nielsen's ratings, Univision is now the fifth-largest network for prime-time viewers nationwide. Out of the 100.8 million television households in the United States 8.6 percent are Hispanic.

Who We Live With

Four states with the largest minority populations—California, Texas, New York, and Florida—are home to nearly half of all U.S. mixed marriages. Nearly one of every four such couples lives in California.

months after falling in love, and *ay Dios mio*, all hell broke loose once they discovered that love was not going to be enough. While yours may not be a Hollywood romance, the film had moments that reflected just how messy it can get when two worlds meet. So, *mija*, before you rush in, arm yourself with the facts.

With the help of dozens of Latinas who've gone white, I devised this eight-point quiz. Give it to your honey. It's not foolproof, but this checklist will help you and your beloved get to know each other in ways you never imagined.

1. CAN HE FIND ECUADOR ON THE MAP?

Give him a map of Latin America and have him point to your family's homeland. Did he pass, or was he clueless? It may sound silly now, but if your man slept through his sixth-grade geography class, he might find it helpful to take a refresher course. I remember my friend telling me about a *blanquito* she was sweet on. She (a Boricua and a Cuban girlfriend would tease each other—in front of her white *amor*—about which island had better music, food, guys, and so on. This went on until one day he pulled her aside and asked, "What's up with the Puerto Rico–versus–Cuba jokes? Isn't Puerto Rico part of Cuba?" No need to tell you that the sweet turned sour faster than you can order Chinese takeout.

But what does this geographically and historically challenged guy have to do with you and your honey? It's simple: knowing about the land where you or your parents or *abuelos* came from is knowing and respecting a part of what makes you who you are. Your white *papi* will need to recognize that you have roots that go beyond Kansas, the Bronx, Los Angeles, or wherever your native city is, and that these roots are important, an integral part of your Latina identity. It's vital that he knows that your family has its roots in a beautiful country with distinct traditions and a unique and rich history.

That's why I think that, besides brushing up on geography, your honey might want to freshen up on Latin American history. In fact, if you can afford the trip, it might be a great idea for both of you to take a trip to your homeland. (That is, of course, after you've gone there by yourself. See chapter 11, "Going Home—to Your Roots.")

But a little geographical ignorance on his part doesn't mean he's not marriage material. If you are willing to be a "teacher" and share all the great things your homeland and heritage have to offer, and if he has the interest to learn, go ahead and take out the chalk. The point here is about ensuring recognition of roots—deep, rich roots that are a big part of you.

2. WHO WAS CARMEN MIRANDA?

If your gringo sweetheart thinks Carmen Miranda was a typical Latina, *hermana,* you are in for *muchos problemas.* The sexy Brazilian who balanced a basket of tropical fruit on her head while swinging her hips and rolling her *r*'s wasn't typical, even in her heyday, more than fifty years ago. But the character she created is only one of the many stereotypes that still plague us and remind us that we don't live in a bias-free society. Until we do, there are some very serious things that your man must understand about you and your people. The first thing is this: discrimination is real.

I'll assume that if your guy has popped the question and you've said yes, he himself is cool. That said, *'mana,* your Anglo honey will never know—no matter how Latino acculturated he is, no matter how much *salsa* or *merengue* he can dance, no matter how spicy he likes his food— the experience of being a Latina in the United States. It's not his fault, and it doesn't make him bad, but it is a fact, and it *can* be a problem.

High on the list of *quejas* from Latinas who went with *blanquitos* was that their non-Latino partners just didn't "get it"—they didn't understand how Latinas experience racism. With a Latino, there are certain *cositas* that don't need explanation. It's like those old *abuela* sayings that are not translatable to English. Simply because a Latin male has lived a Latin life in the United States, it is sometimes easier to for him to "get it."

My friend Maria told me a story about vacationing in a rural town in the southern United States with her white husband. It was two A.M. when they arrived at a small inn, and her husband, who was driving, asked her to go and check for vacancies. Maria refused, thinking, "In 'redneck' country, they see a Latina face roll in at two A.M. and all of a sudden there are no rooms available." Maria's husband mistook her refusal to risk humiliation at that hour of the night for laziness. "He just didn't understand, and frankly, I was too tired to explain."

A white male goes through life with privilege, not having to think much about his race, ethnicity, or gender. This unspoken privilege gives your *papi* access and authority in society. Again, it's not his fault, but it's real, and it will creep up in your life as a couple.

A white guy is usually not subject to racial profiling while driving along the border or down U.S. highways—unlike his browner Latina sweetie (that's you), her siblings, parents, aunts, uncles, and other relatives. When he visits a department store, he's probably not tailed by undercover store security, as many of us have been. He's more than likely paid at least 43 cents an hour more than you are, even if both of you have equal training.

If he's never experienced these unfair conditions himself, it may be hard for him to acknowledge that they're real; a certain naïveté comes with leading a privileged life. You may want to ask yourself what his reaction will be if you're faced with discrimination, however subtle. His ability to feel your rage and soothe your injured soul will be important. Therefore your partner's opinion on larger Latino race-relations issues will eventually affect you.

WILL HE UNDERSTAND YOUR PAIN?

A key factor in a strong relationship is having the comfort that your partner understands, empathizes with, and can console you.

To appreciate where your man stands on these issues, bring them up in casual conversation. Even the best-intentioned white guy can honestly believe that Charo or Jennifer Lopez are representative Latinas if his life hasn't brought him much contact with the real thing. But check out other negative stereotypes that might have seeped into his subconscious. It might be a good idea to share with him newspaper articles about racial bias against Latinos. Ask his opinions about these news events. You might be surprised by what you learn about each other from these discussions. The idea is not to "catch" your partner having racist thoughts but to get him to see life from your perspective, so that the two of you will share in the outrage if an event ever requires it.

You might reach a point where you have to accept that he simply will not understand some things, and hopefully you can be okay with that if you're happy with the rest of him. In Maria's case, she found a support group of Latina friends and family that she could gripe with. "He's naive about Latino racial politics, but he's great about everything else."

3. WHO IS THE *VIRGENCITA* IN YOUR LIVING ROOM?

Does he understand that the crucifix, the statues of *La Virgen de la Guadalupe,* Santa Barbara, San Lazaro, and the fruit and candles adorning these altars in your or your parents' living room are not kooky decor or some other exotic voodoo stuff?

There is no subject Latinos take more seriously than religion (see chapter 5, "Centering Your Soul"). My deep sense of *fé* is evident smack in the middle of my living room: Santa Barbara, the patron saint of powerful *chicas,* greets all my visitors. My altar is always adorned with fresh flowers, and sometimes red wine and apples. Once a white *papi* I was sweet on walked into my place, saw my altar, said, "Wow, cool," and grabbed the apple! I snatched it from his hands before he bit into it. He thought he'd just walked into some funky retro–chic–Nuevo Latino museum exhibit. And I quickly showed him the exit sign, too!

Your faith, whatever it is, is very much a part of you. If you are not practicing at the moment, your family is. And what you or your family believes, whether practicing or not, is not open to ridicule—it's embedded in your soul.

Even if both of you share the same faith, for instance, Catholicism, the truth is that Latino Catholics worship God very differently than non-Latino Catholics do. When was the last time you saw thousands of Irish Catholics crawl on their bloody knees to pay tribute? What will he think of your visit to an *espiritista* for a much-needed *consulta*? Will he consider it freaky when you roll out the *pan dulce* and skeleton candy for your *Día de los Muertos* celebration? We express our faith *en Dios* more publicly and dramatically, and it's not just about language.

Diosas de las Américas

Ix-chel is a Mayan goddess whose name means "She of the Rainbows." Among the Maya of the Yucatán peninsula, this was the name of the snake goddess of water and the moon, of childbirth and weaving. Once, it was said, she took the sun as her lover, but her grandfather jealously hurled lightning at them, killing her. Grieving dragonflies sang over Ix-chel for thirteen days, at the end of which time she emerged, whole and alive, and followed her lover to his palace.

If your relationship does progress from puppy love to a more serious stage, faith becomes an even more important issue. Make sure you discuss and agree upon how you will praise your God and bring up your children *before* you say "I do."

4. WHAT DOES HE THINK ABOUT *LA FAMILIA*?

Since love is ultimately not just about two people, family—his and yours—will play a very important role in your life as a couple. Does he understand the importance of *abuela, mami, las tías, y los tíos* at every family gathering? How does he define family? For Latinos, getting together with family is not just for "the holidays." My brothers, sisters, and I visit Mom on a weekly basis, some of us daily. Even in our worst mother-daughter struggles, there was that obligatory call to check in. And who does not get that mom call after three days, "*¿Ya te olvidaste que tienes madre?*"

It may sound stereotypical, but in my weekly or semiweekly family visits, there is always music, banter (we try to outtalk each other), children running all around, and, of course, *mucha comida*. My mom is always telling me how *flaca* I look and how I should have second and third helpings. (Believe me, I'm no *flaca!*) Someone foreign to that world might confuse my mother's home with a madhouse, because to non-Latino ears, it may seem a bit loud. A man who dates me will have to find a way to fit it in, to feel comfortable in all

The Non-Christian Papi

For Christian Latinas marrying men of a non-Christian faith, the test will depend on how much give-and-take there is between the two of you. The most important part of the test for a non-Christian *papi* is—you guessed it—the *Virgencita* in your living room. When two very different religious worlds come together, it will be a topic of discussion for both of you (and your families), from the planning of the ceremony to the holidays to how you raise your kids.

In the end, the most important factor in an interfaith relationship is your mutual willingness to embrace and respect each other's religious and cultural worlds. This won't be an easy journey, but it's one that can work if you both commit to it, and renew your commitment every day. Of course, that's the formula for *any* successful relationship!

the noise, and to understand the sense of comfort it gives me to be there.

In the end, it's not so much about whether or not your Anglo honey can understand your mother's limited English (though that would mean a lot), or even whether he likes her *tamales*. In the end it's about his comfort level in your madhouse.

There's also the fact that we take on our family's problems as our own. That's why we are family, right? You have to make sure that your new mate understands that, in a funny way, he is marrying your family as much as he is marrying you.

You have to ascertain whether your man will feel comfortable in that environment or just "put up with it." Will he understand the importance of that "fortress" in your life? Take him to as many gatherings as you can, and see how he reacts.

His Anglo family also plays an important role in your relationship. He may not be as close to them as you are to yours, but their opinion and acceptance of you will be important. (Remember that famous George Bush quote about his "little brown ones"—the grandchildren from his son Jeb and Mexican daughter-in-law, Columba?) You will want to meet his family and spend time with them too. Their acceptance of you and your comfort level with them is just as important as his is with yours.

5. WILL HE SAY "*TE QUIERO*"?

Can he roll his *r*'s? Does he know how to say "*Te quiero*" without sounding like George W. trying to speak Spanish?

I dream in Spanish, and as I've said before, I make love *en español*. I've had to define these sexy love words, said in the throes of passion, for my white *papi*. (I got tired of being a Berlitz class after a while.) But hey, to each his own. Even if you don't speak it, the right of those who want to is very *importante*. And if he doesn't speak Spanish, you better check out how he feels about the language, and how comfort-

When Your Honey is African American

Throughout the Jennifer Lopez–Puffy Combs relationship I heard tongues wagging, *viejitas* sitting on stoops wondering out loud why a *muchacha tan bonita* was doing *de novia con ese negro feo,* meaning Puffy. I can't begin to tell you what those hateful *comentarios* would do to my blood pressure. We've all heard the expression, when a relative married a *blanquito,* "*Va a mejorar la raza.*" Of course we now know how racist it is to think that by marrying white, our race would "improve," but ours is, sadly, a very color-conscious community. Check out some Univision *novelas:* all the good girls are blond; the black girls are maids.

So when your *papi* is African American, only part of the quiz applies. He more than likely knows about racial profiling. He'll probably appreciate your curvy body, sense of family, and religious fervor. On top of that—and I know this sounds stereotypical—he can probably learn to do a mean *salsa* in no time. However, if he's American, he may need to take that geography, food, and Spanish part of the test.

The most important test for your chocolate honey is the family test—your family. Bringing home any man your family considers "different" will raise issues, but while bringing home a gringo is controversial in many Latin *familias,* and bringing home an Asian American or Arab American will give them palpitations, bringing home an African American, I'm sad to say, can be tantamount to heresy. Despite the mélange of races and ethnicities that make up "Latino," race hatred is still incredibly pervasive among us. (When my ex-husband—a Latin man, mind you—visited my Puerto Rican family on our way back from our honeymoon, he exclaimed, "I didn't know you had black relatives!" That's part of the reason why he's an ex. Hadn't he ever noticed my nose, my hair, my lips, and my butt? What did he think?) As disturbing as this is (and should be) to you, remember: this is a test of your family, not of your *novio.*

Many of our Latino family members are not in touch with their own African roots. A Dominican friend of mine tells me that her dark-as-night father says he is *indio* (or Indian-looking), as if that makes him less black. Our racism, an ugly legacy of colonialism, is a serious issue that we must face head-on. And of course, there is *his* family. Will he be judged as "trying to go white" with a Latina wife? Maria, married to an African American man for five years, told me that his black southern family still has a hard time understanding that her Latino-ness is not necessarily whiteness.

able he is when others speak it around him. Heck, check out his stand on bilingualism!

6. CAN HE DANCE?

I've dated several Latinos who could not dance to save their lives. They proved to me that we don't have the corner on dancing or rhythm. But if you like to dance and he has three left feet, how comfortable is he with the idea that you want to dance with others? Or will he be willing to learn to dance—seriously learn? You have to ascertain this now or forever be left sitting with your *blanquito* husband on the sidelines as your *hermanas* who married guys who can dance *salsa* the night away.

7. CAN HE CHEW A JALAPEÑO WITHOUT CRYING?

Does he understand that Taco Bell is not Latin food? Does he eat spicy food or have tolerance for those who do? Food comes up in every area of Latino lives, and it will in yours. That is why every Latin fiesta always ends up in the kitchen.

So will he make all kinds of crazy faces when your mother (and maybe even you) roll out the cow-tongue fricassee? Will he be disgusted (or, worse, call the animal-rights group) when you bring him to a family gathering and he sees a pig roasting in the backyard? (That happened to my sister's friend.) It's perfectly okay for your white honey not to want to dig into that *morcilla*-type of blood sausage, but— a *big* but—find out his tolerance level for a weekly Latin foodfest. This is a very important part of the test, unless you don't plan to eat Latin food in your home as long as you're married to him.

8. DOES HE THINK JENNIFER'S BUTT IS BIG?

When Jennifer Lopez's derriere got so much attention a few years ago, my girlfriends and I were surprised by all the hoopla. I mean, what's the big deal? Our bodies, especially those of us from Caribbean backgrounds, no matter how *flacas* we are, have meat. Our men love meat on our bones, and their appreciation of our natural *curvas* is comforting. Does your man relish your well-upholstered

---

A fierce Latina who made U.S. history . . .

 After almost sixty years as an educator and activist, **Antonia Pantoja** still exhibits a passion for life that is inspiring. Born in Puerto Rico on September 13, 1921, to an impoverished family, Antonia often went to sleep hungry, but from an early age she understood the importance of education and action as tools of empowerment and social mobility. She earned a teaching certificate in 1942 from the University of Puerto Rico. Two years later she emigrated to New York City, where she graduated with a bachelor's degree from Hunter College in 1952. She later received both a master's degree from Columbia University's School of Social Work and a doctoral degree from the Union Graduate School. In 1958, she joined young professionals to form the Puerto Rico Forum. Three years later she founded ASPIRA, an organization that empowers young students to become educated leaders. While teaching at the University of California at San Diego, she was chosen as the director of the School of Social Work's undergraduate program. While in San Diego, she founded the Graduate School for Community Development, a freestanding institution, and became its president. In 1984, she decided to return to her native Puerto Rico, where she created Producir, Inc., an organization that serves the island's poor in the hills. Her hard work and community involvement have not gone unnoticed: in September 1996, Antonia became the first Puerto Rican woman to receive the Presidential Medal of Freedom, the highest award bestowed upon a civilian by the U.S. government. Antonia's forthcoming book entitled *The Making of a Nuyorican: Memoirs of Dr. Antonia Pantoja* is to be published in 2002 by Arte Público of the University of Houston, Texas. In the midst of writing a book, Antonia organized an archive on the history and contributions of Puerto Ricans in the City of New York.

Latin body? Our sense of what is beautiful thankfully includes a curvier woman, and I hope that your man really appreciates that, or you'll be left asking that age-old question: Am I fat?

Even if you are *flaca*, you don't want to be hanging with a man who thinks that Jennifer's butt is fat. And if you are? *Ay, Dios mio!* You'll have to go back to page 1 and start reading this book all over again—and this time, pay attention!

CHAPTER TEN

FINDING PROFESSIONAL SUCCESS: The Get-Ahead Guide for the Nueva Latina

*P*rofessionally, Latinas continue to be chronically underpaid and underemployed. We are collectively at the bottom of the pay scale. A 1998 study (the latest one available) found that for every dollar earned by white men, white women earned 78 cents; African American women earned 67 cents; and Hispanic women earned 56 cents.

Discrimination is real. Sexism is real. Racism is real. I don't need to tell you that if you are brown, have a Spanish surname, and are female, sometimes it can be like getting up to bat with three strikes against you before the first pitch is thrown. We may not *always* be up against discrimination, racism, and sexism in every situation, but it does happen often—all too often.

Count yourself lucky if you yourself haven't been on the wrong end of an "ism" or if it's been a long time since the last time you were. However, not having disturbing and demeaning judgments made against you because of your name, color, or gender doesn't make discrimination against Latinas a thing of the past. If it happens to another Latina, it happens to me and it happens to you.

Even so, despite the "strikes" we have against us, despite the ugliness of discrimination, I have faith in the ultimate goodness of the human spirit, and in the strength we have as *mujeres*–individually and as a *raza*–to rise above it. And one of the best ways to do so is Latina networking.

"MY MAID READS IT."

Let me tell you a story.

At the pinnacle of my magazine career, racism stared me in the face and slapped me a couple of times to remind me how alive it was.

I was at a posh Lincoln Center gala event, dressed in my Sunday best–a beautiful black dress. The event was a tribute to Duke Ellington, one of the immortals of jazz. I was then the proud editor of *Latina,* sitting at a table with the crème de la crème of the magazine industry, among them the executive director of the Magazine Publishers of America and the president and CEO of *Essence* and *Latina* magazines. There were celebrities and VIPs everywhere.

I was making the kind of small talk you make when you are trying to network with very important people. The executive director of the MPA, a white man in his sixties, asked me how *Latina* magazine was doing. I eagerly and proudly responded, "Very well, thank you. Circulation is up *and* advertising is up." (Those are two barometers of a magazine's health.) I mentioned that the magazine had reached a million readers to date–no small task for an upstart.

I thanked the nice white man in the tuxedo for asking, and inquired whether he read the magazine. After all, he was the head of the MPA, the industry's "watchdog" and regulator. And the nice white man in the tuxedo answered, "No, I don't read it. My maid does."

"Don't jump to anger," I thought to myself. "Think of something positive." "Gee," I

White women earn 75.7 percent of what white men earn.

Black women earn 83.7 percent of what black men earn.

Hispanic women earn 85.7 percent of what Hispanic men earn.

responded, "what a smart maid you have." This nicely dressed white male proceeded to tell me that his maid reads Spanish–*good* Spanish, not the Spanglish spoken by Puerto Ricans or the choppy Dominican Spanish he often hears.

My eyes opened wider and my jaw almost dropped. "Okay," I thought, "either *este esta borracho* or high on crack." I tried to slide his foot gently out of his mouth, explaining that there's no such thing as "good" Spanish spoken by *boricuas* or "bad" Spanish spoken by Dominicans; I said that Spanglish was a good thing, proof that our language is very much alive.

But the very elegantly dressed white man wasn't interested. He went on to tell me that his maid actually no longer worked for him, but that before she'd left, she'd written him a very beautiful letter in Spanish. And he said that although she was from Colombia, she was no drug dealer, and he repeated that she wrote and spoke excellent Spanish.

My eyes must have been popping out of their sockets. If I hadn't had witnesses (my boss's daughter Nicky and her date were sitting between this man and me), I wouldn't have believed my own ears. He kept going. At some point, I decided it was all a joke, and I was waiting for the punch line–as if he'd been pulling my leg and was about to say "Gotcha!" However, it was no joke. Trying again to steer this man from further embarrassment and humiliation of *mi gente,* I said, "Your maid's letter was in Spanish–good Spanish. So can I assume that you read Spanish?"

In a very matter-of-fact tone he said, "Well, I used to speak it on the farm when I was growing up with the wetbacks in California." By then, I thought the insults were too obvious and this *pendejo* wanted

How much Dinero Do we make?

In 1997, U.S. Hispanics' mean household income was $43,098. If current growth continues, Hispanic purchasing power will be approximately $1 trillion by 2050.

Swing the vote.

The voter registration rate for Hispanics increased from 31% to 34% between 1994 and 1998.

5.5 million Latinos participated in the presidential election in 2000. That's up from the 4.9 million that participated in the 1996 election.

trouble. I felt I had two choices: I could get ghetto on the man—throw my wine in his face, tell him how obnoxious and rude he was, call him a *cabrón,* and walk out—or I could leave without saying a word. There was probably a middle way—calmly but forcefully disagreeing with him, explaining to him the error of his ways, logically reasoning him out of his idiotic and ugly racism—but I was so angry that I knew I'd lose it completely if I opened my mouth again. If it were just him and me, that would have been fine by me, but I didn't want to ruin the evening for the people there whom I respected and cared about. So I just cut out, before the free dinner was served.

The next morning I got a phone call from *el jefe grande,* Ed Lewis, the angel who'd put up the money to start *Latina* magazine. He'd heard about the whole exchange from his daughter and was just as stunned by it as I was. Mr. Lewis asked me to explain what had happened, which I did, in detail.

I'm sure that he was shaking his head; I could hear it in his voice. He couldn't believe it, he said; this guy was married to an Asian woman. But why, Mr. Lewis wanted to know, didn't I *say* anything? *He* would have set the man straight after the first remark!

Diosas de las Américas

Tonacacihuatl is an Aztec goddess who's name means "our lady of flesh." She is a creatrix who gives life to all things and to whom the spirits of children return at death. She is the wife of the creator god Tonacatecuhtli. Together they had four children, Tlatlauhqui Tezcatlipoca, Yayauhqui Tezcatlipoca, Quetzalcoatl, and Huitzilopochtli. According to this creation myth the couple and their four children didn't do much for the better part of six hundred years. One day they decided to create the earth and their four children got together to decide what to do and what laws they would follow. From this came the creation of earth, the sun and the moon, and the first humans that inhabited earth.

I explained that first of all I was in shock; secondly, I didn't want to spoil the magical evening for the group, which I knew would have happened if I'd let myself go. (I imagined myself leaping across the table and grabbing Mr. MPA by his satin lapels: "*Pendejo . . . !*") Mr. Lewis, a self-made millionaire African American man who I'm sure had lived through more than his share of racist incidents, said that this was simply not acceptable—I should have stood up for myself, or at least asked for help from Mr. Lewis himself. But, he said, it was this man's offense that was truly not acceptable.

The next call I got was from the culprit himself. An apology call. To his credit, he sounded genuinely troubled by the effects of his words. "I'm sorry I offended you. It wasn't my intention," he said.

I told him why what he said was offensive, and how he'd offended not only me but also an entire community of readers and other people.

He explained how he'd come by his ideas: "I'm a white man who grew up in a different era, listening to all kinds of things, common talk among white folk. I understand now that these are not only politically incorrect things to say about people but wrong and offensive." He finished his apology by saying that while he is an old dog, he's not too old to learn new tricks—and if I ever heard him say anything slightly inappropriate anywhere, I should please stop him dead in his tracks. He said he'd appreciate that very much!

The lesson Mr. Lewis taught me was priceless: Stand up to racism whenever it rears its ugly head. Never stay quiet, no matter where you are or who's hurling the brick. Stare it down and bring it down, diplomatically but honestly, and always have a response. That frank conversation with Mr. MPA taught me something, too: racism really is ignorance. But ignorance can be challenged, and should be challenged.

We all face the possibility that we will be seen through the distorted lens of popular and demeaning stereotypes about *la raza* in general and Latinas in particular. That's why the first get-ahead rule is so simple: **Recognize that racism and sexism exist.**

I know that before anyone gets to know me, professionally or socially, they've been infected with popular misconceptions about me simply because I am a Latina, a Puerto Rican. In addition, if they know a bit about me, I will be further stereotyped by the fact that I'm a single mother. Now, just because I recognize this doesn't imply that I run around with a chip on my shoulder or try to blame any *caca* that happens to me on that reality. But accepting the presence of these attitudes arms me with the ability to look racism in the face and call it what it is—stupid! It also helps me not to be blindsided or thwarted. I have the upper hand if I already know what someone else might be assuming about me because of my gender, nationality, race, and single motherhood. That knowledge gives me power.

Another rule I apply to my professional life is the recognition that, whether in the classroom or at work, **as a Latina I have to work harder, play harder, and be smarter.** It's unfair, it's not right, but, *mujer,* it is *la verdad*—at least for now.

Notwithstanding all the clichéd ideas about gender and culture that can stymie personal and professional success, many of the roadblocks we have to overcome are self-imposed. I call these cultural *complejos*. See how many of them you recognize in your life.

1. "*NO ME LO MEREZCO*," OR "I DON'T DESERVE IT," SYNDROME

Marc Anthony has a song with the same name, but while his *no me lo merezco* is all about love, this *complejo* is all about entitlement.

For many years, I had a serious case of "I don't deserve it" syndrome. I'd get flare-ups during job interviews, exams, and stages in my life where I was being tested or getting close to tasting sweet success. The syndrome reared its ugly head by way of an inner voice that made me doubt my talent, skills, and entitlement to some of the prizes and privileges of the United States. While the little voice sometimes humbles people to a reality check, for me the voice was more like a matador that stabbed me in the heart with huge doses of insecurity.

As an immigrant child, I felt different, and we all know how "different" in America is criticized, demonized, attacked, and ridiculed. I came to this country at the tender age of nine, and the only English I spoke were six words in a song taught to Puerto Rican children learning English: *pollito,* chicken; *gallina,* hen; *lapiz,* pencil; *pluma,* pen; *ventana,* window; *piso,* floor.

When I entered Mrs. McGuire's fourth-grade class, I was scared and lost. Think of how grown-ups sound in the Charlie Brown cartoons and you can imagine my first two semesters in school. I was placed in a program called Sink or Swim. Metaphorically speaking, I was expected to either drown or float by the end of the school year. I was one of the lucky Latino children in the school, and by the second semester I could defend myself in a broken but usable New Jersey English. But the effect of sitting in the back of the classroom, lost, feeling different, and not understanding the language would stay with me into adulthood.

My sense of not belonging was also reinforced at home. Whether or not Mom did it to protect us, she constantly reminded us that America was not home, that we came from a great island with a beautiful cultural tradition. *Nosotros no somos americanos*—we were proud Puerto Ricans, and as soon as she'd saved enough money, we'd return. So from very early on I saw this country not as my home, but as a temporary sanctuary. On top of that, we were poor and on welfare, so here I was living on borrowed land, being fed with government money. See how that "I don't deserve it" *complejo* can multiply?!

Now add to that mix the one-dimensional representation and outright *mis*representation of Latinos by Hollywood and the news media. I was constantly reminded that my people and me were "less than." Ultimately, I came to believe that this country belonged to "John and Mary," not "Juan and Maria"—and that by extension all the benefits, rewards, and entitlements were not really mine to have. I was a second-class citizen in a society that kept telling me the opposite—on paper. The funny thing is, I never really thought about these issues, and how my perception of not belonging would affect my life and career, until my son's first day of second grade.

I watched all his classmates in this public school—90 percent Anglo, sons and daughters of lawyers, activists, and doctors, businessmen and -women—scamper about the classroom, claiming things as their own: "my desk," "my book," "my chair," "my crayon," even "my teacher." My son, meanwhile, never left my side to claim anything.

I could almost hear my family proudly crowing that my son was displaying *respeto* about "other" people's property, and those gringo kids sure weren't. I was raising BJ with values that embraced "*lo ajeno se respeta*"—respect what is not yours. I told him just to stake a claim on his little desk, but he grabbed my leg tighter. It wasn't until his teacher went up to him and showed him "his" desk that he felt a little "ownership." Days later, it finally hit me: I was raising a little boy who was respectful of *lo ajeno* but shy about what was rightfully his. I had passed on "*no me lo merezco*" syndrome to him!

As I meet more and more U.S. Latinas, I've learned that too many of us have been afflicted and conflicted with the same cultural insecurities about the privileges and wealth that we are just as entitled to as any other nonbrown citizen is.

Maria Echaveste is one example. As the highest-ranking Latina in the Clinton White House, she had achieved a tremendous career milestone. During a casual conversation at a journalism conference several years ago, I asked her what was the biggest lesson she'd learned after four years on the job. Her response: that she needed to have "*thicker codos*," or thicker skin, as if she had to elbow her way to the front of the picture.

"These white guys in the office," she said, "subordinates and supervisors alike, have a sense of entitlement," which she defined as a need to be heard, "to speak with authority that I didn't have." They—white males—were confident that their point of view was important and must be shared. They *belonged* there. And Maria,

The Latina Politician

National Level:

In 2001, 73 women served in the U.S. Congress, an all time high.

13 women in the U.S. Senate

60 women in the House of Representatives.

6 Latinas served in the House of Representatives

None served in the U.S. Senate

Of the 73 women serving in the 107th U.S. Congress, 20, or 27.4 percent are women of color. In addition, an African American woman and a Caribbean woman serve as delegates to the House from Washington, D.C., and the Virgin Islands, respectively.

State Level:

The number of women in statewide elective executive posts is 87, or 22.4 percent.

Only 2 Latinas have been elected to statewide executive posts: Patricia Madrid, the New Mexico Attorney General, and Rebecca Vigil-Giron, the New Mexico Secretary of State.

Of the 88 women serving in statewide elective executive offices, 5, or 5.7 percent, are women of color.

Of the 1,663 female state legislators serving nationwide, 266, or 15.9 percent, are women of color. All but 8 are Democrats. They include:

73 State Senators

92 State Representatives

Of the 1,663 female state legislators serving nationwide, 55 are Latina.

Women of color constitute 3.6 percent of the total 7,424 state legislators.

despite being a manager, having a law degree, numerous achievements, and talent to match or pass any of them, would many times keep her opinion to herself. She confessed that there was this little inner voice that came up every so often to caution her about her opinion, her talent, and her "belonging" there.

Maria surmised that she must have picked up the "*no me lo merezco*" clues from her years on a farm helping her parents work the harvest. She resolved to acknowledge how unfounded her pangs of inadequacy were, and then to work on ridding herself of them. She said every time she'd get a bout of "*no me lo merezco*," she'd remind herself that President Clinton had seen something special in her: she belonged there, she had a gift and something important to contribute to this nation. That affirmation and reminder gave her a new sense of freedom.

A Hispanic woman, no matter how light or dark, will be perceived differently. In professional settings, I've often heard stupid comments like "You're not like the rest of them," meaning I was a different kind of Latina—I spoke well and dressed well, I was well mannered, so I wasn't a threat. People who told me things like this often thought they were paying me a compliment by saying I wasn't one of "them"— you know, the *raza* mass. How much would I have to hate myself and my people to feel good about a remark like that?!

But it's not always easy to resist internalizing the stupid ethnic and gender assumptions made about us. To get over this *complejo*, you have to arm yourself with the facts and have a historical sense of identity.

Learning about my individual Puerto Rican history was liberating. Studying the collective Latin American history in the United States and in our homelands has clarified the truth and given me a sense of pride and strength in myself and my people. Whenever I'm having a moment of doubt about my entitlement to the good things this country has to offer, I look at this quote I copied out of Juan Gonzalez's brilliant book *Harvest of Empire: A History of Latinos in America*:

If Latin America had not been raped and pillaged by U.S. capital since its independence, millions of desperate workers would not now be coming here in such numbers to reclaim a share of that wealth; and if the U.S. is today the world's richest nation, it is in part because of the sweat and blood of the copper workers of Chile, the tin miners of Bolivia, the fruit pickers of Guatemala and Honduras, the cane cutters of Cuba, the oil workers of Venezuela and Mexico, the pharmaceutical workers of Puerto Rico, the ranch hands of Costa Rica and Argentina, the West Indians who died building the Panama Canal and the Panamanians who maintained it."

As that quote makes so painfully clear, the sweat and tears and hard work that my parents, your parents, and other Latino and Latina immigrants put into the building of this country entitles us to its riches. Their *sacrificios* here and in our home countries—in the fields, in the factories, in the cabs, in the battlefield, cleaning rich people's toilets, or in countless office and professional jobs across this nation—make it very clear that this is mine and yours to reap.

AFFIRMATIVE ACTION? AFFIRMATIVE!

Many people here refuse to accept Latinos as America's legitimate children, and that is their problem. We're here (many of our families have been here for a lo-o-o-ong time!), we're not leaving anytime soon, and we are *entitled*.

One enormously effective tool for getting what we're entitled to has been affirmative action; unfortunately, it's also an area of real confusion and pain for many of us. Many college students suffer subtle and direct taunts that they got to college because of affirmative action; many plague themselves with self-doubt about the same question (yet another version of *no me lo merezco*). One pained undergrad from the University of Oklahoma, a *tejana* whose family had been in Texas since the state belonged to Mexico, asked me for tips on handling comments she got from her Anglo classmates about getting into the university because of a "Hispanic" quota. Another woman, a Latina doctor, told me about an incident not too long ago when she walked into an elevator at her hospital and an aging gringo looked at her name tag closely and then, clutching it, said, "So, you are the Hispanic who took my son's place in medical school." Stunned, she was left speechless. *Mujeres,* we need to have a comeback for those *cabrones* and *cabronas* who refuse to accept that we are capable and smart and that we belong!

Whether about college, a job, *lo que sea,* my advice to those who sneer is this: Tell 'em straight to their faces that Anglos too get to places through affirmative action. It's called who you know–*padrino* privilege, white privilege. People rarely talk about how those other quotas, the ones dictated by class, skin color, and economic advantage, almost ensure educational success for whites and a foot in the door when it comes to the job hunt. And we almost *never* talk about the most secret white quota of all, the "legacy"–the set of quotas that just about guarantees children of alumni or politically connected *padrinos* admission to our great educational institutions. (Even the president of the United States admits he would never have gotten into Yale otherwise!)

I was a *proud* beneficiary of affirmative action, and I suspect that at some points in my career I was let through the door because of quotas. For me, that leveled the playing field, because all I needed was a foot in the door to show that I'm as good as anybody–and I wasn't going to get to college without government intervention!

Got a job because the company needs to fill a token "Hispanic" position? Make the most of the opportunity. And remember: companies don't practice diversity because they want to be nice but because it's good for business. So just do your best, and be a team player–and never let yourself believe for a second that you're not worthy of being there or that you're not entitled.

2. "DON'T CHALLENGE *LOS VIEJOS*" SYNDROME

I was raised in an autocratic household, where *los niños se ven, pero no se escuchan*–children are seen but not heard. While *mucho mucho cariño* was lavished on the kids in my family, we never got to choose a dinner menu, what sneakers we wore, or which prime-time shows we'd watch (at 8:00 P.M., we *all* watched *las novelas*).

Children who talked back were slapped in the mouth. To look my mom in the eye when she admonished me was truly to look for trouble. Latino children who challenged adult opinions were considered disrespectful and invited a beating. There was no "time-out" in my childhood. My father would ask me to smell the belt whenever he wanted to get me back in line. He figured the scent of leather alone would remind me of the whipping that was to come if I didn't shape up. And we all know the "look" that only Latina mothers can give their children without saying so much a word: these *miradas que matam* say "*Esperate a que lleguemos a la casa*"–Wait till we get home. There was no "let's see what the children think" before decisions that would affect our lives were made. Do you think that my mom consulted her kids about moving to New Jersey? No. Whenever I butted into adult conversations, my mom would always say (and *still* says), "*Los niños hablan cuando las gallinas mean*"–Children speak when hens pee. I later learned that, of course, hens never pee.

Now as a rule, *los niños y las niñas* play and dream and, yes, even annoy the heck out of adults, but *gracias a Dios,* we don't burden them with decisions that moms and dads need to make. I wouldn't

Daily affirmation

The power of daily affirmation is profound. Practice saying this in front of the mirror: "I'm smart, my *raza* is good, I want my share. It belongs to me." Say it with confidence. Repeat it once a day, at least. Write it down. Talk to your family or friends about it. Laugh, cry, be angry, and give yourself room even to doubt that you deserve it, that you're smart, that your *raza* is grand.... Then forgive yourself for doubting it. Practice this as you get ready to go to work or to take a test. Do it in front of the mirror before you go to sleep. Chew and digest these words. One day, you won't need to say them anymore or to even pretend you believe them, because you'll know them–by heart.

have it any other way. And the rule that adults, parents, grandparents, even that drunk *tío* are never challenged or talked back to is one of the things I love about our culture and proudly pass on to my kid; it's *respeto* for the life wisdom of our people.

The danger of this *respeto* comes later in life, when we transfer that unquestioning authority from our parents and family elders to our college professors, bosses, or just plain authority. While a boss or professor is (probably) not your mother or father, questioning them can be as difficult for Latinas, since we never really learned the tools of challenge or negotiation at home. And many of us are uncomfortable with challenging authority. But to achieve personal power and success, we must learn to challenge those in authority—diplomatically.

My breakthrough came when I was in my late twenties, and it started at home. Like most Latina mothers, mine continued to meddle in my life way into adulthood. She'd often unintentionally say hurtful things, and I would stay quiet and respectful. Then one day I politely and respectfully stopped her dead in her tracks when she said something to the effect that just because I had a college degree didn't mean that I was better or smarter: "In fact, you are still *mierda*." At that moment, I decided that I would never let her say something that hurt me, criticize me, or meddle in my life without standing up for myself.

I took a deep breath, ignored the butterflies in my tummy, and said, "Just because you're my mother doesn't give you the right to call me names. If you ever want to see me again, if you want to have a relationship with me, you have to start respecting me." And I walked out. Months later, we made up. I don't remember if she actually apologized or not, but our relationship has been wonderfully respectful ever since. I was willing to walk away from someone I love in my deepest heart, because having a relationship that fostered constant meddling or verbal abuse without the right to fight back or challenge was too hard on my soul.

That episode was great practice for acquiring personal and professional power. For me, to question the queen bee of my family was to break with cultural tradition, risk a slap in the face, and invite family *crítica*. But in doing it, I was standing up to my future. I figured, *si lo hice con mi madre*–if I did it with my mother, if I could draw the line in the sand and stand up for myself to her–I can do it with a stupid boss or an arrogant professor. By standing up to an elder, I acknowledged that I am worthy of respect, from my mother, elders, supervisors, professors, friends, *novios,* and any other "power figures" who come into my life.

Learning to question and challenge *con diplomacia* is key to your success. But just how *do* we get over that fear of standing up to authority?

First ask yourself, "Is this an issue for me? How did I handle authority figures growing up?" Ask yourself if you were given the tools as a child to negotiate with authority figures. Think about your current familial situation. When was the last time you respectfully challenged a family elder who you thought was dead wrong? Now consider whether the dynamics of family power struggles have transferred over to your current work or school situation.

While the turning point for me was standing up to my mother one powerful time, for Lee, a Manhattan assistant district attorney, it's something very different. As a prosecutor, Lee "challenges" judges and other attorneys for a living; according to her, the key is practice, practice, and more practice. So don't drop this book and tell off your mother or father, or storm into your office and give your boss a good licking–everybody's experience with this will be different. Just think about how you negotiated conflict with authority figures in your childhood, and about how you might want to change your techniques to suit your circumstances now.

Latinas who stand up to authority always risk being perceived as aggressive (belligerent and inconsiderate of others) rather than assertive (self-confident in expressing their opinions and beliefs). You can't control other people's thoughts, but you *can* influence them, and the key to this is diplomacy.

If it's a promotion you wanted that you didn't get, good opening questions might be: Why didn't you get the position? How did your boss make the decision? Explain, don't complain; and listen, don't fume. But remember: if you don't challenge authority for yourself, no one else will do it for you.

3. *"ME DA VERGÜENZA TO ASK"* SYNDROME

I come from a very proud line of workingmen and -women. Outside help, merited or not, was always seen as a "handout" and not easily accepted. (You can imagine how traumatic it was for us to be on welfare when I was a kid!) Somehow, somewhere along the line, I confused asking about a job with asking for a handout. Call it misplaced pride.

As a child I'd get my ear pulled or get pinched *en el brazo* if I went to someone's house–*casa ajena*–and dared to ask even for a glass of water. No matter how thirsty I was, I had to wait until I was invited. I later read in Marta Moreno Vega's book *The Altar of My Soul* that this is an unspoken code of behavior in poor communities. You never know if your neighbors have enough to eat, so you don't want to embarrass them by accepting even a glass of *agua*. It makes sense in those circumstances, but it can haunt us later. Many times in my own career, I felt that the office or college campus turned into a *casa ajena–*

Diosas de las Américas

X-tah, of Mexico and Central America, is the Guatemalan goddess of rain and water. Her rain bears constructive, fulfilling energy to maintain the gardens of our spirit with spring's growth-centered magic.

---

don't ask till you are offered! No job offers, no asking if there is one available.

Casually asking a colleague or an old associate about a job was impossible. Inquiring about freelance work was torture. *Se me caia la cara de vergüenza*–my face would just turn red with embarrassment. And forget about dropping my résumé off with someone I knew just in case there was an opening. It was somehow *humillante*. It may sound silly, but there I was, educated, with great connections, and without the guts to "hint" about a job to further my career.

No one will know you're looking for work if you don't tell them. Sending the people you know an error-free cover letter and résumé to let them know about your job search can be a great start. Then follow up the letter with a telephone call. It's getting the word out, sending out messages that you are looking or need advice. Think of it this way: you are standing outside a door and want to get in. If you don't knock, no one will even know you're there. By sending the résumés and calling to follow up, you are knocking, and your chances of getting in are better; someone will at least crack open the door and know you are there.

Lilly Maestas, a career specialist at the University of California at Santa Barbara, has worked in career development for twenty years. She advises young women who are just starting out to build their personal networks, then their professional ones. "Put yourself out there," she says. And her formula is a lot easier than you may think, since networking begins with the people you know.

"It starts with the people right next door, the people who sit next to you at church and on the bus. Networking can be very spontaneous, but you have to have your career antennas on. It's not just

Cyber Latino Spending

Reuters reports that Hispanics in the United States were seen spending $42.6 million over the Internet in 2000, a growth of 100 percent over 1999.

The leading merchandise purchased online by Hispanics includes CDs (15 percent), airline tickets (11 percent), electronics (11 percent), books (9 percent), and software (9 percent).

According to Reuters, about 38 percent of Hispanics surveyed spent more than $100 during a three-month period (April–May 2000), compared to 16 percent of Anglos, 11 percent of Asians, and 6 percent of African Americans.

Eleven Habits of Every Successful Latina

El que madruga, Dios lo ayuda

As the dicho goes, early to rise, God is by your side. Timeliness is a very sound habit to pick up, especially considering our "Latino time" stereotype. Be the first to arrive as often as you can; whenever possible, try to leave after the *jefe* leaves and be open to clocking those extra hours and overtime. While being right on time and leaving at the sound of the bell will rarely get you noticed, making it before others and staying past 5:00 P.M. consistently will score some points. It shows dedication and professionalism. And I don't need to tell you what habitual lateness or skipping out early can do for your reputation and your career. In many places, it can mean a death sentence in the eyes of your supervisor.

No por mucho madrugar, amanece más temprano

Another of my mother's favorite *dichos:* Just because you rise early does not mean that morning will be here faster. I think this can definitely apply to a professional situation, since just because you are at work early does not necessarily mean you get noticed. This habit is about being there on time *and* being "ready" and prepared for the task at hand. You have to be very able to do your job, and that means to staying on top of your game. If we can borrow anything from professional athletes, it should be their dedication to improving their game, their focused discipline to get better. That means you not only have to have the degrees and the certificates for the job but must continue the education and preparation process after college. Find out the latest in your field, take special training courses, do anything that can help you perform your job better. If your company reimburses tuition, what are you waiting for? Take advantage of the freebie now. It might not help you immediately, but it can be noticed within the company or help you land a better job elsewhere.

Los amores cobardes no llegan hacer historia

While Cuban crooner Silvio Rodríguez was singing about cowardly lovers who refuse to take risks in matters of love, he could have been singing about those employees who refuse to take risks at their jobs too. Think creatively. Approach your job with an open mind, and always think outside the box. That doesn't mean reinventing the wheel, but you should look for fresh ways to do what you do. Innovative and ingenious minds are noticed and do make history; regular minds don't. And, *mi hermana*, Latina professionals cannot afford to be just average. *¿Me entiendes?*

Dress to impress

This does not mean you should get a Gucci this and a Prada that (especially if you can't afford it). People judge you, to some degree, by the way you dress and speak (see below). This excellent habit is about always looking neat, clean, and together and paying attention to the fashion culture of your environment. Every industry has a dress code, whether it is spoken or not. That nose ring and those hip-hugging pants may fly well in the club, but they won't go over in a boardroom. Neither will stilettos or spandex—unless, of course, you work in an industry that is all about that. Adhering to the dress code does not mean that you have to lose your individuality and dress like every Tom, Dick, Mary, and Heather. No, *mija*, it's about showing your keen fashion sense and individuality by working within the office or environment dress code. The last thing that you want is for your taste in clothing and accessories to be used against you, or to give the impression that you don't mean business or can't be taken seriously. I am also not a big fan of dress-down Fridays. It's for the *blanquitos*. Why? One too many Latinas have shared their stories for being confused with the "cleaning lady" or messenger. Nothing wrong with that; in fact, it should be a source of pride (at least for me, since that is what Mom had to do to put clothes on my back). However, it can be rather irritating to have to explain to the security guard—as you walk in with your *gringa* assistant—that you are the vice president of marketing and this chick's *jefa*. Truth is that many times even when dressed to the nines, we still get confused with the help, so you can imagine what dressing down could do for your image and career. Dressing professionally is a particularly important habit to pick up because we are fighting against the sexy-spitfire image in pop culture, and Lord knows we are not about to fulfill anyone's stupid stereotype about us.

Speak to impress

Eloquence is an art and a common trait among all the successful Latinas I know. The way you speak says a lot about you. Just as there is an office dress code in your work environment, there is a "work lingo" you must learn. As the saying goes, talk the talk, *mujer*! Now, I am not saying that you should affect a British accent, as Madonna recently has. Your accent—if you have one—should be a source of pride. This habit is about clear professional speech and knowing the lingo around you. It's about leaving the *mija* this and *sister* that for the private and personal space. It's true what that Hooked on Phonics commercial cautions: people judge you by the way you speak.

Have you heard of Gumby?

This fictional character was very pliable, and so should you be when it comes to your job description. When your supervisor asks you to perform a task that is obviously outside your "job duties" (assuming it is a legal request, of course), never say that it is not in your job description. Speaking as a manager, I can tell you that rolling out your job description instead of pitching in when you are needed damages your reputation as a team player and a cooperative employee. All the successful Latinas I know have never just strictly performed just what the job called for. Now, that doesn't mean that you should do three people's jobs for months without saying a word or getting an extra cent or day's work for it. It's not about exploitation; it's about collaboration. Be open and willing to go the extra mile. The job description—in most, if not all, twenty-first-century jobs—represents a skeleton of your expected responsibilities, and, much like the Bible, it should not be interpreted literally.

Know and understand your competition

This should be an obvious habit but one that must be repeated. Being aware of what your competitors do and how they do it will affect your employer's bottom line and, by extension, your job. Read the trade journals about your industry. Keep abreast of who is doing what and when. And keep your boss informed. Be a fountain of solid information and, yes, *mujer*, you will get noticed. Knowledge is power, and it can actually translate into to a promotion or a better job.

No te quejes; instead be a problem solver

There are two kinds of employees: those who complain and do nothing about it, and those who don't complain and get the job done. You want to be the latter. Don't nag about a problem; instead, use the energy to find a solution. If things are falling through the cracks and you have a solution, why complain when you can do something about it? But be cautious: don't ever "solve" anything before running it by your supervisor. Let your boss know what you see happening, offer your suggestion, and propose to implement it if she or he likes the idea. While *jefes* don't have all the answers, sometimes they think otherwise, and your efficient problem-solver attitude can be confused with trying to do your boss's job. You don't want to make him or her feel incompetent. (Even if you think otherwise.) Your initiative to improve a given situation, more often than not, is truly a welcome attitude in any job setting.

Stay away from office *chisme*

Amparo Silva, a New York college counselor and career coach, says that being *chismosa*-free is a major habit that you want to pick up. While it is important to know what is happening in your work environment, you want to stay away from the personal and crude stuff about *la jefa* and other colleagues that sometimes goes around. In addition, if you hang with the *chismosa* in the office, chances are that your own stuff is all over the place too. Your reputation is priceless in your work environment and, of course, everywhere else. Keep in mind this wise *dicho: Dime con quien andas, y te diré quien eres;* birds of a feather flock together.

Give *and* expect respect, and know your rights

You set the tone of how people will treat you, including your *jefa* and colleagues. Yes, the law prohibits racial, religious, national, gender, and age discrimination, but it doesn't protect us from screaming and hollering supervisors. However, that does not mean you have to take their *humillaciones.* No, sister, you set the tone of *respeto.* As Amparo reminds us, even if the law doesn't protect you, "you have the right to be treated with dignity and respect." Nip a disrespectful colleague's (or boss's) attitude in the bud by standing up the first time it happens. Do it politely and diplomatically. It's not about inviting them outside to settle the matter or getting your posse to kick some butt. No. If your parents didn't treat you like that (or even if they did), no one has the right to disrespect you now—on the job or elsewhere. All the successful women I know set the tone for how they wanted to be treated from the get-go, never giving any signals that said, Please, walk all over me. Nope, *a mi se me respeta* is what your tone should intuitively say. Know your legal rights, treat people with respect, and demand it in return whenever anyone crosses the line.

Your personal *problemas* stay in your home

We all have lives outside work. (If you don't, you should; balancing your life with things besides work will make you a better employee. So get started if you are all about your job!) We also have issues that don't involve work, and these problems should stay precisely where they belong—at the entrance to your workplace. There is nothing more damaging to your career than continually bringing your personal issues to your job. Sometimes my private world would be falling apart—my kid was sick, money was running low, and my ex-husband was acting *como un pendejo*—but none of my colleagues ever knew it. My attitude was always a *nadie le importa*—it is none of their business. This was sometimes hard, but the fact was and is that business is business. A great positive attitude can do wonders for your professional growth and success.

Ask for a Promotion Without Shame

So, you were overlooked for a promotion or raise? It has happened to all of us at one point or another. The lazy colleague and major brownnoser down the hall got shamelessly promoted while you, Señorita Martyr, who happens to be an excellent employee who plays by the rules, was overlooked *otra ves*. It's time to stop watching great things happen to lesser coworkers and to arm yourself with the proper "negotiating" tools that will get you your much-needed raise, bonus, or advance.

Amparo Silva summed up her twenty-year career experience this way: "*Si hay una persona blanca* doing the same job—*lo mismo*—it takes much less effort for this person to get a raise." And at least one study by the National Committee on Pay Equity confirms what Amparo has seen, that the median earnings for a Hispanic woman with a college degree is $2,843 less than the median earnings for a non-Hispanic white man with a high school education. Notwithstanding the unfair bullshit we have to deal with, Amparo says there are ways to get the *respeto* and the well-deserved step up the ladder.

First, a Reality Check

You must do some deep career and professional soul searching before you start demanding anything or even thinking about suing for discrimination. Look within. Ask yourself if you are comfortable with your job. Is it difficult? Do you know what is expected of you? Are you confused by it? Do you feel prepared to do it? Amparo says that sometimes we are ill prepared or confused but are too afraid to ask for help or a better explanation or training out of fear of looking stupid or getting fired. And she warns there is no such thing as a stupid question, *especially* if it is going to help you do a better job. Ask for training, advice about expectations, and help if you feel you need it. Moreover, she adds, it will eventually show if you don't know what you are doing or are just getting by.

Do you love your job? Do you respect the nature of your industry?

Sometimes we may be just getting by at a job or miserable because we are not happy with the nature of the job or we'd rather do something else. For instance, Amparo explains, some women have their hearts in the not-for-profit world and hate the dog-eat-dog world of the for-profit sector. The competitive demeanor and "profit, profit, profit" philosophy of everyone around you might be a turnoff if what you really want is to be a social worker. Everyone knows an artist trapped in the accounting office. Examine your feelings about your job and your business and make sure you love and respect what you and your colleagues do for a living.

Prepárate Bien

Be prepared to do an excellent job. And I don't need to remind you that we—Latinas, you and me—have to be better prepared than Anglos. Sorry, but it is *la mera verdad*. I didn't make up the rules; I just see how things are played in the real world. Develop your skills and take no prisoners. Ascertain what, if any, degrees, experience, certificates, or special licensing and training you may need to continue improving your performance, and then make sure you get them.

What Is Your Reputation at the Job?

Are you the gossip in the office? The problem solver or the whiner? Are you the one person your *jefa* counts on when something major must be done? Or are you the one who runs for cover? Whether it is fair or not, your reputation with your supervisor *and* your colleagues plays a major role in how far you will get, and in what happens at bonus and raise time. If you don't know how you are faring, ask a trusted colleague for feedback. Hold a mirror to your face at work. What do your colleagues say behind your back? Ask yourself if people work with you or against you. The great thing is that if you don't like what you see or hear you *can* change it—slowly, deliberately, and one day at a time.

Be a Document-Everything Queen

Jot down everything you do, from the extra hours you log on a weekly basis to the extra project that brought in a new client. Amparo says that most of the time you do something and your boss thinks, *Bien hecho!* But your supervisor is so busy with her own drama that she forgot who saved her butt the last time a major project was due. If you have written backup, Amparo says, that *bien hecho* becomes your calling card when it's time to get more money, a better office, or a bonus.

What Does Your Boss Think About You?

You should have an idea of where you stand with the person who supervises you. Does the *jefe* count on you or not? Does he think you are lazy or does he recognize your talent? Is your boss working with you or against you? Bosses are humans and, yes, they are fallible. He or she may not like you—and for no apparent reason. It happens. And, yes, some of us have had to work with freaks, insecure and incompetent managers. Sometimes I think that managers are like *caca*—and you know how fast that rises to the top. Regardless, you know this person best, and you need to ask yourself honestly what his or her perceived *or* real opinion of you is.

Do Your Homework on Salaries and Promotions Within

Figure out how others have gotten promotions in your job. What skills, experience, or connections did they have that you may not know about? Compare the salaries of other people in your industry in your position. Keep in mind that salaries vary by region because of the cost of living; the size of the company is another factor. Figure out the pay scale within your organization and the "true" economic health of your company.

Bueno: you did some introspection, you love your job, you respect the nature of it, you feel excellently qualified, you have a good rep—and still no *dinero,* still no office with a view? Then, as Amparo says, it's time for war.

Ask for a meeting with supervisor first

- **Be prepared to explain why you feel you deserve a raise or a promotion.** Have a figure in mind; if you have done your homework, this part should be easy.

- **Present your case clearly.** To quote Cuban songstress La Lupe, *drama no es necesario;* leave that for *el teatro.* You want to know why you have been overlooked. Is it something that you are not doing? Is it an innocent oversight?

- **Watch your tone as you speak.** Be conversational, not accusatory. You are not there to accuse anyone; you are there on a fact-finding mission and to present your request.

- *Please* **keep your emotions in check.** I know how difficult this is, but we just can't take this stuff too personally. Amparo advises that you don't lose what you've got going for you by crying or making an *escándalo* when the boss starts spewing *barbaridades* about your performance.

- **Learn to breathe.** I have learned to count to ten silently and slowly in my head in English, then in Spanish (sometimes even in my rudimentary French) when things are not going my way. Women already have a reputation for being too emotional. Knowing how to calm yourself by breathing can allow you to have a detached and cool, comfortable demeanor—key to ensuring that you drive your point home flawlessly.

- **Let your boss speak while *you* listen.** Don't interrupt. See what he or she has to say. Listen and listen carefully. You may not have an answer to all her questions or you may think it's just unfair. You may even vehemently disagree with everything being said to you and about your job performance. If you feel a need to respond to it, just wait till he or she is finished. Remember, this is not about defending yourself; you're just stating your point of view.

- **Take notes.** Yes, you will feel better if you at least jot down some things that your altered *nervios* will make you forget.

- **Go into the meeting with an open mind.** Amparo says, "Give the boss the benefit of the doubt." Sometimes, even if our little voice is telling us that he is just a big *chingón*, your being overlooked may be a careless snub on his or her part, and he should know that you know and you have done your homework.

- **Give your boss time to digest the request.** Amparo says a month is enough time to get back to you. However, ask how much time your boss needs to process what you have landed on his or her lap.

- **Thank your boss for the meeting.** This, of course, shows good manners, that you were raised right, and that you appreciate the time for an audience.

- **Still no *dinero*, no answer in a month?** Meet with human resources and find out the written "rules and protocol" of raises and promotions. There are rules, and then there is the real world. Many times the two are in conflict. You need to know what your company pledges on paper. Ask what you can do to continue being challenged and rewarded. Is there any special training you need? Degrees, experience? Let HR know that you want to keep moving up, are ready and willing, and have met with your supervisor about it. Maybe there are other positions available elsewhere too. The bottom line is that you want to keep rising and you need their assistance.

- **Nothing still?** Don't despair; you have options, *mujer*—don't give up. Don't ever feel as if you have no options, because you do.

If you love your job, stay and resolve the situation from within.

Or stay *and* actively look for another job where you will be appreciated more.

Or leave, especially if you are miserable. You will find a better job. Sometimes, Amparo says, we find ourselves *entre la espada y la pared* and feel we have no where to go. But if you have training, the energy to rise up to a challenging position, and the dignity to stand up for your rights, you will be fine. Besides, if you stay in a miserable place, you can only get sick from the stress that it will undoubtedly cause you.

E-Latinos

Home computer use:

Whites: 72.6%

Blacks: 65.6%

Hispanics: 59.6%

12.9% of Latino households have access to the Internet, compared to 32.4% for white non-Latinos.

20% of households earning less than $20,000 have home computers.

80% of households earning more than $75,000 have home computers.

being at the right place at the right time but knowing that it is the right place and the right time. Any place can be the right place if you realize it is the right opportunity."

She teaches a seminar in Santa Barbara entitled "Is Your Net Working?" and finds that many people try to network with important people, but that is not always the best approach.

"Start with everyone you know. And never leave a contact until you ask, 'Is there someone else you know I could benefit from talking to?'"

A word of caution: sometimes your telephone calls will be refused or not returned, and doors will be slammed in your face. It's happened to me, and to every Latina I know, more than once; count yourself lucky if it hasn't happened to you. But as hard as it is not to take it personally, you must fight against internalizing the rejection. Knock on a different door. The more doors you knock on, the higher the chances you have that one will open. Don't assume anything, and don't let rejection stop you. Be open about the possibilities that await you once those doors swing open.

NETWORKING AND YOUR CAREER

Considering that in today's market up to 40 percent of jobs are landed the old-fashioned way, through connections, networking is a professional necessity, not a luxury, and it often goes hand in hand with friendship.

"Who you know is *extremely* important in landing a job," says headhunter Manuel Boado, president and founder of SpanUSA, an East Coast company that places bilingual professionals and executives. "It is the number one way to find a job in today's market."

He says that most of the "great" jobs are not advertised because when companies have an opening, they consider people internally or they let their friends know and get recommendations. Someone looking for a job should network with the people within their company as well as former bosses and friends in other industries and beyond. In other words, your net of contacts should span the globe.

There is a Latina working in every single field today, somewhere in America. We are everywhere: lawyers, public service workers, engineers, scientists, artists, writers, journalists, teachers, secretaries, college professors, and doctors, to name a few. No matter what field you're interested in pursuing or switching to, you should be able to find a Latina there if you look hard enough. There are many way to go about finding these *hermanas*, but three great ones are sororities, professional organizations, and mentors.

SORORITIES

The number of Latina sororities at the university level tripled from 1990 to 1998. Many were formed for support and from a sense of community, and they vary in mission from political to cultural. Latina college students today are lucky to be able to choose from sororities and cultural associations. These are great ways to build networks that can provide future opportunities, not to mention professional support.

The Latina Businesswoman: La Jefa

Do you know which industries had the most popular businesses owned by Latinas in 2000? If you guessed restaurants and hotels, you lose. Our sisters opened all kinds of businesses. And we just bust one myth after another. Only 4 percent of the Latina-owned businesses in 2000 operated hotel and food services. The majority of the firms were in the goods-producing sector, followed by transportation and warehousing, business services, and other professional services. From 1986 to 1997, Latina-owned firms increased by 206 percent, representing the fastest driving force in today's economy. Check it out:

Construction   Transportation
Accounting   Warehousing
Engineering   Hotels
Manufacturing   Restaurants
Agriculture   Bars

Best Careers for Bilingual Latinas

Health care   Marketing
Public service   Financial services
Technology   Professional services
Sales   International services

According to Graciela Kenig, career consultant and author of *Best Careers for Bilingual Latinos,* these are the fields for bilingual Latinos because they are "expected to remain healthy in spite of recent or foreseen major changes, to endure based on population needs and behavioral trends, and to offer continued high demands for employees in general, and bilingual Latinos in particular."

In college I always told myself I wasn't the sorority type (whatever that means), but about a year ago I found out what I'd missed out on when I was asked to speak at the Lambda Pi Chi annual convention. Wow—these Latinas were on fire! There were attorneys, journalists, college students, professional working mothers, and a congresswoman. They had come together in college with a mission to help one another, and now their mission was to give back—to strengthen themselves and the Latino community. The amazing power and energy of a group of Latinas organized with common goals is awesome for the individual, the community, and the country.

These women help one another with career concerns and open doors for each other. As one sorority sister told me, "I won't hire a sorority sister just because she pledged; I'll hire her for talent and hard work." But, she added, "It would help that she was a sister, because it would mean she comes from a shared experience. And, besides—we only pledge fly and smart sisters!"

HISPANIC PROFESSIONAL ORGANIZATIONS

One of the best ways to find a job, or even just keep on top of an industry, is through the vast network of professional organizations. To get ahead in any career, you need to have connections with like-minded professionals. If the organization is Latino, great; if not, that's fine too. As far as I know, there's a Hispanic professional organization for just about every line of work out there. But if there isn't one, start one!

I belong to both the National Association of Hispanic Journalists and LIPS. (See chapter 10, "Finding Professional Success: The Get-

Ahead Guide for the Nueva Latina.") In both, I have an instant network when I'm looking for a job myself or looking to hire someone.

THE POWER OF A MENTOR

Many of us have had mentors growing up, though we probably didn't call them that. In our culture, elders play an important role guiding and, for better or worse, teaching us the ropes. In my life there was the sister who showed me how to do the hustle and taught me all about boys, the sister who taught me about my body, the *abuelito* who taught me about the sea, and on and on. Mentors serve the same purpose in the professional world, whether you are just starting out or have already been working for years.

The power of having several mentors, professional and personal, guiding you through your career is remarkable. But like good jobs, mentors don't usually come knocking at your door. You have to go out and look for them.

I've been blessed with many mentors. Have you?

CHOOSING A MENTOR WHO IS RIGHT FOR YOU. If your are fortunate enough to work in a company with a mentorship program, take advantage of it! Pairing up with someone who shares your cultural background can be helpful, but it doesn't guarantee an instant connection. And watch out for reverse prejudice; white males can be cool, too!

Of course, mentoring doesn't bear beautiful fruit every time. A friend told me that the mentoring program at her job didn't work out at all. Her mentor was a white male in the amusement-park business, and she didn't see any connection between his work and hers, as a music television producer, though they were employed by the same corporation. "We didn't click at all." "There were no white guys in my inner circle growing up. I just don't know how to feel safe and comfortable around them." Still, she said that in hindsight, maybe she should have stuck with it longer and been more open to whatever it was that she might have learned from him.

The Greek-Latina Way

For an updated list of Latina sororities and Latino fraternities, visit Latino Greeks at www.latinogreeks.com, and while surfing check out these sororities:

Alpha Pi Sigma
PO Box 15224
San Diego, CA 92175-5224
www.alphapisigma.org

Alpha Rho Lambda Sorority, Inc.
Alianza De Raíces Latinas
www.alpharholambda.org

Alpha Sigma Omega Latina Sorority, Inc.
c/o Doris Maldonado Fernandez
12 Inwood Lane
Hillcrest, NY 10977

Delta Phi Mu
1001 Stewart Center, Box 631
West Lafayette, IN 47906
e-mail: dphi@expert.cc.purdue.edu
www.expert.cc.purdue.edu/~dphi/index.html

Delta Tau Lambda Sorority, Inc
www.umich.edu/~deevee

Gamma Phi Omega
International Sorority, Inc.
National Headquarters
3329 South Western
Chicago, IL 60608
e-mail: jacosta@butler.edu
www2.uic.edu/stud_orgs/greek/gpo/

Hermandad de Sigma Iota Alpha
www.hermandad-sia.org

Kappa Delta Chi
www.clubs.asua.arizona.edu/~Kdchi/

Kappa Delta Chi® Sorority, Inc.
National Headquarters
PO Box 4317
Lubbock, TX 79409
e-mail: info@kappadeltachi.org
www.kappadeltachi.org

The reality is that there will hardly ever be an instant lovefest between you and the mentor chosen for you. It may be feel like you two have nothing in common. But hang in there and try it out. It's like Dr. Seuss's *Green Eggs and Ham*. It may not look or smell the way you think it should, but if you try it, you might find that you like it! I believe that everyone enters your life to teach you something; sometimes the lessons aren't obvious to the naked eye.

Kappa Delta Chi Sorority, Inc.
www.utexas/edu/students/kdchi/

Lamda Pi Chi
Latinas Promoviendo Comunidad
PO Box 3182
Grand Central Station
New York, N.Y. 10163
e-mail: jeanette.rodriguez@pfizer.com
www.geocities.com/wellesley/5640/delta.html
ucsu.colorado.edu/~latina/

Lambda Pi Upsilon Sorority,
Latinas Poderosas Unidas, Inc.
www.lpiu.com

Lambda Theta Alpha Latin Sorority, Inc.
44 High Street, Apt. 17
Perth Amboy, NJ 08861
National voice mail: 609-219-4326
www.lambdalady.org

Lambda Theta Nu
La Mesa Directiva
PO Box 232026
Sacramento, CA 95823
www.lambdathetanu.org

Sigma Alpha Chi
www.angelfire.com

Sigma Lambda Alpha
www.sigmalambdaalpha.homestead.com

Sigma Lambda Gamma Sorority
www.ukans.edu/~gammas97/

Sigma Theta Psi
www.sigmathetapsi.org

Zeta Phi Gamma
PO Box 4339
Lubbock, TX 79409
e-mail: zetaphigamma@hotmail.com

Zeta Phi Gamma Sorority, Inc.–Alpha Chapter
www.members.tripod.com/zetaphigamma/zphi.html

If your company doesn't have a mentorship program, ask the human-resources person to establish a program for young and new employees. Then volunteer to help establish it. The company is not open to it? Start a Latina brown-bag lunch. No Latinas in the company? Start a group of people for women of color. Or a secretaries' mentoring program, or one for middle managers . . .

I survived my three years at a local Fox television station by team-

The entrepreneuri al Latina

From the mid-1980s to the mid-1990s, the number of Latina-owned firms jumped more than 200%.

Total sales by those companies soared 534%, to $67.3 billion.

ing up with the only other Latina in the office. By combining our efforts, we were able to do more Latino stories and get more Latina experts on the air than we ever would have otherwise. Our informal network also included African American women, and while we've all moved on to bigger and better things, we've maintained our network, telling one another about openings we hear about and keeping one another up on the inner industry *chisme.*

Hispanic professional organizations also have mentorship programs. During her first year in law school, my district attorney friend Lee was paired up with a Latina attorney. "It was the best thing that could have happened to me," Lee remembers. "I was able to get to know a fellow Hispanic woman who shared my working-class Latina background. She got it—she got me. And I thought, If she could do it, so could I."

Professional mentors are not your therapists; they are pros and peers who can share and help in your professional growth. If you get lucky and find a friendship in a mentor, that's great. *Pero* keep the intimate details of your life between you and your *comadres.*

Don't think you can find a mentor only through a formal program; potential mentors are probably all around you. The secret about them is that they are not the distant people we might imagine them to be; they surround our lives. The most important thing is to be open. Just think of this Buddhist proverb: When the student is ready, the teacher will appear.

USING YOUR CULTURE TO GET AHEAD

We are the largest ethnic minority in this nation. What that means is that in this new economy and marketplace, our culture and background affect the bottom line: we have buying power. And as more and more companies try to reach this long-ignored market, people with bilingual or bicultural skills are ahead of the competition. You can bank on that.

But just *how* can you bank on it? By marketing your knowledge.

Language skills and a bicultural background—understanding the nuances of our Latino brothers and sisters nationwide—are two very marketable skills in this new economy. A 2000 study that examined the income levels for bilingual and English-only Hispanics in ten metropolitan areas nationwide with high percentages of Hispanic immigrants found that in Miami; Jersey City, New Jersey; and San Antonio, bilingual Hispanics earned more than those who communicated only in English. In Miami, for example, they found fully bilingual Hispanics earn nearly $7,000 per year more than their English-only counterparts.

4. *SACRIFICADA* SYNDROME

Like many of us, I grew up with a mother who is a case study in the *sacrificada* syndrome. She gives, gives, and gives so much of herself and "just" expects people (mostly her children) to notice. (In recent years she has gotten better at stating her needs and not assuming that everyone recognizes her efforts.) Her model is one lived by so many mothers, and all too often passed down to daughters. We usually see how counterproductive this model is when we find ourselves living it at work.

Many of us are socialized to be selfless mothers, wives, and daughters at home, and we transfer those distorted notions of selfless giving (and hoping the beneficiaries of our giving will notice) to the workplace. We assume, incorrectly, that the employee who works the most, *que se sacrifica* the most, will be the most rewarded. No way— that's just not the way it works in real life.

It's important to do things on time with the right attitude and get the details right; it's also good to do things without being asked—sometimes. But doing extra work all the time and hoping someone will notice is a recipe for stress. And it will get you only so far.

Much has been written about this *abnegada,* or *marianismo,* complex that seems to be handed down from Latina mother to daughter. (For more on this, see chapter 5, "Centering Your Soul.")

In *The Maria Paradox,* authors Dr. Rosa Maria Gil and Dr. Carmen Inoa Vazquez describe the syndrome this way: "*Marianismo* is about sacred duty, self-sacrifice, and chastity. About dispensing care and pleasure, not receiving them. About living in the shadows, literally and figuratively, of your men—father, boyfriend, husband, and son—your kids, and your family." While this may be true in our private struggle as Latinas, we have to watch that it does not transfer to the workplace, that we do not "work in the shadows," so to speak. We have to learn to get ourselves noticed. It may sound impossible if that's not the way you've been doing things, but here are two practices you need to make habits:

1. Call attention to a job that someone else has done well.
2. Take credit for what you do yourself; that is, become your own public relations person.

In other words, we have to learn to give and *collect.* Your employers may notice that you're working hard and putting in long hours, but they won't necessarily reward it. It's up to you to transform the vicious cycle of endless giving into a healthy cycle of giving, pointing out, and receiving.

As I mention in the sidebar included in this chapter, in a professional setting, you should never assume that people notice or reward good work. Keep a record of your excellent labor, be a team player, be timely, and never complain. And at bonus time or review time, you'll have a record of your contributions to the company.

5. CULTURAL GENDER GAMES

Most of us are raised to go to school and "*no meter las patas*" (not have premarital sex, let alone get pregnant, especially as a teen). The expectation behind this is that as soon as it's appropriate, we *will* get married and start having children. But what happens after college if you want to start a career before getting married? Or if you've gotten married, but you want to solidify your career before you have kids? Those of us who break the "Latina rule" and place career before fam-

Stand Up to the Sexists and Racists Dolores Huerta Style

"The growers complained about me; they were not used to dealing with women," Dolores says, during an interview for a PBS series on the Chicano civil rights movement, recalling the atmosphere during the tense negotiations to end the grape workers' strike in the 1970s. However tense the battle, this fierce Chicana, a cofounder, with Cesar Chavez, of the United Farm Workers Union, was relentless, so much so that the growers gave her the nickname Dragon Lady.

She remembers that some of her colleagues told her, "We have to be polite; they are attorneys, so you have to be polite." However, Dolores remembers responding, "Why do we need to be polite to people who are making racist statements at the table or making sexist comments? When they do that, you have to call them on it, because when you do that, you are educating them in the process so that they can stop that kind of behavior."

ily face painful *crítica* from *la familia* and sometimes from well-meaning *comadres*. The key to dealing with this pressure in a healthy way is straight out of the Serenity Prayer—striving for the serenity to accept the things we cannot change.

I've come to accept that my family just does not and probably never will accept some of my life choices, such as my being a "career girl." I try first to be comfortable with my own decisions, and second, to be aware of when those decisions might offend those with more traditional expectations. But in the end I have to live my own life, and I can't convince others to share my values, just as no amount of criticizing or yelling at me will convince me to share theirs.

6. UNDERSTANDING THE POLITICS OF THE WORKPLACE

My friend Ana says that we Latinas are still learning how to "play the politics" in a work environment, that as a community we are still very young at the game. Having worked closely with major political and labor leaders, Ana has learned the power plays that go on close to the seat of power. She's taught me that in the subtle game of office politics, it's not always the *jefa* who holds the ultimate power. Study your company structure, and be strategic about who holds the power and your relationship to that person. Have an overall strategy for success at that particular job. Chicago-based career consultant Graciela Kenig says, "Office politics is essentially about power: who has it, who wants it, and who can control its transfer at any given moment."

Get to know *todo el mundo* where you work, from the mail-room delivery personnel to the president, and be careful about the people you connect with: a true friend always has your back, but a friendly colleague is not always your friend.

Be conscious of good work, celebrate individual and department victories, and give the right people a shout out, a pat on the back.

We're all used to celebrating the big moments in our colleagues' lives—promotions, marriages, engagements, pregnancies—but we seldom celebrate the everyday little things. If you notice a clean floor, let the person who cleaned it know that you notice. This is *respeto,* and it takes only a second, but it lasts much longer. Pointing out other peoples' good work won't get you a serious promotion, but it tells everyone that you take notice and value people and all their contributions.

As the sidebar on asking for a promotion or raise says, get to know how others perceive you. If you don't like what you hear, change it. Attitude is the key.

Whatever you do, *don't complain.* If you don't like the way something's being done, do it better yourself, propose how you think it could be done better, or let it go. And *don't explain* when you haven't done something properly or on time—tell your boss that it's not done, state a realistic estimate of when it will be done, and work to do it right. Finally, do the job, whatever it is, with a positive attitude. This is for you: you have to do the job, whether you're happy or miserable, and you'll enjoy it much more if you can find the positive in the experience.

Diosas de las Américas

Chalchiuhtlicue, "She of the Jade Skirt," is an Aztec water goddess associated with rivers, lakes, lagoons, and the sea. According to the *Leyenda de los Soles* (Legend of the Suns), she gave birth to the world in the Fourth Sun, in the era known as Four-Water. During her regency, the sky was made of water, and it fell on the Earth, precipitating a great flood.

A fierce Latina who made U.S. history . . .

 **Gloria Anzaldúa** has been essential in bringing the literature of women of color to the forefront of mainstream society. She is a Chicana lesbian-feminist poet, writer, and cultural theorist. Gloria was born on September 26, 1942, on a ranch called Jesus Maria of the Valley, Texas, to a family of Mexican immigrants. Her book *Borderlands/La Frontera: The New Mestiza* (1987) was chosen as one of the Best Books of 1987 by the *Literary Journal.* Gloria has won the prestigious NEA Fiction Award, the 1991 Lesbian Rights Award, the 1992 Sappho Award of Distinction, the Before Columbus Foundation Book Award, and the Lambda Literary Best Small Press Book Award. Gloria is also the author of *Interviews/ Entrevistas* (2000) and the children's books *Friends from the Other Side/Amigos del Otro Lado* (1993) and *Prietita and the Ghost Woman/Prietita y la Llorona* (1996), as well as the editor of *Making Face, Making Soul/Haciendo Caras: Creative and Critical Perspectives by Feminists of Color* (1990). She is also well known for *This Bridge Called My Back: Writings by Radical Women of Color* (1983), which she co-edited.

CHAPTER ELEVEN

GOING HOME—
to Your Roots

. . . in Spanish I tell my daughter
stories
of an island that thinks
it is a continent, floats
somewhere between heaven and hallucination,
where the blind think
they see
and the mute hope to sing.

    —From *My Daughter,* by Alejandro Anreus,
      Cuban-born and New Jersey–raised poet

There's a line I love from the beautiful poem *"Boricua en la Luna"* by Puerto Rican poet Juan Antonio Corretjer, which was turned into an equally beautiful song by Roy Brown. It goes, *"Yo sería borincano aunque naciera en la luna"*—I would be a Puerto Rican even if I had been born on the moon. I love those words, because for me they speak to the truth of my Puerto Rican identity. But I also believe that the poem

¿Donde está mi compadre?
Concentrations by Group

Mexican: Los Angeles, Chicago, Houston, San Antonio, and Phoenix.

Puerto Rican: New York, Chicago, and Philadelphia

Cuban: Hialeah, Miami, New York, Tampa, and Los Angeles.

Central American: Los Angeles, New York, Houston, Miami, and San Francisco.

South American: New York, Los Angeles, Chicago, and Miami.

speaks in metaphor to our collective Pan-Latino truth, because across other American cities and homes, *boricua*-ness, Dominican-ness, *colombiano*-ness, and Latino-ness in general are affirmed and reaffirmed for generations, in countless private and public ways. You can replace "*boricua*" in the song with any other Latin American nationality and it would be just as true. We can all lay claim to this heritage, even if we were born in icy cities like Fargo, North Dakota, or Chicago, Illinois, or in cement metropolises like New York or Los Angeles.

"Home" is such a complicated issue for so many of us. What does it mean to "go home" when your ancestral home is now part of the United States? What does it mean to go home if your home is Albuquerque or Houston, and not Mexico City or San Salvador? I've come to understand that for me there are two kinds of homes—the physical kind and the spiritual. America is my physical home and Puerto Rico my spiritual home; and neither is more important than the other. They're both what makes me me, just as your two homes make you you. In a sense they are your parents; if not for both of them, you wouldn't be here.

In her memoir *Borderlands/La Frontera,* Chicana author and thinker Gloria Anzaldúa writes, "We are a synergy of two cultures with various degrees of mexican-ness or anglo-ness . . . I have so internalized the borderland conflict that sometimes I feel like one cancels out the other."

To know and feed the other culture within me before the Anglo one cancels it out, I often pick up my *maletas* and head south of the border to that Caribbean island I left as a child, where my ancestors are buried, where my mother has retired, and where some of my aunts and distant cousins still reside. These trips nourish my soul, strengthen me, lift me, and ground me, all at the same time. If *you* want to connect your two cultures, if you want to discover yourself, a trip to your spiritual homeland is essential. Visiting our ancestral countries of origin, as my friend Tania points out, connects us to a lifeline that goes back in time. You feel the layers of history that speak to your past. If you haven't done so already, it is a must!

It's very American to want to forget, to assimilate, but it's very Latino to want to remember. This remembering through songs, *cuentos,* and *comida* in many ways has been like a protective shield that has allowed our ancentors to survive here, amid these strange customs and racism and humiliations. This is why I feel so strongly about the journey home. Going home will be about reclaiming, reaffirming, remembering, and rediscovering yourself all over again.

YO, LA FAKE PUERTO RICAN

When I went to Puerto Rico during summer vacation in my teenage years, I was considered different, but I didn't mind. It was the kind of different that made me popular with the local kids, not the kind I feel in America sometimes, that defines me as an "illegal alien." In the eyes of my relatives and other islanders, I was a *gringita,* a *blanquita, de allá*–from over there, not an authentic Puerto Rican. My cousins would make me repeat words in Spanish and then laugh because my Spanish sounded cute and funny to them. It never bothered me to be different there. My accent told them—and reminded me—that I was indeed different. To be different back then, in that small pueblo, was to be a rare jewel.

But everything got twisted around one summer when I went "back home" as an adult, for a conference. I had won an Emmy Award, and I found myself a guest of honor at a conference hosted by

Puerto Rico–based journalists. It felt great when they were celebrating my accomplishment and claiming me as one of their own, but throughout the week-long conference something didn't feel right; I came face-to-face with the *rechazo* that an illegitimate child lives.

The culturally arrogant, curious about my accent and background, thought they were paying me a compliment me when they said (with real surprise), "Oh, your Spanish is not so bad!" Now, I know that my accent speaks of my snowy history, not sandy beaches. It speaks of skyscrapers and barrio life. It speaks of *el norte.* But this time my accent defined me, it seemed, as a *gringa,* a Jerseyrican, as something not just different but illegitimate. My *hermanos y hermanas boricuas* had bought into the stereotypes of those of us *en el norte*– they noted all the differences between me and them, and then went on to make crazy assumptions based on those differences. It was a reverse version of the cultural arrogance we face here in the States, when someone thinks they know all about you once they see your face or hear your name or the way you talk. But in a way it was more painful, because I had thought I was home; the truth is, I was only half right. Has this ever happened to you?

In my spiritual home, on the island where I was born, I had to explain my Latino-ness, my *boricua*-ness, all over again; I had to defend it. As much as the experience hurt, it also awakened something in me: a consciousness of the duality I live. I am completely part of the skyscrapers and tenements, *and* completely a part of the tropical rain forest and *cuchifrito* joints. In a soulful and profound way, that trip reaffirmed my Latino-ness: I was a Puerto Rican sister from New Jersey (who, by the way, had just won an Emmy, thank you very much!).

THE PILGRIMAGE

Going back to your parents' or grandparents' (or, in some cases, your great-grandparents') homeland can be as spiritual a pilgrimage for you as going to Mecca is for a Muslim. Even if you feel like a tourist at first (and you definitely will!), your visits will undoubtedly change your life. And depending on what your expectations are, this can be positive or negative. The only guarantee is that "going home" will touch your soul.

For one woman who visited Cuba, the island where her mother was born but left as a child, the trip completed a circle. "If nothing else," Margaret told me, "the trip was about connecting to my parents. It told me so much about why they are the way they are."

It was a similar coming full circle for my friend Nina, whose father was born in Puerto Rico and whose mother is Jewish of European descent. When she was growing up in New York, Nina says, her dad made little of his heritage, something she understood as a rejection of it. But while his silence about who he was seemed like a negation, in his expressions, his color, the cadences of his speech, and his essence, he was Puerto Rican. In one euphoric experience she remembers, "I was in a *cuchifrito* place with lots of people dancing and eating, talking and hanging, just a normal Friday night for them. And then like a flash, in one moment, I recognized all these aspects of my dad. I found bits and pieces of him and me in *la gente.*"

If a single moment can change your life, this was it for Nina. She no longer felt like a sham in claiming her *boricua*-ness. She had often feared that one day she'd be unmasked, that the identity she'd cooked up for herself—a *boricua,* born and raised in New York, who spoke little Spanish—was fake. In that instant she no longer felt like a tourist in her father's homeland. Her dad may have downplayed his Puerto Rican–ness, yet his daughter recognized parts of him—his essence—on that faraway island. And for the first time in her life, she felt that his island, with its spirit and style so profoundly familiar to her, was her second home.

That's how it is with these trips: you reconnect with parts of yourself that are profoundly familiar. For Adriana, who identifies herself as a *colombiana* born in New York, the trip back to the land that her mom and dad were born in also gave her clarity about her identity.

Home for me is not a place, it is *la familia*—a feeling of having an inside joke with your immediate family and community. Home is like going to get a *cafecito* in Versailles (Calle Ocho in Miami) and hearing the waitress call me "nena" and my husband "nene." That feeling connects us like a thread and it tells you that you belong.

—Cecilia Betancourt Corral, Miami-born Cuban American writer

Diosas de las Américas

Alaghon: A Mayan *diosa*, she created the human ability to think, reason, and mark time. Using those skills, she also designed the intangible parts of nature, which take us beyond concrete realities into the world of the goddesses and its magic.

"It's a subtle and subliminal thing that fortifies you," Adriana says of her pilgrimage. "I came back [to Long Island] with a new strength." Growing up so far away from Colombia, in the two-car-garage suburbs of middle-class America, Adriana needed to connect the cultural-identity dots. Before her trip, she had always felt a strange void at her core. "You have to be able to explain yourself in [the United States]," she tells me. What's great about these trips is that they help you explain yourself to yourself first, and then to others.

Adriana remembers one particular trip, at age fifteen, when she was walking around Buga, her father's hometown, near Cali. Serendipity happened: "'Oh, my God,'" she remembers thinking. "'Everyone here looks like me!' I wasn't so special or so different anymore. I blended in. We always feel so *sobresaliente* in the States. Here I'm just like everybody else."

Tania had visited her parents' Cuba as a child, but the trips ended with the U.S. embargo. When she went back at age fifty, the trip turned out to solidify her sense of self. "I feel more secure in my identity—the one that I forged for myself in the States. I'm not sure that I ever doubted it, but certainly after this trip—no more."

THE *POCHA* DILEMMA

Here, on the mainland, I was never fully an *americana,* and there on the homeland that I was claiming, I was never fully a *boricua.* I know that that's what many of my *mejicana* and *tejana* sisters experience too—here never quite American and in Mexico *una pocha,* a *tejana,* or a *chicana,* but never quite Mexican enough. Feeling a part of both places without really being accepted by either can leave you in the state of a cultural castaway, rejected by two worlds that can't or won't understand the women we have become.

There is a moment in the movie *Selena* when Edward James Olmos, who plays Selena's father, is spelling it out for the young *tejana* star played by Jennifer Lopez, who's about to perform in Mexico for the first time. "You are a *pocha, mija,* and what that means is that when you're in Mexico, you can never be Mexican enough; and when you're in the United States, you can never prove yourself American enough." I find as much truth in this line as I do in the line from Corretjer's poem. And of course it doesn't apply only to those whose family roots are in Mexico.

But despite the cultural frictions we sometimes feel with the "homeland," the idea that you belong to something with deep roots is powerful. My friend Ana's philosophy of cultural ownership is the healthiest form of identity I know: she may not necessarily be welcomed by her *hermanos y hermanas boricuas,* but she feels welcomed by the land itself—the mountains, the sea, and the air. The land itself makes her feel like a daughter who has returned to her Mother Earth.

THE TURLINGTON LAND AFFAIR

I was once on a cover shoot with model Christy Turlington, whose mother was born in El Salvador but raised in California. I still remember what Christy said to me as we stepped off the plane in San Salvador and she breathed in the tropical air: "There is something about the way El Salvador smells that makes me feel so warm inside." We were traveling to the Central American nation, taking Turlington and her Salvadoran mother back to the land that Christy had visited as a child, to do a cover and a fashion layout for *Latina* magazine's

Going to a Forbidden Home: The Cuban American Dilemma

"I will not go to Cuba until Fidel dies" is what a Cuban American friend born and raised in Miami tells me. While the trip home for most other Latinas is mired with emotional complications, a trip to Cuba for many of our Cuban sisters is an even more complicated affair. Ceci, whose parents fled with their parents to Miami as children, tells me that even *thinking* about going to the land her parents and grandparents had to flee is fraught with politics, nostalgia, and fear.

"Visiting Cuba would be disrespectul to the elder members of my family," she says. Akin, I think, to *una bofetada.*

"You don't want to support a system that proved to be so painful for them," she adds. Ceci's grandmother left Cuba with a purse, her husband, their three children, and the clothes on their backs. She did not have the opportunity to say good-bye to any of her friends and relatives. "My grandmother walked and never looked back, and I in some way have to honor that profound pain of so many things lost," she says.

These issues run so deep in the exile Cuban community that another friend tells me that, even before he could crawl and speak, before he knew who Mickey Mouse was, he learned about an "evil dictator named Fidel Castro." Cuban American children in exile grow up bathed in nostalgic tales and tears of a life and land that is forever lost. Tales of pre-Castro Cuba are

January 1999 issue. The issue—"New Year, New You"—turned out to be one of my favorites. It was all about connecting and remembering and coming full circle.

I remember that Turlington wanted to know right away when she would get to eat her favorite Salvadoran food—*pupusas.* The food also gave her a sense of warmth. I couldn't help noticing that this beautiful international icon stood out and yet fit in. The comfort, ease, and pride she exuded said that she had something to share with a crew of mostly non-Latino fashionistas. We shot on location in different what ground many of the elders and feed the passion to topple the Cuban president. In many ways, the memories and passion of returning home is what keeps the elders going. And because of such intense memories, many of the Generation ñ *cubanas* refuse to set foot there. As one woman told me, "I just want to honor the Cuba of their memories, and not the real Cuba, the decaying Cuba, that I am sure to see if I go. I'm afraid to see the real Cuba."

The only Communist country in the Americas is forbidden twofold. While Cuba seems to be an "in spot" for some, it is still illegal for American citizens to vacation in Cuba—another reason other Cuban Americans will not go to the island nation. (The United States likens vacationing in Cuba to trading with the enemy, because it has had an embargo against the island nation since the Kennedy administration.)

Many Cuban exile children who have heard of the torture, jailings, and political harassment of dissidents fear that they too will fall victim to similar experiences if they travel there, legally or not. "It may sound paranoid, but I'm afraid that I would get arrested and disappear," Ceci says.

Yet despite all of the family and political implications, more and more Generation ñ *cubanas* are visiting the island their parents love so much. Risking a family fight, *deshonra* and being called a *comunista* by her *tíos, tías,* and *familia,* another friend—who asked that I not use her real name—said that as much as fighting communism has been part of her parents' life, it's not her battle. She needed to see Cuba for herself, *"para que no me lo cuente nadie."* And after the emotional trip to Cuba, she understood more profoundly the pain and the passion of her family and many in the exile Cuban community in cities like Miami and Union City and in Puerto Rico.

For those *amigas* not ready to go to the "real" Cuba, I recommend a visit to mini Cubas: Miami or Union City. As Ceci tells me, the only Cuba she has ever really known is located in Florida, and it's a city called Miami.

places where she and her mother and sisters visited, places with mother memories and daughter memories. Mother and *hija* were so proud. Though Turlington spoke very little Spanish, it didn't really matter—she was *salvadoreña.* During our shoot we also visited aunts and cousins that Christy hadn't seen or spoken to in years. Her relatives hosted a party for her and her mother, and the crew was invited. Very Latino, I thought, a family fiesta. Though Turlington hadn't grown up with her cousins, *tías,* and *tíos,* they immediately claimed her as one of their own—*sangre, raza.* I saw the easy way the Calvin

Klein model blended in with her blood. It seemed to me that for this international cover girl and actress, who has visited so many lands for work and play, El Salvador represented a deep connection to her past, and maybe even her future. I hoped she would keep going back.

Now, before you pack your suitcases, sundresses, and bikinis, here are some *consejitos*.

PLAN, PLAN, AND PLAN

First of all, *plan* your trip. This is a vacation like no other. Don't let the places you visit and the experiences you have be determined by the cousin you are visiting. Identify some things you want to do that are part of your search, and figure out how to get there. You should, of course, allow for spontaneity and serendipity, but have a concrete idea of your logistics.

Interview your parents and *abuelos* (or another family elder) if they are still around, about some of the places that are important in your family history. Where did your parents meet? Your *abuelos*? Where were they born? Where did they go to school? What church did they go to? Which beaches? If they took you there as a child, find out about those places, too. Memories you think you must have lost are only locked away, waiting for you to find the key. Knowing your family history will tell you where you need to visit. Find out when your parents or grandparents made *their* pilgrimage to the States, and why. For many of us, the family's reasons for immigrating are very clear—war, political strife, natural disasters, oppression. But for others, it's not that black and white. It's important to learn their history there.

My mother left Puerto Rico at the height of the 1973 economic recession, when the sneaker factory she worked at closed up shop and relocated to Taiwan. She was one of the many seamstresses and factory workers who left the island looking for economic relief. Knowing details like that before you go can make the experience that much richer. You will be able to get a sense of where your parents were living. It also gives concrete answers to the memories that you grew up with.

Besides family history, I encourage you to learn about your country's history. This is important in general, but especially if you have

---

The Stolen Mexican Lands

What happens when your ancestral homeland is now a mall on Interstate 66 in Arizona? If, as Gloria Anzaldúa says, not even the cemetery is ours, if home is not south of the border but now part of the U.S. of A.? My friend Adelita tells me of her *bisa-abuela* who one day was a Mexican citizen and the next morning, a second-class American citizen.

For many Mexican Americans whose heritage dates back to the time when California, Texas, New Mexico, and Arizona were part of northern Mexico, going home is laden with political and emotional strife, different in kind from the Cuban experience, but not in degree.

This situation requires that the definition of "home" be readjusted again to fit an understanding more familial than political. Ownership of the lands that were part of the 1848 Treaty of Guadalupe Hidalgo is still being fought by the heirs in the highest tribunals of the land, with stories of stolen lands and stolen pasts. Yet it's like Anzaldúa says: "These are our lands and no imaginary border will erase our histories there. This is our home."

Investigating your family history and locating the place and landmarks where your ancestors came from is what this trip will be about. But I believe that after you've visited landmarks and places that are today part of the U.S.A. *and* part of your Mexican history, your journey will be incomplete without a trip to *el pais* that is still *Méjico*. If the border was drawn and your people were divided as a result of wars, a visit to Mexico, south of our U.S. border, is a trip worth taking. For all that has been lost on this side of the border, much has been preserved on the other side. And just as you can connect at the carnival during Fiesta or a Cinco de Mayo celebration up north, you will find a completely different experience connecting to *la raza* in a *zócalo* or a *mercado* in some remote pueblo where, a long time ago, a leaf in your family tree may have fluttered to the ground.

little or no blood connection. As significant as land is, you won't find your roots by simply smelling the soil or rolling on the sand, as my friend Ana points out; you have to know your country's story. Choose a book written about your country: fiction, history, or biography; the genre doesn't matter. Each and every one of our twenty Spanish-speaking Latin American nations has such a rich history, and each thing you know about it will make your visit resonate even more. Rent movies made in your home country—the cinema says so much about the culture of a place. The Internet is also another great source to help plan your trip: key the name of any Latin American country into a search engine, and you'll get a brief history of the country, at the very least.

BET YOU CAN'T GO JUST ONCE

There's something sweet about repetition. The first time you go, you may feel like a tourist, especially if you don't speak Spanish or you have no relatives or connections there. Don't think for a moment that you'll land and instantly feel that *esta es mi casa.* You are a tourist, girl—maybe a tourist with blood connections, but a tourist nonetheless. Be conscious of that: you're a visitor, you're different, you carry dollars. You carry the mixture of sweet apple pie and spicy enchiladas in your blood. You may get sick from the water, just like those other tourists do, and you will need time to connect.

It wasn't until Nina's fifth trip that she had her wonderful epiphany and started recognizing parts of herself in other *boricuas.* "I made a conscious decision not to do anything 'touristy.' I behaved like I was a local *boricua,* going to the clubs, restaurants, and *mercados* like my *boricua* sisters did. And this was when I made this magical connection: I saw the family tree, the connectedness that is my dad, my Puerto Rican *abuela,* and me."

All the women I spoke to who made the pilgrimage say that repeat visits are crucial. Margaret, who planned her second trip to Cuba just months after her first, likens it to watching a movie twice. "You always pick up something you missed the first time." While she said the connection she felt was so intense that she could imagine living there permanently, the second visit was like the second chapter in the novel that began with her first trip.

SPEAKING SPANISH

It's the Spanish, *comadre* . . .

Your accent in Spanish speaks volumes about who you are. *Ay, Dios mio,* how embarrassing it is when you get there and you can't communicate, even though you have called yourself *dominicana, colombiana, cubana, mexicana, boricua,* or the like for so long. But no matter how embarrassing, it isn't the end of the world. While speaking Spanish may be the icing on the cake—you can connect more deeply if you speak the native tongue—not speaking it doesn't necessarily keep you from feeling the vibe of your *hermanas y hermanos.* Don't let your language "deficiency" stop you from visiting or delving right in. You may have to walk around with an English-Spanish dictionary, *pero qué importa?* My son BJ can't speak Spanish—in fact, he's failing it as I write this chapter!—but he can communicate in the elementary Spanish he does know, and he can connect in the cadence and the rhythm of the words that he's heard and become accustomed to from knowing his grandparents and *tías,* and living with me.

"The moment that I opened my mouth in Colombia," Adriana tells me, "I found myself saying things like '*soy colombiana,* but I was born en Nueva York'!" Nina's Spanglish embarrassed her so much that she tried to avoid speaking as much as possible. "I didn't want to sound dumb," she told me. Speaking the language opens up other doors for you,

¿Hablas español?

As much as 20% of the total Hispanic population in the United States does not speak Spanish.

but don't be embarrassed if you don't have that particular key. Nina's monolingualism didn't keep her from connecting; feeling "home" was much more meaningful for her than language.

You can still connect at a spiritual level, a cultural level. If you want to share in the style and the spirit and the energy of this land, not knowing it's language won't stop you. And besides, you can start learning it any time.

MEETING RELATIVES

Meeting cousins was weird for Nina. "People just claim you. It's so bizarre to be claimed," she laughs, "by people who don't even know you." Nina's mother—who is not Latina—would always say that family is what you make it, but there on that island, if you are blood, no matter how distant, you are claimed. Being claimed by your relatives gives you carte blanche on the block, in the pueblo. Even if you are meeting them for the first time, even if they can't quite understand you, they make you feel like you're one of them. *Eres sangre*—you're blood—and that is such an important thing for us.

For Adriana, though, the relative connection is always fraught with guilt. While she fit in with them, she always felt what she calls "the guilt of privilege." They see themselves in her, and she sees herself in them, but there is still an invisible wall—a wall put up by her privileged life in America.

I know exactly how Adriana feels, because I live the wall every time I visit my *tías*. Things don't change that much in the small town they were born in and never left. The warmth I feel when I go back is pure magic; I feel fortunate that I can live that magic and that not much changes in this town. But a part of me feels sad and guilty, because I have things—material things—that make my life as a woman, a mother, and a professional easier. I have access to comfort that they don't. And that guilt is ever present during my short stays.

You may feel the guilt of privilege, too, but just as with language, do not let that stop you. Look for that family tree, the distant connections, the distant blood, and claim your family as they may claim you.

WHEN IN GUATEMALA . . .

. . . it almost goes without saying, do as the *guatemaltecos* do. Keeping a tourist mentality about the trip—staying by the hotel pool, going only to tourist spots with no real familial connection—won't give you the journey. You won't find soulful connections sipping piña coladas, working on your tan, and getting the standard guided tour of your homeland. The trick is to get out, get around, and move in the circles that the locals move in. Be open to the energy and the ways that people there live their lives. It's certainly understandable if you don't want to drink the water for fear of getting sick, but if you hang out in restaurants that serve Americanized *rancheras,* how will you ever feel like anything but a stranger in a strange land?

Whenever I stayed at hotels in Puerto Rico, I felt bitter at how tourism personnel—the ones being paid to explain the local ways—presented such watered-down and false versions of Puerto Rican–ness. I always secretly hope that tourists will have the sense to explore the lush land, the people, the food, and the children. You will never get to know yourself in the lobbies of the hotels. Only in the *mercados,* the churches, the buses, the plazas, the local cafeterias, even the malls, can you get a small taste of what this land—and you—is all about. In these places you won't find the pretensions that are served on platters to "other" tourists.

SURVIVING CULTURE SHOCK

When Margaret traveled to Cuba, the poverty shocked her. Cuban women had so little of what she had and too often took for granted. "Luxury" became a relative term: for Cuban women it means toothpaste, tampons, soap, and toilet paper. Another thing Margaret found painful was the policy (in many Latin American nations, not just Cuba) of segregating the locals from the tourists. I have witnessed it myself, to varying degrees, in all the Latin American countries I've visited.

This can (and should) be really disturbing, whether you know to expect it or not. In the Cuba Margaret visited, the tourists (she and her family) could choose from various ice-cream flavors; for locals, there was one flavor. Poverty is usually the biggest component of culture shock during the visit "home." We all know that there's plenty of poverty in America, but Third World poverty can be shocking to the fainthearted, and distressing even to the most politically aware *hermana*. The shacks, the lack of running water, and (sometimes) the begging will hit you hard, even if you don't recognize parts of yourself in the beggars who ask for your dollars.

As tempted as you might be to distance yourself from what you see, this is not the time for the princess or goddess within to come out. I urge you to keep that *chica* in check, and expect the unexpected.

FALLING IN LOVE WITH A "NATIVE"

Oh boy, love is always such a hot potato. I try to embrace it most of the time, but this is one version that gives me serious pause. Love on the road happened to Wendy, a Dominican from Washington Heights, New York. We all can see why: "The men over there are definitely different—in *los detalles*," she says. "They are more romantic and attentive to women. *Más cariñosos*, more mature, *más hombres*." The man she fell in love with was thirty-three, and so serious. To Wendy, who was used to the informal ways we form relationships here, the seriousness of the affair was striking. If you have a romance there, chances are that for you it's exactly that—a "romance." But the man is likely to take it far more seriously; romance for Latinos *is* a more serious affair. In America we have grown to assume that most romance begins with the leisurely process of "dating," but over there

Wendy discovered that the minute she went out with this love interest one time she became his woman. The concept of dating *no existe*. The traditional notion of love was intoxicating for Wendy. Her affair lasted a year and a half, through letters, hours-long phone calls, and many trips, hers and his. It's over now, but she thinks of it as having been a worthwhile experience.

While it was all about love for Wendy, it isn't always that way. Men, both here and abroad, often have agendas when they see a woman alone with "dollars"; you could be someone's ticket out of the country. Don't for a second, in the sweetness of tropical nights and lovely serenades, be blind to that possibility. I know a young *peruana* who poured her heart and wallet into a south-of-the-border Señor Right for two years. She spent energy, time, and money trying to make the long-distance relationship work until he could join her in Florida. Once his documents were settled, she was left high and dry—and broke. Smart women can still make dumb choices.

So does that mean you should always avoid romance when you make the pilgrimage? *Pues claro que no.* Never say no to love. Go for it but with, as my mom says, *con un ojo abierto y otro cerrado, mija.* While your *papi chulo* may seem like your soul mate, I can only offer the wise *abuela dicho* that *amor de lejos es de pendejos.* Remember, time itself is the truest prophet. *Héchale* slowly, *con cuidado*, and enjoy the voyage.

MOVING TO LATIN AMERICA

For some women, the visits back were so powerful that they moved abroad. Evelyn was born in New York to Dominican parents. At twenty-four, she moved to her parents' "home," having found liberation, empowerment, and the feeling of belonging she had always sought. "The first thing that made me move back to the Dominican Republic was a sense of national pride and passion. After my trip in 1998 (it had been eleven years since my last trip to D.R., when I was eleven), I loved everything that was Dominican." Evelyn was so proud of the change and development she saw on the trip she made as an adult that she wanted to take part in it. She decided that she wanted to move back and immerse herself entirely in its society. But living and working in the Dominican Republic hasn't been as warm and fuzzy as she expected.

"The most difficult part is that, just as in the States, where you don't quite feel that you belong, you realize that here it is the same thing. It's not quite 'like home,' and it takes some getting used to." It's that cultural synergy again—no matter where we are, here or over there. So for Evelyn and the many Latinas who make the pilgrimage south of the border and stay, the last part of the process is often to come home *again,* this time to the home north of the border, to reconnect with parts of the soul.

TRAVELING *SOLA*

This is another little big thing to consider before getting on that plane. In almost every country, a woman traveling alone is a walking target. Your appearance invites curious glances, stare downs, sometimes angry words and even violence. And while we don't have to be covered from head to toe, as do some of our sisters in the Middle East, India, and Africa, our *hermanas* south of the border do live a subtle gender apartheid in public (and private). In many of our home countries, especially in the small towns, women don't do things in public alone. A *turista,* meaning you, alone in any corner of Latin America will provoke curiosity of all sorts. Be prepared to stick out like a sore thumb, even if you look just like the woman next to you.

There is also the dangerous issue of political violence in many of our home countries, which makes us targets of rape, kidnappings, and other crimes, especially if we're traveling alone. The State Department issues travel warnings from time to time about countries it deems particularly dangerous for Americans. (See the sidebar on travel safety resources.) If you are lucky enough to have relatives in your home country, they can help you determine how safe it is for you to travel alone.

The best thing you can do is learn how the local women dress and pack clothing that is conservative and comfortable. That means leave your hot pants, *mini-faldas*, high heels, gold, and *diamantes* at home. Forget about your designer best, and please, don't buy fancy clothes for this trip—save them for a local spot you are familiar with. Subtlety is the dress code when you're traveling to the homeland. You'll already be standing out from the crowd; there's no reason to make yourself a walking target.

There are more basic travel tips for women traveling alone, especially as they relate to safety in Latin America. Look at the sidebar on travel safety resources, and make sure that you are familiar with them.

TO GO ALONE OR *ACOMPAÑADA*

For many of us, myself included, traveling alone is challenging. I don't do it often, and it's still scary to me when I do. But for these trips, the experience

Travel Safety Resources

The U.S. State Department

Travel warnings are issued when the U.S. State Department recommends that Americans avoid a certain country it considers too risky because of terrorism or violence. The information is accessible via the U.S. State Department website, www.state.gov/index.cfm.

Besides warnings, you will find information called "consular sheets" for every country in the world. In them you can find information on such matters as health conditions, crime, unusual currency or entry requirements, any areas of instability, and the location of the nearest U.S. embassy or consulate in the particular country.

Other Useful Websites

www.corporatetravelsafety.com

www.womenstravelclub.com

www.gravelroads.com

Excellent website for women travelers:
www.Journeywoman.com

Books

Safety and Security for Women Who Travel, by Sheila Swan and Peter Laufer (San Francisco: Travelers' Tales, 1998).

Gutsy Women: Travel Tips and Wisdom for the Road, by Marybeth Bond (San Francisco: Travelers' Tales Guide, 1996).

will be enriched if there is no buffer between you and what you are going to experience. If you're traveling solo, you can talk to the *tamalera* all you want, without worrying if your buddy is hungry or ready to move on to the next landmark. It's all about you and the experience. You don't have to worry about anyone else's schedule but your own.

If you're not ready to travel alone and you take a best friend along, make sure she understands that the trip is not about frozen daiquiris or tanning; it's about the pleasures of the soul and the humble plazas and the forgotten schools. It's about the cemeteries and the parks—and all the familial landmarks that are yours to enjoy.

Traveling in packs generally makes trips safer, but it also waters down the experience because it does involve others. When Tania went to Cuba, she felt alone on a great adventure: "Without children or my fiancé, there was no buffer between me and what I lived." But she did have one *consejo* about men. "Be aware of the men who will offer all kinds of services to a pretty lady traveling alone. Weigh how much you really need those services—taxis, guides, *compañía*—and move on."

FITTING IN OR NOT: CULTURE SHOCK

In his moving memoir *Days of Obligation*, Mexican American author Richard Rodriguez writes about the alienation he felt with when he visited Mexico to connect to his father's homeland and himself. How could he be a part of this land when the water made him sick, when he couldn't speak the language, when everyone looked like him but no one looked at him? I think that he was suffering from a severe case of the culture shock of not fitting in where you feel you should.

Maybe you'll feel that you are part of this land—but not fully. You may have the pleasure and privilege of being embraced by long-lost relatives and even strangers. You may even be "claimed," as Nina was, by relatives you never knew you had. You may be whisked from home to home to be shown off, if you are one of the lucky ones. You may look like everyone else around you, but while this *sentimiento* of home may feel good, the truth is that you are different. You're an Americana from *el norte,* and this trip is not like buying a dress in your size. I liken it more to buying a pair of jeans. The more you wear them, the more they are yours; the more you embrace this land, the more it will feel like your own. It's that simple.

THE ULTIMATE LUXURY: TAKING YOUR MOM OR DAD ON THE TRIP HOME

This *will* be a luxury—time, money, and willingness on their part. If you can take a parent with you on this pilgrimage, do it. Convince your mom, for example, that you want to go back with her and have her show you where she grew up, where her relatives came from, to relive the memories with you. It's like walking down memory lane with a life narrator. What a treat that will be for your connectedness.

Fíjate . . .
Did You Know?
The Hispanic middle class grew by 80% from 1979–1998.

My friend Ana traveled with her mom to Puerto Rico; it was the first time in twenty years that her mom had been in the small town where she was born and raised. "After that trip," Ana said, "I have another level of information about my mother, myself, and my identity." They walked in the plaza where her father *enamoró,* or serenaded, her mom. They visited a photography studio where her mom had had a picture taken with her as an infant. "I was standing in front of this stupid photography studio for such a long time," she laughs. "My roots became more solid [after the trip]." They walked into the church, the plazas, the local bakery, around the school where her mother had taught, and found her mother's childhood friend. Her mom even spotted the corner where her dad had kissed her for the first time. "I could picture it all. It was wonderful."

Going with a parent on this discovery can deepen the whole experience; it can make it simply unforgettable.

One final "warning": visiting your ancestral lands—whether you do it alone, with a parent, a best friend, your boyfriend, your husband, your child, or your children—will place you at risk of emotional upheaval. Every woman I spoke to said it was a strong emotional trip. One of them summarized it best when she said, "It will be your soul's revolution; it will awaken the warrior woman in you."

A fierce Latina who made U.S. history . . .

Don't mess with **Mia "the Knockout" St. John.** The Chicana-boxing champion has a mean right hook and drop-dead gorgeous looks that can leave the weak dizzy. Born Mia Rosales St. John in San Francisco, California, to Mexican parents on June 24, 1967, she is one of three children. Mia has been a fighter most of her life. At age six she began competing in tae kwon do and earned a black belt with an impressive 27–1 record. This warrior isn't just strong, she is absolutely beautiful. She modeled in magazines and calendars to put herself through California State University, Northridge, where she graduated with a bachelor's degree in psychology. However, her passion lay in the sport of combat, and she decided to pursue it fulltime in 1996, when she became a professional boxer, knocking out her opponent seconds into the fight— a real life *Girlfight* chica. Mia has kept an impressive undefeated record that has earned her well-founded nickname. One of the biggest sources of strength is her mother, Maria Rosales, who can be seen coaching her daughter during her fights. Her *mami* also stood by her when Mia decided to pose for *Playboy* in November 1999. In the summer of 2001, Mia, thirty-two years old, had been undefeated in twenty matches. To top things off, Mia, who lives in Calabasas, California, has two children, Julian, nine, and Paris, seven. The persistence, passion, and discipline that have brought Mia this far are sure to take her to unprecedented heights in women's boxing.

CHAPTER TWELVE

LA FUTURA:
Taking Care of Our Little *Hermanitas*

To awaken and unleash the Latina heroine who lives within each of us is the greatest gift we can give ourselves. The path that unleashes this heroine is long and full of mystery, pain, and joy. And once you've found her, feeding and nurturing her becomes an everyday responsibility. Like everything worthwhile, it starts with loving yourself as a sacred soul, but it doesn't end there. How can my heroine within fully enjoy soaring to new heights when she looks behind and sees so many of our little girls in pain and struggling to find their way?

I asked a twelve-year-old Latina girl I met a year ago what her life-long dream was. She looked at me quizzically and responded that she had no dream. She wasn't being shy—she simply had no dream of being anything in particular when she grew up. I was saddened and dumb-founded. When I was a little girl, my dream of being a writer kept me alive, curious and searching. I had fortitude in my family, and big sisters who encouraged me. *Pa'lante nena,* they would say. You can do it—do anything. Economic poverty was not a hindrance when I had people who loved me and cheered me on. I had teachers who reminded me of all the things I could be, drowning out those racist teachers who told me that I would never make it past high school. Further along the way,

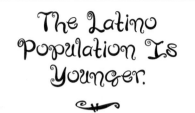

The Latino Population Is Younger.

Almost 75 percent of our people are under forty:

39.2% are under twenty.

35.5% are twenty to thirty-nine.

18% are forty to fifty-nine.

6.6% are sixty to seventy-nine.

9% are over eighty.

The average American age:

Latino: 28.8

Anglo: 38.5

African American: 32.3

Asian: 32.9

Others are older:

29.5% are under twenty.

30.2% are twenty to thirty-nine.

24.6% are forty to fifty-nine.

13% are sixty to seventy-nine.

2.7% are over eighty.

Percent under eighteen:

Latino: 35.7%

Anglo: 24%

African American: 33.4%

Asian 26.7%

I had mentors and friends whose support nurtured the young warrior within. Education and books took me to new worlds, even worlds of my own creation. And as special as I thought I was, I always assumed that *every* little girl has her dreams.

That's why the hopelessness of that seventh grader stunned me. I tried to imagine who could have robbed this precious young woman of her dreams. Who stole her faith in a future of personal and professional success? She couldn't visualize a rich life full of twists and turns, fantasies and personal freedom. Somehow she had lost hope in the greatness that life has to offer her. But she is in my life today because her dreamless future became my wake-up call. As I live this Nueva Latina life, I am trying to show her what she can be if she chooses. I share all kinds of things with her: books and movies, Latina heroes of the past and the present. Above all, I share time with her. All this to remind her of the simplest and most important fact she can ever learn: that she is important.

This little girl is but one of millions of Hispanic girls growing up in American suburbs, border towns, and urban centers, whose dreams have been squashed. They're not having an easy time. Think about the suicide statistics I mentioned in chapter 1, "Surviving Your Mother, *la Familia,* and *el Que Dirán* Without Going *Loca*!": two out of ten Latinas between the ages of fourteen and eighteen attempt suicide—dramatically more than African American and Anglo girls of the same age. Experts say that the reasons for these suicide attempts run the gamut from family and acculturation dramas to societal alienation and economic poverty. But there are other ways a girl can foreclose the possibilities of her life—like dropping out, getting pregnant, or both. Again, the reasons are wide-ranging—from not having enough information on contraception to economic poverty and wanting someone to love and need them. Twenty-six percent of Latina teens never graduate from high school—they make up the highest number of girls in the U.S. to drop out of high school. (African American females have a 13 percent drop out rate while Anglo girls have a 6.9 percent rate. The situation with our young men is grimmer, with 31 percent of Hispanic boys dropping out without a high school diploma, compared to 12.1 percent of black boys and 7.7 percent of white boys. We have twice the rate of African American teens and nearly four times the rate of Anglo students. The same study, "Latinas in School," published by the American Association of University Women, found that Hispanic girls leave school earlier than all other groups of young people, male or female, and are the least likely to return.

"We definitely have a very schizophrenic framework and concept where you have both the Old World model of what a female should be and then that conflicts with the modern-day version, the Americanized version that tells us you can be a mother and have a career. . . . There is a lot of confusion and a lot of identity crises going on in the young Latina psyche," said Congresswoman and former teacher Ileana Ros-Lehtinen in a *New York Times* interview.

Esta Juventud

In 2000, of all Latinos aged sixteen to twenty-four:

> 1,586,000 were not enrolled in college.

> 1,228,000 were not enrolled, but were employed.

> 322,000 were not enrolled and were not employed.

Who teaches our kids?

4.3% of all teachers at the elementary- and secondary-school levels are Hispanic; 14% of all public school students are Hispanic.

Mentoring

Mentoring a young Latina or Latino can many times mean the difference between the failure or personal and professional success of the youngster. If you are interested in feeding a young soul as well as your own, there are many local, national, and regional organizations helping our youth attain academic and personal success. Please make sure that you specifically request a Latina or Latino youngster.

MANA

MANA is a national nonprofit Latina advocacy organization founded in 1974. The original intent was to provide a voice for Mexican American women at the local, state, and national level. However, the organization has expanded to serve the diverse U.S. Latina population in all political, social, and professional areas. One of their more popular mentor programs, *Hermanitas*, teaches young women leadership and life skills. Visit their website: www.hermana.org

Girl Scouts of the U.S.A.

Girl Scouts was founded in 1912 in Georgia and has become the world's largest organization exclusively for girls, serving more than 2.7 million of them in the United States and around the globe. The programs are designed for girls from five to seventeen years of age. To volunteer or start a Latina Girl Scout troop, visit their website: www.gsusa.org

ASPIRA

The ASPIRA Association is the only national nonprofit organization devoted to the education and leadership development of Puerto Rican and other Latino youth. Taking its name from the Spanish verb *aspirar*, to aspire, the foundation was established in 1961 to address the exceedingly high drop out rate and low educational attainment of Puerto Rican youth. Visit their website: www.aspira.org

Big Brothers Big Sisters of America

Big Brothers Big Sisters of America (BBBSA) is the nation's oldest mentoring organization, serving youth in this country since 1904. BBBSA provides one-to-one mentoring relationships between adult volunteers and children at risk. BBBSA currently serves more than 100,000 children and youth through more than 500 agencies throughout the United States. Visit their website: www.bbbsa.org

The National Mentoring Partnership
The National Mentoring Partnership (NMP) advocates for the expansion of mentoring initiatives nationwide. Visit their website: www.mentoring.org

Boys & Girls Clubs of America
The Boys & Girls Clubs are neighborhood-based buildings specifically for youth programs and activities. Every club is staffed by full-time, trained youth development professionals, providing positive role models and mentors. Volunteers provide key supplementary support. Visit their website: www.bgca.org

National Dropout Prevention Center
The National Dropout Prevention Center, established in 1986, serves as an information-clearing house on issues related to school reform and dropout prevention. The center helps community and corporate leaders and teachers in K–12 education by supplying leadership in technical assistance, training, and resources. Visit their website: www.dropoutprevention.org

America's Promise
America's Promise, led by General Colin Powell, is a national organization that serves as a youth advocacy group in the public, private, and nonprofit sectors. Visit their website: www.americas-promise.org

Points of Light Foundation
This foundation's goal is to encourage more people to become volunteers. Based in Washington, D.C., it works in communities throughout the United States through a network of more than 500 Volunteer Centers. Visit their website: www.pointsoflight.org

Junior Achievement
Junior Achievement is a nonprofit economic education organization. The programs are taught

by classroom volunteers from the business sector in the United States and nearly 100 countries worldwide. Junior Achievement reaches more than 2.6 million students each year in America's cities, suburbs, and rural areas. Visit their website: www.ja.org

Tutor/Mentor Connection

Based in Chicago, the Tutor/Mentor Connection builds and sustains a "village" of tutor and mentor programs. It works to ensure that tutor/mentor programs are located where they are needed and have the resources each needs to help the youth it serves. Visit their website: www.tutormentorconnection.org

National 4H Council

The National 4-H Council is a not-for-profit organization that uses private and public resources to build partnerships for community youth development. Visit their website: www.fourhcouncil.org

HOSTS Corporation

HOSTS Corporation is best known for its Structured Mentoring Program in language arts. The program targets students (K–12) who need assistance in reading, writing, thinking, and study skills. HOSTS matches students with trained business and community volunteer mentors, as well as cross-age mentors. Visit their website: www.hosts.com

Poverty, alienation, and cultural, societal, and family indifference and expections crush the dreams of millions of Hispanic girls. Latina teenagers are screaming for our help. But what can we do?

Well, one Latina alone can't do a thing to change that disturbing trend. But one woman alone *can* make a difference in one little girl's life—remember "each one teach one"? What if each of us grown-up sisters made it her business to help out just one *hermanita*—can you even imagine what the cultural reverberations of such radical compassion would be? Wouldn't it be great to find out?

Part of my responsibility as a Nueva Latina is to become a dream catcher. In fact, it's *our* responsibility. We have to start seeing the younger *hermanitas* as part of our extended *familia*. Our voices must be louder than the voices of those who threaten their success. As we make our own rules for success without making excuses for our heritage and our right to be our own women, we owe it to the younger ones to show them how far they can soar.

So, how do we bring out the hero who lives in the heart of each Latina girl? It seems like a daunting task if you look at the whole picture. It isn't really when you look around you.

Do you have an hour a day? One day a week? One day a month? It doesn't take much time, and it doesn't even take being part of an institution, in case that's not your style; Latina girls at high risk are all over, and that includes our own families. Consciously giving back *should* start in your own circle, so look at the young girls in your family: cousins, sisters, nieces, even neighbors. But if your personal world does not have a Latina girl in need, there are always more formal mentoring programs for Latina professionals who want to light the way for a *hermanita* who's struggling in the dark.

I know another twelve-year-old girl. This

The Latino Master and Doctor

In 1998, about half a million (514,000) Hispanics age twenty-five and over had an advanced degree (e.g., master's, Ph.D., M.D., or J.D.).

The Latino College Grad

In 1998, there were 15.5 million students enrolled in college.

70.8% were white.

12.6% were black.

6.5% were Asian and Pacific Islander.

8.8% were Hispanic.

By 1998, of people at least twenty-five years old who completed a college education:

11% were Hispanic.

25% were white.

one is my niece Cristina, who dreams of being the next Selena *and* Marion Jones, combined. She sings, dances, and runs a mean hundred-yard dash. Her future is tied to mine; I hold her hand and remind her that she can achieve anything she wants. She'll need discipline and education first and foremost. But she also needs to see a little of the world—through books and other cultural experiences, and, when she's older, through travel and exposure to other kinds of people. I take time to hang out with her, and I teach by doing.

Ruben Blades once said that we cannot expect Hollywood to write our stories for us; we have to write our own. We Latinas are part of a story that is larger than our individual stories, and we owe it to our *hermanitas* (as well as to ourselves and our collective future) to give them a sense that they're part of a story larger than *their* own.

I hope this book will help you unleash and feed the ancient warrior spirit within. I also hope that you will take the time to grab the hand of a Latina girl and restore her faith in her future, your future, and the future of our Latina nation.

Diosas de las Américas

Ixchebel Yax: In Guatemala, this goddess bears a striking resemblance to Ix-chel in that she teaches spinning, weaving, and basketry to humans. More important, she is a mother figure who watches over all household concerns from the moon, her home.

Notes

INTRODUCTION: THE JOY OF BEING NUEVA LATINA

page 2. Gonzalez, Juan. *Harvest of Empire: A History of Latinos in America* (New York: Viking, 2000), p. 206.

page 3. Rodriguez, Richard. *Days of Obligation: A Conversation with My Mexican Father* (New York: Penguin Books, 1992), p. 173.

page 5 and subsequent. All population statistics cited throughout this book are derived from U.S. Census: "Hispanic Population in the USA," March 2000. "Detailed Tables for Current Population Report," February 2001, pp. 20–535.

page 19. Bibliographical information on Josefina Sierro de Bright obtained from www.cambios.org and www.yale.edu/ynhti/curriculum/units/2000/4/00.04.08.x.html#c.

CHAPTER ONE: SURVIVING YOUR MOTHER, *LA FAMILIA,* AND *EL QUE DIRÁN*

page 26 and subsequent. All goddess research information derived from Lurker, Manfred. *Dictionary of Gods and Goddesses, Devils and Demons* (New York: Routledge & Kegan Paul, 1995) and Telesco, Patricia. *365 Goddesses: A Daily Guide to the Magic and Inspiration of the Goddess* (San Franciso: HarperSanFrancisco, a division of HarperCollins, 1998).

page 28. Centers for Disease Control and Prevention, www.cdc.gov.

page 33. Letter to mamá translated by Clara La Rosa Ribbeck.

page 34 and subsequent education statistics. All education statistics cited are derived from U.S. Census: "School Enrollment in the United States—Social and Economic Characteristics of Students," October 1999, issued March 2001.

page 47. Biographical information on Evelina Lopez Antonetty provided by United Bronx Parents, Inc., 834 E. 156th Street, Bronx, NY 10455, (718) 292-9808.

CHAPTER TWO: *QUE BELLA SOY*

page 49. U.S. Census: "National Consumer Expenditure Survey," 1997.

page 50. Adamy, Janet. "From Milk to Perfume, Latinos Are Marketed To." *Contra Costa Times,* August 29, 2001.

page 54. Pachón, Harry, Louis DeSipio, Rodolfo de la Garza, and Chon Noriega. *Still Missing: Latinos In and Out of Hollywood* (The Tomás Rivera Policy Institute, May 2000).

page 55. U.S. Census: "Hispanic Population in the USA," March 2000. "Detailed Tables for Current Population Report," issued Feb. 2001, pp. 20–535.

page 56. National Consumer Expenditure Survey, 1997.

page 58. Office on Women's Health. "Eating Disorders Information Sheet: Latina Girls." p. 1.www.4woman.gov/BodyImage/bodywise/uf/Latina%20Girls2.pdf

page 58. Robinson, T.N., J.D. Killen, I.F. Litt, L.D. Hammer, D.M. Wilson, K.F. Haydel, C. Hayward, and C.B. Taylor, "Ethnicity and Body Dissatisfaction: Are Hispanics and Asian Girls at Increased Risks for Eating Disorders?" *Journal of Adolescent Health,* Vol. 19, No. 6 (December 1996), pp. 384–93.

page 58. Fitzgibbon, Marian and Melinda Stolley, "Minority Women: The Untold Story," www.pbs.org/wgbh/nova/thin/minorities.html.

page 59. Turner, Sherry L., Heather Hamilton, Meija Jacobs, Laurie M. Angood, and Deanne Hovde Dwyer. "The Influence of Fashion Magazines on the Body Image Satisfaction of College Women: An Exploratory Analysis," *Adolescence,* Vol. 32, No. 127 (Fall 1997), pp. 603–15.

page 61. Anzaldúa, Gloria. "Don't Give in, Chicanita," *Borderlands: La Frontera, The New Mestiza* (San Francisco: Aunt Lute Books,1999), p. 224.

page 75. Biographical information on Ileana Ros-Lehtinen obtained from www.house.gov/ros-lehtinen/.

CHAPTER THREE: THE HEALTHY LATINA

page 76. Carrillo, J. E., F. M. Trevino, J. R. Betancourt, and A. Coustasse. *Health Issues in the Latino Community,* "Latino Access to Health Care. The Role of Insurance, Managed Care, and Institutional Barriers" (Jossey Bass: San Francisco, 2001), Chapter 3.

page 77. Simmons Market Research Bureau, "National Hispanic Survey, 2000," released on December 6, 2001.

page 82. www.cancer.org and The National Women's Health Information Center, www.4woman.gov/minority/index.cfm.

page 84. SAMHSA, Office of Applied Studies, "Summary Tables from the National Household Survey on Drug Abuse," 1999, G13–16, G30–32, G75–76, G84, G89.

page 86. Mora, Pat. "Coatlicue's Rules: Advice from an Aztec Goddess" in *Goddess of the Americas: Writings on the Virgin of Guadalupe,* edited by Ana Castillo (New York: Riverhead Books, 1996), pp. 88–91.

page 92. U.S. Census: "Detailed Health Insurance," March 2000, and "Detailed Tables for Current Population Report," P60, Table H101, issued March 2001.

page 93. Centers for Disease Control and Prevention, www.cdc.gov.

page 100. Mishell, Daniel Jr., M.D.; Morton A. Stenchever, M.D.; William Droegemueller, M.D.; Arthur L. Herbst, M.D. *Comprehensive Gynecology, Third Edition* (Mosby-Year Book, Inc., 1997), Chapter 5, p. 146, Table 5-1.

page 108. Bibliographical information on Emma Tenayuca obtained from: Delgado Campbell, Dolores. "Shattering the Stereotypes: Chicanas as Labor Union Organizers," *Berkeley Women of Color* (Summer 1983), pp. 20–23, and Hardy, Gayle J. *American Women Civil Rights Activists: Bio-Bibliographies of 68 Leaders, 1825–1992* (Jefferson, NC: McFarland, 1993), and Telgen, Diane and Jim Kamp, editors. *Notable Hispanic American Women* (Detroit: Gale Research, 1993), and Zophy, Angela Howard. *Handbook of American Women's History* (New York: Garland, 1990).

CHAPTER FOUR: TALK CIRCLES

page 110. Center for American Women and Politics: "Women in Elected Office 2001: Fact Sheet Summaries," Eagleton Institute of Politics–Rutgers, The State University of New Jersey, www.rci.rutgers.edu/~cawp/facts/cawpfs.html.

page 112. Kenig, Graciela. *Best Careers for Bilingual Latinos: Market Your Fluency in Spanish to Get Ahead on the Job* (McGraw Hill: New York, 1998).

page 116. Fradd, Sandra and Thomas Boswell. "Creating Florida's Multilingual, Global Workforce," a joint project of the University of Florida, the University of Miami, and the Florida Department of Education, 1998.

page 127. Biographical information on Ellen Ochoa obtained from the National Aeronautics and Space Administration, www.jsc.nasa.gov/Bios/htmlbios/ochoa.html.

CHAPTER FIVE: CENTERING YOUR SOUL

page 129. Monsivais, Carlos. "Dreaming of Utopia," NACLA Report on the Americas, 19:3 (Nov./Dec. 1995), p. 41.

page 129. National Opinion Survey Research Center, Survey 1997, www.nsf.gov/sbe/srs/ssed/sedmeth/html.

page 131. These are preliminary findings from a national telephone survey of Latinos conducted in 2000 as part of a study by Hispanic Churches in American Public Life (HCAPL). In collaboration with the Alianza de Ministerios Evangelicos Nacionales (AMEN) and the Mexican American Cultural Center (MACC), The Tomás Rivera Policy Institute (TRPI) designed and conducted the HCAPL study, which was funded by a grant from The Pew Charitable trusts.

page 139. Castillo, Ana. *Goddess of the Americas: Writings on the Virgin of Guadalupe* (New York: Riverhead Books, 1996), p. xv.

page 150. Biographical information on Selena Quintanilla Perez obtained from www.q-productions.com/selenabio.htm.

CHAPTER SIX: SECRETS OF LATINA DATING

page 157. Association for Hispanic Advertising Agencies, www.ahaa.org.

CHAPTER SEVEN: LATINA SEXUAL MYSTIQUE

page 181. Villarruel, A. "Cultural influences on the sexual attitudes, beliefs, and norms of young Latina adolescents," *Journal of the Society of Pediatric Nurses,* Volume 3, Number 2 (April-June 1998), pp. 69–81.

page 193. Romero, Gloria J., and Wyatt, Gail E. "The Prevalence and Circumstances of Child Sexual Abuse Among Latina Women." *Hispanic Journal of Behavioral Sciences,* Vol. 21 Issue 3 (Aug. 1999), pp. 351–68.

page 212. Biographical information on Dolores Huerta was obtained from the United Farm Workers, www.ufw.org/dh.htm.

CHAPTER EIGHT: LOVE AND RELATIONSHIPS

page 216. Anzaldua, Gloria. *Borderlands: La Frontera, The New Mestiza* (San Francisco: Aunt Lute Books, 1987), p. 38.

page 218. Niolon, Richard. "Domestic Violence in Gay and Lesbian Couples," www.psychpage.com/learning/library/gay/gayvio.html.

page 218. "Dating Violence in Gay and Lesbian Relationships" obtained from www.rutgers.edu/SexualAssault/16.html.

page 224. García Márquez, Gabriel. *Love in the Time of Cholera* (New York: Penguin Books, 1988).

page 231. Biographical information on Rosemary Casals obtained from: International Tennis Hall of Fame, www.tennisfame.org/enshrinees/rosie_casals.html and Women's Stories, www.writetools.com/women/stories/casals_rosemary.html.

CHAPTER NINE: MARRYING OUTSIDE *LA RAZA*

page 233. Association of Hispanic Advertising Agencies, www.ahaa.org.

page 236. Catalyst (www.catalyst.org), "Women of Color in Corporate Management: A Statistical Picture," 1997, and U.S. Census Data, 1994–95. *Catalyst, The Glass Ceiling in 2000: Where Are Women Now?* Labor Day Fact Sheet.

page 243. Biographical information on Antonia Pantoja obtained from www.aspira.org/about_assoc.html.

CHAPTER TEN: FINDING PROFESSIONAL SUCCESS

page 245. Earnings information provided by Catalyst, www.catalyst.org.

page 253. Center for American Women and Politics Women in Elected Office 2001: "Fact Sheet Summaries," Eagleton Institute of Politics–Rutgers, The State University of New Jersey, www.rci.rutgers.edu/~cawp/facts/cawpfs.html.

page 261. Association of Hispanic Advertising Agencies, www.ahaa.org.

page 282. Biographical information on Gloria Anzaldúa obtained from voices.cla.umn.edu/authors/gloriaanzaldua.html.

CHAPTER ELEVEN: GOING HOME

page 283. Anreus, Alejandro. "My Daughter," from an unpublished collection of poems, *In This Our Exile*.

page 303. The Tomás Rivera Policy Institute, www.trpi.org.

page 304. Biographical information on Mia "the Knockout" St. John derived from www.miastjohn.com

Index

About the Author

Sandra Guzmán is an award-winning journalist and former editor-in-chief of *Latina* magazine. She is the founding content director of soloella.com. A writer and producer who has produced hundreds of stories for Fox Television's morning show *Good Day New York* and Telemundo, Sandra won an Emmy for a half-hour special, "Embargo Contra Cuba," which aired on Telemundo's New York affiliate. A popular motivational speaker among the college circuit and Fortune 500 companies and a recipient of numerous community awards, she is a national leading expert in journalism targeting the U.S. Hispanic population. Born Sandra Rodríguez-Gonzalez in Puerto Rico, she was raised in Jersey City, New Jersey. She lives in New York City with her teenage son, BJ.